T0350624

Africa's Demographic Transition

Africa's Demographic Transition

Dividend or Disaster?

David Canning, Sangeeta Raja, and
Abdo S. Yazbeck,
Editors

A copublication of Agence Française de Développement and the World Bank

© 2015 International Bank for Reconstruction and Development / The World Bank
1818 H Street NW, Washington, DC 20433
Telephone: 202-473-1000; Internet: www.worldbank.org

Some rights reserved

1 2 3 4   18 17 16 15

This work is a product of the staff of The World Bank with external contributions. The findings, interpretations, and conclusions expressed in this work do not necessarily reflect the views of The World Bank, its Board of Executive Directors, or the governments they represent, or the Agence Française de Développement. The World Bank does not guarantee the accuracy of the data included in this work. The boundaries, colors, denominations, and other information shown on any map in this work do not imply any judgment on the part of The World Bank concerning the legal status of any territory or the endorsement or acceptance of such boundaries.

Nothing herein shall constitute or be considered to be a limitation upon or waiver of the privileges and immunities of The World Bank, all of which are specifically reserved.

Rights and Permissions

This work is available under the Creative Commons Attribution 3.0 IGO license (CC BY 3.0 IGO) http://creativecommons.org/licenses/by/3.0/igo. Under the Creative Commons Attribution license, you are free to copy, distribute, transmit, and adapt this work, including for commercial purposes, under the following conditions:

Attribution—Please cite the work as follows: Canning, David, Sangeeta Raja, and Abdo S. Yazbeck, eds. 2015. *Africa's Demographic Transition: Dividend or Disaster?* Africa Development Forum series. Washington, DC: World Bank. doi:10.1596/978-1-4648-0489-2. License: Creative Commons Attribution CC BY 3.0 IGO

Translations—If you create a translation of this work, please add the following disclaimer along with the attribution: *This translation was not created by The World Bank and should not be considered an official World Bank translation. The World Bank shall not be liable for any content or error in this translation.*

Adaptations—If you create an adaptation of this work, please add the following disclaimer along with the attribution: *This is an adaptation of an original work by The World Bank. Views and opinions expressed in the adaptation are the sole responsibility of the author or authors of the adaptation and are not endorsed by The World Bank.*

Third-party content—The World Bank does not necessarily own each component of the content contained within the work. The World Bank therefore does not warrant that the use of any third-party-owned individual component or part contained in the work will not infringe on the rights of those third parties. The risk of claims resulting from such infringement rests solely with you. If you wish to re-use a component of the work, it is your responsibility to determine whether permission is needed for that re-use and to obtain permission from the copyright owner. Examples of components can include, but are not limited to, tables, figures, or images.

All queries on rights and licenses should be addressed to the Publishing and Knowledge Division, The World Bank, 1818 H Street NW, Washington, DC 20433, USA; fax: 202-522-2625; e-mail: pubrights@worldbank.org.

ISBN (paper): 978-1-4648-0489-2
ISBN (electronic): 978-1-4648-0490-8
DOI: 10.1596/978-1-4648-0489-2

Cover photo: © Sarah Farhat / World Bank. Further permission required for reuse.
Cover design: Debra Naylor, Naylor Design Inc.

Library of Congress Cataloging-in-Publication Data has been requested.

Africa Development Forum Series

The **Africa Development Forum Series** was created in 2009 to focus on issues of significant relevance to Sub-Saharan Africa's social and economic development. Its aim is both to record the state of the art on a specific topic and to contribute to ongoing local, regional, and global policy debates. It is designed specifically to provide practitioners, scholars, and students with the most up-to-date research results while highlighting the promise, challenges, and opportunities that exist on the continent.

The series is sponsored by the Agence Française de Développement and the World Bank. The manuscripts chosen for publication represent the highest quality in each institution and have been selected for their relevance to the development agenda. Working together with a shared sense of mission and interdisciplinary purpose, the two institutions are committed to a common search for new insights and new ways of analyzing the development realities of the Sub-Saharan Africa region.

Advisory Committee Members

Agence Française de Développement
Jean-Yves Grosclaude, Director of Strategy
Alain Henry, Director of Research
Guillaume de Saint Phalle, Head of Research and Publishing Division
Cyrille Bellier, Head of the Economic and Social Research Unit

World Bank
Francisco H. G. Ferreira, Chief Economist, Africa Region
Richard Damania, Lead Economist, Africa Region
Stephen McGroarty, Executive Editor, Publishing and Knowledge Division
Carlos Rossel, Publisher

Sub-Saharan Africa

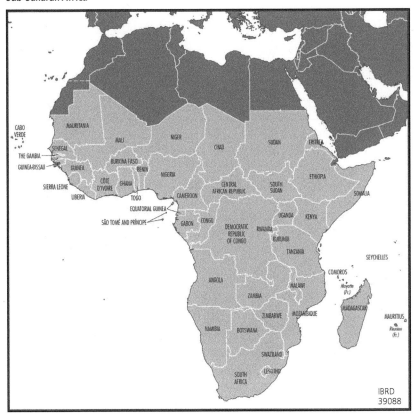

CABO VERDE
MAURITANIA
SENEGAL
THE GAMBIA
GUINEA-BISSAU
GUINEA
SIERRA LEONE
LIBERIA
MALI
BURKINA FASO
CÔTE D'IVOIRE
GHANA
BENIN
TOGO
NIGER
NIGERIA
CHAD
CAMEROON
EQUATORIAL GUINEA
SÃO TOMÉ AND PRÍNCIPE
GABON
CONGO
CENTRAL AFRICAN REPUBLIC
DEMOCRATIC REPUBLIC OF CONGO
SUDAN
SOUTH SUDAN
ERITREA
ETHIOPIA
SOMALIA
UGANDA
RWANDA
BURUNDI
KENYA
TANZANIA
ANGOLA
ZAMBIA
MALAWI
COMOROS
Mayotte (Fr.)
SEYCHELLES
MADAGASCAR
MAURITIUS
Réunion (Fr.)
ZIMBABWE
MOZAMBIQUE
NAMIBIA
BOTSWANA
SWAZILAND
LESOTHO
SOUTH AFRICA

IBRD
39088

Titles in the Africa Development Forum Series

Africa's Infrastructure: A Time for Transformation (2010) edited by Vivien Foster and Cecilia Briceño-Garmendia

Gender Disparities in Africa's Labor Market (2010) edited by Jorge Saba Arbache, Alexandre Kolev, and Ewa Filipiak

Challenges for African Agriculture (2010) edited by Jean-Claude Deveze

Contemporary Migration to South Africa: A Regional Development Issue (2011) edited by Aurelia Segatti and Loren Landau

Light Manufacturing in Africa: Targeted Policies to Enhance Private Investment and Create Jobs (2012) by Hinh T. Dinh, Vincent Palmade, Vandana Chandra, and Frances Cossar

Informal Sector in Francophone Africa: Firm Size, Productivity, and Institutions (2012) by Nancy Benjamin and Ahmadou Aly Mbaye

Financing Africa's Cities: The Imperative of Local Investment (2012) by Thierry Paulais

Structural Transformation and Rural Change Revisited: Challenges for Late Developing Countries in a Globalizing World (2012) by Bruno Losch, Sandrine Fréguin-Gresh, and Eric Thomas White

The Political Economy of Decentralization in Sub-Saharan Africa: A New Implementation Model (2013) edited by Bernard Dafflon and Thierry Madiès

Empowering Women: Legal Rights and Economic Opportunities in Africa (2013) by Mary Hallward-Driemeier and Tazeen Hasan

Enterprising Women: Expanding Economic Opportunities in Africa (2013) by Mary Hallward-Driemeier

Urban Labor Markets in Sub-Saharan Africa (2013) edited by Philippe De Vreyer and François Roubaud

Securing Africa's Land for Shared Prosperity: A Program to Scale Up Reforms and Investments (2013) by Frank F. K. Byamugisha

Youth Employment in Sub-Saharan Africa (2014) by Deon Filmer and Louis Fox

Tourism in Africa: Harnessing Tourism for Growth and Improved Livelihoods (2014) by Iain Christie, Eneida Fernandes, Hannah Messerli, and Louise Twining-Ward

Safety Nets in Africa: Effective Mechanisms to Reach the Poor and Most Vulnerable (2015) edited by Carlo del Ninno and Bradford Mills

Land Delivery Systems in West African Cities: The Example of Bamako, Mali (2015) by Alain Durand-Lasserve, Maÿlis Durand-Lasserve, and Harris Selod

Enhancing the Climate Resilience of Africa's Infrastructure: The Power and Water Sectors (2015) edited by Raffaello Cervigni, Rikard Liden, James E. Neumann, and Kenneth M. Strzepek

The Challenge of Stability and Security in West Africa (2015) by Alexandre Marc, Neelam Verjee, and Stephen Mogaka

Africa's Demographic Transition: Dividend or Disaster? (2015) edited by David Canning, Sangeeta Raja, and Abdo S. Yazbeck

All books in the Africa Development Forum series are available for free at https://openknowledge.worldbank.org/handle/10986/2150

Contents

Maps

Tables

Foreword

"Demography is destiny" is both an important message and an inaccurate one. There is little doubt that demographic change can have a deep impact on poverty, economic growth, health, fragility, and human development, and as such it is extremely important. However, the nature of the impact of demographic change is not set in stone. The most important lesson from this book is that the right policies can help countries to reap the benefits of demographic change on the overall development of a nation.

This report lays out a range of policy actions that are needed at the various phases of the demographic transition and uses global and regional experiences to provide evidence on what has worked and what has not. Countries have a menu of options available to speed up the transition, improve investment in the resulting youth cohort, expand labor markets, and encourage savings.

While this study looks at lessons from East Asia, Latin America, and the Middle East, Sub-Saharan Africa currently exhibits two unique demographic characteristics. First, it is the only region in the world that is still at a very early stage of the demographic transition. As such, it can learn from other regions that have gone through the same journey to ensure that demographic change paves the way to deeper and more sustainable prosperity. As this book points out, this path is neither easy nor automatic. Success requires actions in different policy realms that are time-coordinated, adapted to the current level of the demographic transition, and results-driven.

The second unique characteristic of the region's demographic picture is its heterogeneity. While a small number of countries are far along in the transition, with fertility rates that are below replacement levels, many others are exhibiting surprising delays in the transition in the past 10 years. Some countries are showing very little movement along the natural transition and are stuck at very high fertility rates. These large differences argue for differentiated policies that target different sectors and processes. They also argue for country-to-country learning and knowledge sharing.

Sub-Saharan Africa has experienced impressive and sustained economic growth and development. Some of that growth is powered by natural resources and policies that are opening up more markets and attracting investments. The demographic transition—particularly the speed with which it takes place and the economic and human development policies that accompany it—can power the next wave of economic growth with healthier and better educated youth cohorts that enter expanding labor markets and contribute to improved financial markets.

Harnessing the demographic dividend means, first and foremost, empowering women and girls by improving their health, enhancing their human capital through increased investment in education and skills, and providing them with greater market, social, and decision-making power. The full potential of the demographic dividend *can* be realized in Sub-Saharan Africa with proactive policies that can help to make it happen.

Makhtar Diop
Vice President, Africa Region
World Bank

Acknowledgments

This volume is part of the African Regional Studies Program, an initiative of the Africa Region Vice-Presidency at the World Bank. This series of studies aims to combine high levels of analytical rigor and policy relevance, and to apply them to various topics important for the social and economic development of Sub-Saharan Africa. Quality control and oversight are provided by the Office of the Chief Economist for the Africa Region.

This report was prepared by a team led by Sangeeta Raja, together with David Canning, Elina Pradhan, and Abdo Yazbeck. The other members of the core team from the World Bank included Anne Bakilana, Yoonyoung Cho, David Locke Newhouse, Jonas Ingemann Parby, David Robalino, Michael Weber, and Roland White. Non–World Bank staff—Reiner Kingholz, Ruth Müller, and Franziska Woellert (Berlin-Institut für Bevölkerung und Entwicklung); Parfait Eloundou-Enyegue (Cornell University); Jocelyn Finlay, Mahesh Karra, and Akshar Saxena (Harvard University); Donald Hicks and Neelima Ramaraju (LLamasoft); Peter Glick and Sebastain Linnemayr (RAND); and Jean-Pierre Guengant, Supriya Madhavan, John May, Charles Simkins, Bienvenue Tien, Joshua Wilde, and Claudia Wolfe—helped prepare background papers that contributed to the overall report. Additional research support was provided by Carolyn Makumi and Yvette Atkins. The team benefited from continuous engagement with Deon Filmer and David Evans.

The team thanks Ritva Reinikka, Human Development Director for Africa during the early phase of this work, as well as Shantayanan Devarajan, Africa Chief Economist, and Eduard Bos, Elizabeth Lule, and Jean Jacques de St. Antoine, former World Bank staff, during the early phase of this work, for their strategic direction. The team also thanks Trina Haque, Africa Health Practice Manager, and Olusoji Adeyi, Health, Nutrition, and Population Director, for their continued support throughout the process. The team also thanks the current Africa Chief Economist, Francisco H. G. Ferreira, for his support during the closing phases of the work. The team benefited greatly from the communications support provided by Kavita Watsa and Kristina Ifeoma Nwazota.

Several World Bank staff, as well as policy makers, academics, and other stakeholders, provided comments at various stages of development of this report. Wolfgang Fengler, Markus Goldstein, Michele Gragnolati (World Bank staff), and Ron Lee (Berkeley University) provided insightful peer review comments. Any errors or omissions are the responsibility of the team.

The team would like to acknowledge the generous support for the preparation of the report by the Government of Netherlands through its BNPP Trust Fund, The Hewlett Foundation, and the Africa Vice President's Chief Economist Office (AFRCE).

Book design, editing, production, and distribution were coordinated by Patricia Katayama, Stephen McGroarty, Nora Ridolfi, and Janice Tuten in the World Bank's Publishing and Knowledge division. Special thanks to Elizabeth Forsyth for editing the book and Bruce Ross-Larson for editorial support for the overview chapter.

About the Editors and Contributors

Editors

David Canning is Richard Saltonstall Professor of Population Sciences and professor of economics and international health at the Department of Global Health and Population, Harvard T.H. Chan School of Public Health. He has a PhD in economics from Cambridge University and has held faculty positions at the London School of Economics, Cambridge University, Columbia University, and Queen's University Belfast. He is associate director of the Harvard Center for Population and Development Studies. He has carried out extensive research on the impact of health improvements on economic outcomes and served as a member of Working Group One of the World Health Organization's Commission on Macroeconomics and Health. He has also worked on the demographic dividend looking at how changes in fertility and age structure affect macroeconomic performance.

Sangeeta Raja is a senior public health specialist at the World Bank. She has more than 15 years of experience working in reproductive health in Africa and was one of the founding members of the Reproductive Health Supplies Coalition. She holds an MPH from Boston University. Ms. Raja was the task team leader for the demographic dividend study. She also manages several lending operations in Africa. Prior to joining the World Bank, she worked for John Snow Inc. and UNICEF in the field and at headquarters.

Abdo Yazbeck is the health practice manager for Eastern and Southern Africa and a lead health economist. He holds a PhD in economics with a focus on health and labor. His most recent assignment was as a manager in the Europe and Central Asia Department for Human Development. Prior to that, he was the program leader at World Bank Institute's Health and AIDS Team for five years. He previously worked for seven years in South Asia operations as a senior health economist supporting health projects in Bangladesh, India, Maldives, and Sri Lanka. Abdo also worked as a senior health economist in the private sector focusing on Africa, the Middle East, and the former Soviet Union after being part of the team for *World Development Report 1993: Investing in Health* and teaching economics at Rice University and Texas A&M University. He has authored/edited six other books, including *Better Health Systems for India's Poor, Learning from Economic Downturns, Reaching the Poor with HNP Services*, and *Attacking Inequality in the Health Sector*.

Contributors

Anne Bakilana is a senior economist in health at the World Bank, with experience in analytical works and management of health sector projects in Europe and Central Asia and in the Africa Region. Prior to joining the World Bank, she worked as a senior research lecturer at the University of Cape Town's School of Economics. She holds a BS in economics from University College London and an MS and PhD in demography from the London School of Economics.

Yoonyoung (Yoon) Cho is a labor economist at the Social Protection and Labor Global Practice in the World Bank. Yoon has been working on issues related to labor markets including skills, entrepreneurship, activation and graduation, migration, and labor market intermediation, particularly focusing on the poor and vulnerable. She has worked in the Middle East and North Africa, Asia, Sub-Saharan Africa, and Europe and Central Asia. More recently, she has been focusing on issues related to the design and implementation of labor and safety net programs in Albania, Bangladesh, and Pakistan. She has published papers in peer-reviewed journals and is actively serving as a peer reviewer for academic journals as well as the World Bank's knowledge products. She received a PhD in economics from the University of Wisconsin-Madison in 2005.

Parfait M. Eloundou-Enyegue is professor of development sociology at Cornell University. He holds a PhD from the Pennsylvania State University and spent a postdoctoral term at RAND (Santa Monica). Much of his research in population studies has focused on the mutual linkages between fertility and child schooling in Sub-Saharan Africa, but his current work also addresses the implications of global demographic change in socioeconomic inequalities. With support from the Hewlett Foundation, he coordinates a network of researchers in Sub-Saharan Africa who work on issues related to the demographic dividend in that region.

Jocelyn Finlay is a research scientist at the Harvard Center for Population and Development Studies. An economist by training, but now benefiting from the multidisciplinary environment at Harvard T.H. Chan School of Public Health, Jocelyn's research focuses on understanding the economic consequences of health and demographic change particularly in low- and middle-income countries. Her research fields examine the economic consequences of demographic change, the economics of reproductive health, issues surrounding child and maternal health, and the economics and social responses to natural disasters. Jocelyn works with the Demographic and Health Surveys and has created a database of reproductive health laws around the world from 1960 to the present. In addition to the empirical work, Jocelyn conducts systematic qualitative analysis exemplified by recent work conducted in Burundi and Ghana.

Peter Glick is a senior economist at the RAND Corporation and director of the Center for Research and Policy in International Development within RAND Labor and Population. His research on developing countries spans the areas of health, education, employment, and poverty. His recent projects have examined health risk behaviors among youth in West Bank and Gaza, the impacts of cataract surgery in Ethiopia, and employment in the Kurdistan Region of Iraq. He has also conducted extensive research on HIV/AIDS in Africa, including studies of changes in prevention knowledge and behavior and the impacts of antiretroviral therapy on economic well-being. He has designed and implemented numerous household and provider surveys in Africa and the Middle East.

Jean-Pierre Guengant is emeritus director of research with The University of Paris-I Sorbonne. He holds a PhD in development economics and a masters in demography. He was the resident representative of IRD (Institut de Recherche pour le Développement) in Benin, Burkina Faso, Côte d'Ivoire, and Niger, until 2009. In 2009, he held the post of deputy director of the United Nations Population Division in New York. He is the author of numerous publications, many on Sub-Saharan Africa and the Caribbean, and he has recently given lectures on population and development in Paris at the G20 Parliamentary Assembly, in Brussels for the European Union, and in several African capitals and cities.

Mahesh Karra is a doctoral student in global health economics at the Harvard T.H. Chan School of Public Health and a research assistant at the Harvard Center for Population and Development Studies. His research interests are broadly in development economics, health economics, econometrics and quantitative methods, and applied demography. His most recent work focuses on examining the economics of fertility, and maternal and child health. Mahesh holds a joint honors BA in economics and in Hispanic studies from McGill University and an MS in economics from the Barcelona Graduate School of Economics.

Reiner Klingholz studied chemistry and earned his PhD in molecular biology. He worked as a science and environment editor for *Die Zeit* and *GEO* magazine and was editor of the science magazine *Geo-Wissen*. Since 2003, Reiner Klingholz has been director of the Berlin Institute for Population and Development, a think tank concerned with demographic topics. He has written several books on issues of global change and was a fellow at the Stellenbosch Institute for Advanced Study in South Africa in 2013 and 2015.

Sebastian Linnemayr is an economist at the RAND Corporation, associate director of the RAND Center on Research and Policy in International Development (RAPID), and affiliate faculty at the Pardee RAND Graduate School. His current research focuses on the use of economic incentives and insights from behavioral economics on medication adherence, in particular for people living with HIV in Sub-Saharan Africa. Prior to joining RAND, he was a postdoctoral research fellow at the Harvard School of Public Health. Dr. Linnemayr is leading three NIH-funded projects that investigate how behavioral economics can be used to improve antiretroviral therapy (ART) adherence in Uganda.

Supriya Madhavan is a senior implementation research adviser in the Bureau of Global Health at the U.S. Agency for International Development. She has more than 20 years of experience working internationally and domestically in research and program implementation in family planning and reproductive health, maternal and child health, and infectious diseases. Prior to joining USAID, Supriya worked with Population Services International, the Aga Khan Foundation, Chicago Department of Public Health, and University of California, San Francisco. She is a demographer by training, with a PhD in population and health from Johns Hopkins University and an MPH from Columbia University.

John F. May, a specialist in population policies and programs, is a visiting scholar at the Population Reference Bureau. He is also an adjunct professor of demography at Georgetown University in Washington, DC. For 15 years, he was a lead demographer at the World Bank. Prior to coming to the United States in 1987, he worked on many population projects around the world for UNFPA, UNICEF, USAID, and IUSSP. He was posted in Haiti and New Caledonia for the United Nations. He also worked for the Futures Group International, a U.S. consulting firm offering services in population and HIV/AIDS modeling, policy, and program design. He has a doctorate in demography from the University of Paris-V (Sorbonne). His book *World Population Policies: Their Origin, Evolution, and Impact* (Springer 2012) received the 2012 Global Media Award of the Population Institute for best book on population. In 2013, he was elected an associate member of the Royal Academy of Belgium.

Ruth Müller studied journalism in Hanover and then graduated with a master's degree in Eastern European studies from the Free University Berlin. Her key interests during her studies centered on political transition processes in the postsocialist states, international relations, and communication research. She has been employed as a research associate at the Berlin Institute for Population and Development since 2012. In her work she mainly focuses on worldwide population dynamics and the related link to socioeconomic development.

David Newhouse joined the World Bank's Poverty Global Practice as a senior economist in 2014 and covers Pakistan and Sri Lanka. Prior to that, he was a labor economist in the Social Protection and Labor Global Practice. He has co-led Bank efforts to monitor labor markets in developing countries and analyze the policy response to the 2008 financial crisis. He co-authored three background papers to *World Development Report 2013: Jobs*, and has led the evaluation of the Urban Youth Employment Program in Papua New Guinea. He first joined the Bank in 2007, and worked in the Jakarta office as a task team leader of the Indonesian Jobs Report. Prior to that, he worked for three years as a consultant in the Poverty and Social Impact Analysis unit of the IMF providing policy advice on energy and food subsidies. David holds a PhD in economics from Cornell University, and has published several articles on a wide range of issues relating to labor, health, and education in developing countries.

Jonas Ingemann Parby has been the technical lead on urbanization and the demographic dividend and a separate working paper on urbanization in Africa and its relation to the demographic dividend. He is an urban specialist at the World Bank Group based in Washington, DC. Jonas has 10 years' experience on urban development across Africa, South East Asia, and Latin America. He holds degrees in international development and public administration from University of Roskilde, Denmark. Before joining the World Bank Group, he served as adviser for DANIDA (Danish International Development Agency) and worked in international and local nongovernmental organizations.

Elina Pradhan, born and raised in Nepal, is a doctoral student at the Department of Global Health and Population at Harvard T.H. Chan School of Public Health. She is interested in population health policy modeling, evaluation, and design in resource-limited settings. She works in a wide range of projects on topics such as the impact of national education policies on female education and adolescent reproductive behavior, policies to reap demographic dividend in Sub-Saharan Africa, and mathematical models of the population-level health impact of drug/diagnostic interventions. She holds a BS in chemical engineering from the Massachusetts Institute of Technology and an MS in global health and population from the Harvard T.H. Chan School of Public Health.

Neelima P. Ramaraju is the director of Global Health Applications at LLamasoft, Inc., a global leader in supply chain design software and services. In this role, she works closely with public and private partner organizations with a focus on supply chain and mathematical modeling and analysis to support decision making. She has been involved in projects in Ethiopia, Haiti, Kenya, Mozambique, Tanzania, and elsewhere, focused on restructuring public health supply chains to improve customer service and reduce costs. She has a BS in industrial and systems engineering from the Georgia Institute of Technology and an MBA and MS in industrial and operations engineering from the University of Michigan.

David Robalino, an Ecuadorian national, joined the World Bank in 1999 as a Young Professional. David has been working on issues related to labor markets, skills, social insurance, and fiscal policy and has published widely on these topics. He has worked in several countries in Latin America, the Middle East and North Africa, Sub-Saharan Africa, and Asia. His most recent book is *Social Insurance, Informality, and Labor Markets: How to Protect Workers while Creating New Jobs* (Oxford University Press 2014). David also serves as codirector of the Employment and Development Program at the Institute for the Study of the Labor (IZA). Prior to joining the Bank, David was a researcher at the RAND Corporation.

Akshar Saxena is a doctoral student in global health economics at the Harvard T.H. Chan School of Public Health. He is interested in economics of aging, noncommunicable diseases, and primary care provision in Africa, Asia, and the United States. He is currently working on macroeconomics of aging, analyzing the dynamics between health, retirement, pensions, and insurance. He has previously worked for the Ministry of Health in Singapore. He holds a BA in economics from the National University of Singapore and a master in public policy from the Lee Kuan Yew School of Public Policy.

Charles Simkins was the Helen Suzman Professor of Political Economy at the University of the Witwatersrand in Johannesburg, South Africa for many years. He has retired from that position and now works as a consultant for the Helen Suzman Foundation and the Centre for Development and Enterprise on South Africa growth issues and the promotion of a liberal constitutional order. He has a long-standing interest in demography and associated areas in economics and he has recently completed work projecting the future of school and university education.

Bienvenue N. Tien is a full-time consultant at the World Bank Group. He has a track record in policy-oriented research on labor, poverty, education, and trade, as well as linkage between human capital formation and economic development. Since joining the World Bank Group in 2012, he has worked across several Global Practices: Social Protection and Labor, Education, and Poverty. His most current assignments have been on youth employment, skills, and inequalities of opportunity in postconflict and fragile states in Sub-Saharan Africa and South Asia. He previously worked for a Washington, DC-based economics think tank, DIWDC, where he co-authored peer-reviewed articles published in English and German. Mr. Tien holds an MA in economics from the University of Toledo (Ohio).

Michael Weber is an economist with the World Bank Group's Jobs Cross-Cutting Solution Area. He has published and worked on youth employment, informality, labor regulations, active labor market policies, and social insurance schemes. Mr. Weber has initiated and led innovative projects to explore behavioral and financial interventions, youth's preferences and constraints, enforcement effects of labor codes, or simulations on the effects of labor policies and tax and benefit systems in developing countries. In recent years he has also been active in monitoring global and regional job trends and has contributed research on data quality issues as well as labor market indicators. Prior to joining the World Bank Group in 2008, Mr. Weber worked at a joint research organization of the three main Universities of Vienna on applied research topics. He holds a PhD in economics and master degrees in economics as well as commerce.

Joshua Wilde is an assistant professor of economics at the University of South Florida. His research interests focus on the intersection of demography and macroeconomics in the developing world. Most of his work deals with the macroeconomic effects of fertility decline, and the intersection of infant and maternal health and fertility choices on long-run economic performance. He holds a PhD in economics from Brown University.

Franziska Woellert studied geography with a focus on international cooperation, migration, and resource management at Goettingen University. She completed several traineeships at institutions working in development cooperation before becoming a fellow at the Center for Rural Development in Berlin in 2007. She has worked at the Berlin Institute for Population and Development from 2008 until 2010 and then again from 2013 onwards. From 2010 to 2012 she worked in Namibia for GIZ (German Agency for International Cooperation) in resource management.

Claudia Wolff is a senior health economist at Medtronic. She holds a PhD in economics from Stockholm School of Economics. During her PhD studies, she worked on several research projects at University College London, as well as in Ethiopia and India. Her research focuses on the empirical assessment of health technologies, as well as health and labor policies. She has worked as a consultant in the Labor Group of the Human Development Network of the World Bank as well as for the European Bank for Reconstruction and Development.

Abbreviations

AIDS	acquired immunodeficiency syndrome
CYP	couple-year of protection
DHS	demographic and health survey
FDI	foreign direct investment
GDP	gross domestic product
HIV	human immunodeficiency virus
LCH	life-cycle hypothesis
ODA	overseas development assistance
SAR	special administrative region
TFP	total factor productivity
TFR	total fertility rate
UN	United Nations

Overview

Introduction

The demographic dividend describes the interplay between changes in a population's age structure due to the demographic transition and rapid economic growth. Declines in child mortality, followed by declines in fertility, produce a "bulge" generation and a period when a country has a large number of working-age people and a smaller number of dependents. Having a large number of workers per capita gives a boost to the economy provided there are labor opportunities for the workers.

More important for a sizable dividend, however, are changes in worker productivity. Smaller family sizes mean that both families and governments have more resources to invest in health and education per child. It also means that women are more able to enter the labor force. If the economic environment is conducive, and this large and well-educated cohort finds well-paying work, a first dividend comes as this productive labor boosts family and national income. Longer life spans mean that this large, better-earning cohort will also want to save for retirement. And with the right policies and a well-developed financial sector, a second dividend can come from higher savings and investments, leading to further productivity gains.

Except for a few countries in Southern Africa and some island nations, fertility rates and youth dependency rates in Sub-Saharan Africa are among the highest in the world, exposing the region to higher poverty rates, smaller investments in children, lower labor productivity, high unemployment or underemployment, and the risk of political instability. But demography need not lead to disaster. If the focus shifts from population numbers to population age structures, the prospects for Africa may be positive. Declines in fertility automatically raise income per capita in the short run and have the potential to bring further gains in savings and investments in the long run. With prudent policies, African countries can reap the benefits of this demographic dividend. Policy choices and actions can transform the population of a nation into a healthy, educated, empowered labor force that can contribute to real and sustained economic growth that lifts people out of poverty. As a bonus, a demographic dividend can even accelerate economic growth in ways that spread prosperity across society.

There is definite cause for optimism about Africa's potential to reap a demographic dividend. Child mortality rates, the leading edge of the demographic transition, are declining quickly in a majority of countries in the region. Fertility rates in Africa vary enormously with women's education. For example, women with a high school education in Ethiopia have below-replacement fertility—a total fertility rate (TFR) of less than 2 children per woman—while the national TFR is just fewer than 5 children per woman. The rapid expansion of school enrollments in the region makes it likely that the total fertility rate of the school-age cohort will be lower than that of previous cohorts. There also is renewed interest in improving access to family planning services. And once a substantial fertility decline gets under way, feedback loops can accelerate the process.

To realize this potential, strategic planning and preparation are required in each country. The first and perhaps most challenging step is to speed up the fertility decline in countries where it is currently slow or stalled. An accelerated fertility decline will produce a larger, healthier, and more productive workforce, and these gains in human capital can drive faster economic growth if economic policies create enough demand for labor. Reducing fertility leads to immediate gains in income per capita as youth dependency rates fall. However, achieving the full potential of the demographic dividend requires economic policies that take advantage of the opportunity. Formulating and implementing policies that strengthen financial institutions and encourage saving will channel rising incomes into domestic savings and investments that further fuel growth and development.

The relationship between the fertility transition and human development works in both directions, creating a virtuous cycle that can accelerate fertility decline, social development, and eventually economic growth. Empirical evidence points to three highly interactive accelerators:

- *Health, especially child health.* Child health is a critical input into fertility declines. As children's health and survival rates improve, family demand for more children declines as confidence in child survival increases. Smaller family sizes improve maternal health, which further improves child health, completing a virtuous cycle.

- *Education, especially education for girls.* Female education is a critical driver of lower desired fertility and the transition from high to low fertility. Fertility decline, in turn, has a strong effect on education by allowing for fewer, healthier, better nourished, and better educated children.

- *Women's empowerment, which is clearly related to the first two.* Better educated and healthier women—with more market, social, and decision-making power in the family—are likely to have fewer children (World Bank 2011).[1] And women who have fewer children—as a result of delayed age of marriage, delayed first sexual contact, or more space between births—are much more likely to enter the paid labor market, to have higher earnings, and to be more empowered.

While speeding up the demographic transition can help to deliver more and higher-quality workers, the full economic benefits can be achieved only if there is strong demand for labor: the supply of labor is not enough in the absence of sufficient demand. Moreover, the workforce needs to be productively employed. East Asia reaped the demographic dividend because it combined a rapid demographic transition with export-oriented policies that increased the demand for labor. The best possible outcomes are the result of economic policies that expand the demand for labor coupled with policies that support a healthy, skilled workforce, which can in itself attract investments that create jobs.

After a period of stagnation, the takeoff in economic growth in Africa over the last 15 years creates some optimism for the future. A rise in foreign direct investments (FDI) is compensating to some extent for weak domestic savings. However, not all FDI is the same in creating jobs. Some FDI may support the growth of extractive industries in ways that do not absorb the increase in labor supply. In the short term, the economic dynamism in the region provides some fiscal space for governments to put in place policies to speed up the fertility decline and take advantage of the resulting demographic transition. The longer view hinges on the ability of Africa to continue this rapid growth and to create high-productivity jobs that absorb the youth bulge and the expected increase in female labor force participation in the formal sector.

This report presents a positive agenda for increasing the likelihood of first accelerating the demographic transition and then capturing the potential social and economic benefits to create a demographic dividend in Sub-Saharan Africa. There is a real possibility to realize a rapid demographic transition and a large demographic dividend given the region's rapidly decreasing child mortality, rapidly increasing female school enrollment, increasing demand for family planning, renewed high-level political support for tackling demographic challenges, and rapid economic growth. Reasons for concern include stagnant fertility rates, stubborn pockets of child malnutrition, cultural norms that greatly value high fertility, gender inequality, and low domestic savings. Based on evidence in and outside Africa, the report identifies policies that can begin to tackle the challenges of transition and build on recent successes.

While this report takes a regional approach to outlining the potential for a demographic dividend and presenting broad recommendations, country-level considerations will drive country-specific approaches. There is huge heterogeneity across Africa, making it critical to avoid a cookie-cutter approach. The priority actions listed at the end of this overview are likely to be important in most countries. But country-specific actions must take into account the country's constraints and opportunities. Countries that still have high child mortality and fertility will naturally focus on policies to speed up the demographic transition. Those that have made substantial progress on mortality and fertility and that are seeing a rise in the working-age share of the population—the ratio of working-age people to youth and elderly dependents—will focus on creating jobs for the growing labor force. Countries with larger cohorts of older workers will focus on encouraging savings and investment.

The phrase "demographic dividend" might imply a simple interaction between age structure and economic growth. But the report lays out relationships across several sectors that go to the heart of human, social, and economic development. The sectors needed to encourage the demographic transition and produce a dividend include health, education, population, business development and investment, domestic savings, and trade. The relationships among sectors have the potential to create virtuous as well as vicious cycles. Once the demographic transition gets under way, it can accelerate, with economic growth leading to further demographic change that feeds more economic growth. The interconnectedness and range of issues touched on require national commitment and responses that transcend sector silos and engage broad segments of society.

Demographic Dividend or Disaster

The concept of a demographic dividend was introduced in the late 1990s to describe the interplay between changes in population structure and fast economic growth in East Asia (Bloom, Canning, and Malaney 2000; Bloom and Williamson 1998). The first demographic dividend—or extra boost to the economy—focuses on the labor supply effects of changes in age structure. It can be captured if three things happen. First, improvements in health status, especially child health, increase child survival and contribute to a decline in the number of children born to each family as the total number of children that families want to have decreases. The combination of higher child survival rates in one cohort and fewer children in the following cohorts produces a population bulge—a large cohort that works its way through the age structure—with large macroeconomic effects. Second, investments in health and education are higher in cohorts following the bulge. As families have fewer children, they and the government have more resources per child to invest in the education and health of the surviving children, increasing human capital (Kalemli-Ozcan, Ryder, and Weil 2000; Schultz 2005). And the labor supply gets an additional boost, as low fertility allows more women to enter the labor force (Bloom et al. 2009). Third, an economic environment has to be fostered so that this bulge cohort can find well-paying jobs, rather than simply be unemployed or forced into low-productivity work. If all three steps are successful and well timed, an economic dividend is produced as the large cohort moves into highly productive jobs, boosting family and national income.

In addition to this first dividend based on a productive labor supply, a possible second dividend results from the savings and investments of the bulge cohort as it matures and saves for retirement. This dividend can take place only if policies to promote saving are established and the financial sector is developed enough to attract savings and translate them into productive investments. Later, the bulge cohort ages, leading to a high old-age dependency rate, so savings have to be sufficient to finance this cohort's retirement and health care needs (figure O.1).

A demographic dividend is not guaranteed in every country. If, for example, the birth rate is slow to decline, investments in education are less likely because families and countries will have fewer resources per child. If economic reforms are not successful and high-productivity jobs are not created, the increased labor supply may not be employed productively and incomes will not rise substantially. If the financial sector is not reformed, savings from the bulge cohort will not materialize in large enough amounts to drive investment.

While achieving the dividend is not guaranteed, a failure to reduce family size will expose countries to additional risks. The large youth cohort that appears when child mortality first declines puts an enormous strain on family and national resources. The demographic dividend occurs only when fertility falls and the cohorts that follow are smaller, lowering the youth dependency ratio

Figure O.1 Four Stages of the Demographic Transition in Sweden, 1750–2010

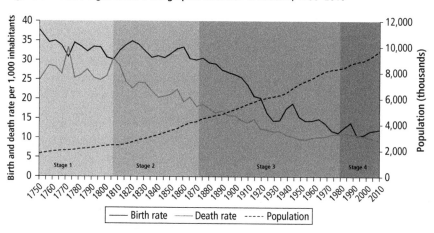

Source: Statistics Sweden.

and allowing larger investment per child. Without a fertility decline, countries will face an ever-growing population base and ever-larger youth cohorts—and children will be further exposed to health risks, malnutrition, and lower public and private educational investments. This will result in higher youth dependency ratios, higher poverty, higher unemployment or underemployment, and greater risks of instability. Demography may be destiny, but countries can shape policies to try to ensure that this destiny produces a dividend and not a disaster.

Demographic Dynamics in Africa

In recent years, Sub-Saharan Africa has undergone profound changes in its population structure. Rapid declines in death rates, particularly of children, have contributed to a rapidly growing population. In East and Southern Africa, life expectancy was rising until the advent of the human immunodeficiency virus (HIV) and acquired immunodeficiency syndrome (AIDS), although the increased availability of antiretroviral therapies has allowed for some recovery. Many African countries have also started to experience lower fertility, particularly among urban educated women. These demographic changes promise to have significant effects on economic performance. But compared to other regions of the world, Sub-Saharan Africa is experiencing an extremely slow decline in fertility. While child mortality rates have declined, fertility rates have remained high, leading to high youth dependency. High youth dependency rates are exacerbated by the heavy burden of HIV/AIDS, particularly in East and Southern Africa, which has increased mortality among working-age adults.

In addition to the two potential economic dividends—increased labor income and increased savings—that a fast transformation in the age structure and decline in dependency ratios can bring about, there are three additional benefits. First, lower fertility is usually associated with delayed age of first birth and longer spaces between births, both of which improve maternal and child health. Second, a lower youth dependency ratio allows larger investments per child in schooling. Third, lower fertility increases the potential for female employment and hence investment in women's education and empowerment. The benefits are worthy goals in themselves, but they also help to facilitate the two economic dividends.

Sub-Saharan Africa faces big challenges, however, in harnessing its demographic dividend. The first is that the demographic transition is projected to occur very slowly. In the 1950s, the three regions in figure O.2 had declining working-age shares in their populations due to falling child mortality rates and higher youth dependency. From 1975 to 2010, East Asia experienced a rapid decline in fertility that reduced youth dependency and increased the working-age share from less than 1.5 to a peak of 2.5 over 35 years. This substantial increase in

Figure O.2 Actual and Projected Ratio of Working-Age Population 16–64 Years of Age to Dependents in Select World Regions, 1950–2100

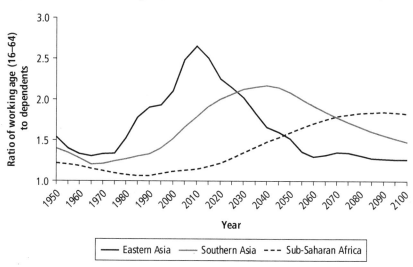

Source: UN Population Division 2013.
Note: Data after 2010 are projections based on medium-variant fertility.

East Asia closely parallels its economic takeoff: about one-third of the increased growth during the East Asian "economic miracle" can be attributed to the demographic dividend (Bloom, Canning, and Malaney 2000; Bloom and Williamson 1998). South Asia is following East Asia's lead, and its decline in fertility means that its working-age share is now rising rapidly and will peak in 2040.

In contrast, the projected decline in fertility in Sub-Saharan Africa implies that the working-age share started rising in 1990 but will not peak until 2080, a period of 90 years. Moreover, the ratio of working-age population per dependent will be less than 2 at its peak. Hence the impacts of the demographic transition on growth are expected to be small and slow in coming in Sub-Saharan Africa. A key question is whether the fertility decline in Sub-Saharan Africa can be accelerated so that the potential demographic dividend is larger and can occur more quickly.

The second challenge is that the potential of the demographic dividend is not always realized. While reductions in the youth dependency rate bring obvious benefits, the full potential for economic growth does not automatically follow. A large working-age population requires a comparably large demand for labor to reap the rewards of the demographic dividend. Without the appropriate social and economic policies, the extra labor supply can result in unemployment and underemployment, which can lead to political instability, elevated crime, and a deterioration of social capital (Urdal 2006). Intuitively, the key determinants of whether a country will capitalize on its demographic opportunity relate to how flexible the economy is and how well it can absorb a rapidly increasing labor force. Latin America and North Africa have both enjoyed substantial reductions in fertility and increases in the working-age share of their populations, but not the economic takeoff seen in East Asia (Bloom and Canning 2003).

Slow Declines in Fertility

The declines in both mortality and fertility have been slower in Sub-Saharan Africa than in other regions. Nevertheless, the under-five mortality rate has decreased substantially in Sub-Saharan Africa over the last 50 years (figure O.3). During 1950–55, 307 of 1,000 Sub-Saharan African children born annually did not survive to see their fifth birthday; by 2005–10, the under-five mortality rate was 126 per 1,000 (UN Population Division 2013). This is a remarkable achievement with little economic growth in most of the period. The health improvements have been driven largely by public health interventions rather than by rising incomes.

Today child mortality in Sub-Saharan Africa is on par with that of North Africa and South Asia in the 1980s. While the declines have been remarkable, the rates are still higher than for any other region in the world, and there are wide variations within the region. Southern Africa has relatively low child mortality rates, with a range of between 17 and 50 deaths per 1,000 live births. Mortality rates are almost twice as high in Middle, East, and West Africa

Figure O.3 Under-Five Mortality Rate in Select World Regions, 1960–2012

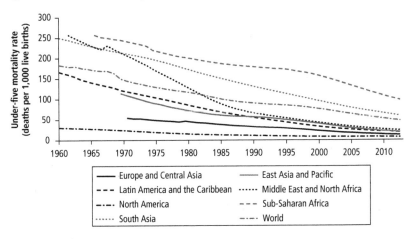

Source: World Bank 2012.

as in Southern Africa, with more than 150 deaths per 1,000 live births in some countries.

The fertility transition has also been slow. Fertility in Sub-Saharan Africa has declined, from 6.5 children per woman in 1950–55 to 5.4 in 2005–10, but much less than in other regions (figure O.4). In East Asia, fertility declined from 5.6 to 1.6 over the same period. Once again, regional averages mask large variations—for example, in the Democratic Republic of Congo and Niger, total fertility rates are rising.

The time gap between the decline in child mortality and the decline in fertility indicates that the population in Sub-Saharan Africa is set to rise rapidly. This rapid pace of population growth contrasts with the slow-growing or even declining populations in other regions, where fertility is much lower. By 2060 there will be about 10 billion people in the world—5.2 billion in Asia, 2.8 billion in Africa, 1.3 billion in the Americas, 0.7 billion in Europe, and 0.1 billion in the rest of the world. Thus Africa is poised to become a much larger part of the world population.

A key question is whether fertility in Africa will continue to decline slowly or whether the speed of the fertility transition will accelerate, as occurred in East Asia (Bongaarts and Casterline 2013). The reason for optimism about the prospects for an acceleration is that, while the decline in fertility has been slow overall, some countries have seen very rapid fertility declines. In addition, even in countries with high average fertility rates, some groups of women—for example, those with a high school level of education—are often close to replacement fertility. High fertility is not a foregone conclusion in Africa.

Figure O.4 Total Fertility Rate in Select World Regions, 1960–2012

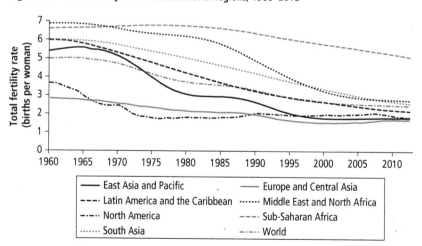

Source: World Bank 2012.

Variations in the Fertility Transition

A group of countries in Southern Africa has total fertility rates of less than 3 (table O.1). Another group, including the Democratic Republic of Congo, Niger, and Nigeria, has very high fertility rates exceeding 6 children per woman. Between these extremes are countries at varying levels of fertility. Ghana and Zimbabwe have total fertility rates between 3 and 4 children per woman, Ethiopia and Kenya have rates between 4 and 5, while Tanzania and Uganda have rates between 5 and 6.

Table O.1 also shows fertility by country income level. There is a clear correlation between higher income and lower fertility in most countries, though there are some outliers to the relationship. In particular, Angola, the Republic

Table O.1 Total Fertility Rate in Sub-Saharan Africa, by Country Income Level, 2012

GDP per capita (quintile)	Total fertility rate (births per woman)						
	1–1.99	2–2.99	3–3.99	4–4.99	5–5.99	6–6.99	7+
1 Lowest				Central African Republic Eritrea Liberia	Guinea Malawi Mozambique	Burundi Congo, Dem. Rep. Somalia	Niger
2				Comoros Ethiopia Guinea-Bissau Madagascar Rwanda Sierra Leone Sudan Togo	Burkina Faso Gambia, The Uganda		
3			Lesotho Zimbabwe	Benin Cameroon Kenya Senegal	South Sudan Tanzania	Chad Mali	
4		Cabo Verde	Djibouti Ghana	Côte d'Ivoire Mauritania São Tomé and Príncipe	Congo, Rep. Zambia	Nigeria	
5 Highest	Mauritius	Botswana Seychelles South Africa	Namibia Swaziland	Equatorial Guinea Gabon	Angola		

Source: World Bank 2012.

of Congo, Nigeria, and Zambia, have high fertility despite having high gross domestic product (GDP) per capita. However, these countries have high levels of income from natural resources, which boosts average GDP per capita but may not translate into higher living standards for most people.

There is tremendous heterogeneity in fertility levels in Africa, as evidenced in table O.1. In Niger, Nigeria, and Zambia, total fertility rates since 1960 have remained consistently high, with at most only very modest declines (figure O.5). In another group of countries, including Kenya, fertility declined rapidly in the 1980s, but stalled after 1995. In still another group, including Ethiopia, fertility declined starting around 1995, while in South Africa, it fell rapidly throughout the time period. In addition to this variation across countries, there is great variability within countries. Fertility is lowest in the capital cities, with slightly higher levels in urban areas (figure O.6). It is highest in rural areas.

That some countries and areas within countries have moved very rapidly to low fertility rates points to possibilities for the continent as a whole.

Speeding up the Transition

Why is the demographic transition, particularly the fertility transition, so slow in Africa, and can its acceleration bring a faster, and larger, demographic dividend? While a faster demographic transition is advantageous, partly for the income gains it brings, people care about things other than income, including their health and the number of children they have. Most of the benefits of the

Figure O.5 Total Fertility Rate in Select Sub-Saharan African Countries, 1960–2012

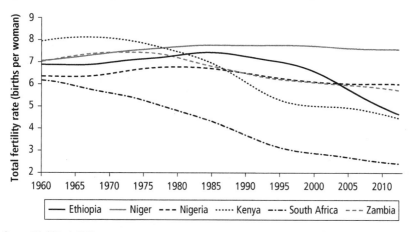

Source: World Bank 2012.

Figure O.6 Total Fertility Rate in Ethiopia, Ghana, and Kenya, by Rural-Urban Residence, Various Years

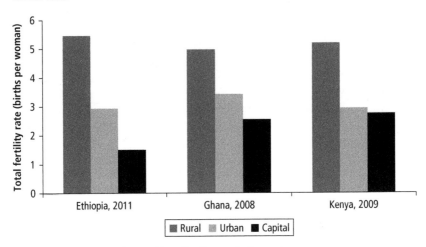

Source: Based on most recent demographic and health survey for the country.

demographic dividend accrue directly to families that decide to delay the age of first birth, improve the spacing of births, and limit the total number of births (Bloom et al. 2012). These benefits come in the form of greater health and work opportunities for women, better health and education for children, and higher incomes and savings for households.

Policies that allow families to make informed decisions and provide the means to implement these decisions are critical. Gender equality is an important part of decision making regarding family size because women bear most of the direct costs of childbearing. All of the policies for accelerating the transition are worthwhile regardless of the potential demographic dividend and independent of their effect on fertility. A healthier and better educated population with the ability to make choices about family structure is an inherent good.

Encouraging Smaller Families

Fertility has five main social determinants: child mortality, urbanization, female education, the time cost of children, and desired investments in children.

A key driver of desired fertility is child morbidity and mortality. One of the strongest empirical regularities in demography is that the fertility transition starts typically after the mortality transition is already well established (figure O.1). Immediately following the death of a child, a couple may choose to have another child in order to compensate for, or replace, the loss. And couples in a high-mortality environment may have many children with the expectation that some of their children will not survive (Ben-Porath 1976; Sah 1991; Schultz 1969, 1976). The correlation between the mortality rate and the fertility rate is clearly positive (figure O.7). Estimates suggest that each child death leads to about one additional birth (Hossain, Phillips, and LeGrand 2007; LeGrand and Phillips 1996; LeGrand et al. 2003). In high-mortality environments, around 25 percent of children die. This implies that in a pretransition society with fertility at around 8 children per woman, completely eliminating child mortality might decrease fertility by about 2 children per woman. The high under-five mortality rate is likely a very important driver of the high levels of desired fertility in Sub-Saharan Africa, and reducing child mortality would thus speed up the fertility transition. Table O.2 provides the information for countries in Sub-Saharan Africa. Some countries, such as Chad, the Democratic Republic of Congo, Mali, Nigeria, and Somalia, still have very high rates of child mortality and fertility; investing in child health may be a prerequisite for reducing fertility in this group of countries.

In agricultural societies where families work their own land, children can add to household production from an early age (Schultz 1997). Even in these rural settings, however, children are usually net consumers from the household's point of view (Lee 2000; Lee and Kramer 2002). In urban areas, the separation between the home and the workplace is greater, and there are fewer opportunities for children to engage in productive activities. Together with the higher cost of living in cities, these factors may explain the lower fertility rates in urban settings.

Figure O.7 Correlation between Under-Five Mortality Rate and Total Fertility Rate in Sub-Saharan Africa and Rest of the World, 2012

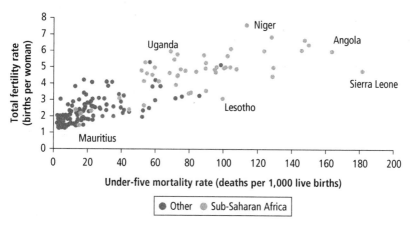

Source: World Bank 2012.

Table 0.2 Under-Five Mortality Rate and Total Fertility Rate in Sub-Saharan African Countries, 2012

Under-five mortality rate, by quintile	Total fertility rate						
	1–1.99	2–2.99	3–3.99	4–4.99	5–5.99	6–6.99	7+
1 Lowest (13.1–55.0)	Mauritius	Botswana Cabo Verde Seychelles South Africa	Namibia	Eritrea Rwanda São Tomé and Príncipe	Tanzania		
2 (58.2–73.1)			Ghana	Ethiopia Gabon Kenya Madagascar Senegal Sudan	Gambia, The Malawi Uganda		
3 (74.8–94.9)			Djibouti Swaziland Zimbabwe	Benin Cameroon Comoros Liberia Mauritania	Mozambique Zambia		
4 (95.5–113.5)			Lesotho	Côte d'Ivoire Equatorial Guinea Togo	Burkina Faso Congo, Rep. Guinea South Sudan	Burundi	Niger
5 Highest (123.7–181.6)				Central African Republic Guinea-Bissau Sierra Leone	Angola	Chad Congo, Dem. Rep. Mali Nigeria Somalia	

Source: World Bank 2012.
Note: Under-five mortality is deaths per 1,000 live births; total fertility is births per woman.

While a couple may prefer to have more children, the costs of an additional child can be high, particularly when considering the high time costs of child care, especially for women. As women's educational attainment and potential earnings rise, they face an increasing cost of childbearing in wages forgone. While fertility tends to rise with increased male education and income, it falls rapidly with increased female education, further reflecting the trade-off. For women with no education in Ethiopia, the total fertility rate is just under 6 children per woman (figure O.8). For women with 12 years of schooling—women who have completed high school—fertility is less than 2 children per woman. An education reform that led to a substantial increase in female education in Ethiopia had similarly large effects on fertility, suggesting that the effect is causal (Pradhan and Canning 2013). Similar causal effects have been found in several studies. For example, an education reform in Kenya that increased the length of primary education by a year had the effect of increasing female educational attainment, delaying marriage, and lowering fertility (Chicoine 2012). Another study in Kenya, a randomized control trial by Duflo et al. (2006), finds that reducing the cost of school uniforms not only reduced dropout rates, but also reduced teenage marriage and childbearing. Osili and Long (2008) examine education reform in Nigeria and find that increasing female education by one year reduced early fertility by 0.26 birth.

The inverse relationship between fertility and women's educational attainment is evident in many Sub-Saharan African countries, including Ethiopia. Currently, education levels are rising rapidly in Sub-Saharan Africa (figure O.9), which means that fertility may decline in the future. But in many countries boys are still much more likely to be enrolled in school than girls.

The rising level of education is very promising, but there is potential for rising inequality as well. Low fertility among the highly educated will mean higher parental investment and smaller families, leading to even better health and education in the next generation. But high fertility among women with

Figure O.8 Total Fertility Rate in Ethiopia, by Female Educational Attainment, 1998–2011

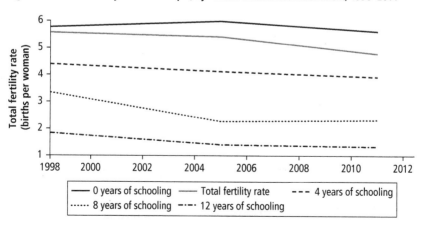

Source: Demographic and health survey for Ethiopia (2011).

Figure O.9 Secondary School Enrollment in Sub-Saharan Africa, by Gender, 1970–2012

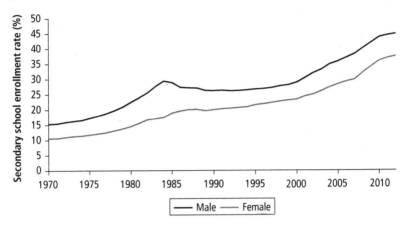

Source: World Bank 2012.

low education and large families may mean correspondingly low investment in children, perpetuating the gap in education, health, and income. This inter-generational transmission of inequality can be broken to some extent by public education and health programs, since public sector investments per child can increase for all children as the national youth dependency rate declines (Eloundou-Enyegue 2013). But there may well be a rise in inequality at the start of the transition, as households with high education and income are the first to move toward low fertility.

The decline in fertility can also be examined with regard to a change in couples' preferences for having many children and making small investments per child to having fewer children and making larger investments per child. As incomes and education increase, couples place more importance on better health and more schooling for their children, which they can achieve by having fewer children. This shift in a couple's preference for fewer but "higher-quality" children is known as the quantity-quality trade-off (Becker 1981; Hanushek 1992). In addition to parental income and education, the returns to education and human capital accumulation also influence parental preferences for having fewer children. If technological progress raises the returns to schooling, families may decide to have fewer children so that they can invest more in the education of each child.

Changing Social Norms and Gender Equality

Complementing the empirical evidence on the links between household characteristics, incentives, and fertility is evidence that changes in fertility reflect shifts in social and cultural norms (Bongaarts and Watkins 1996). When environmental or social changes that affect the fertility of some groups do take place, they may have spillover effects that permeate through the entire community. For this reason, changes in fertility behaviors may be more readily observed and studied at an aggregate level. Moreover, the presence of spillover effects at the societal level may help to explain why the fertility transition is slow to get started in some countries but picks up quickly once the transition gets under way.

The importance of social norms in fertility decision making highlights the need to design policies and programs that are tailored to address them (Bongaarts and Watkins 1996). Political leadership in discussing fertility and family size can help to set social norms. Media messages demonstrating the health and economic benefits of smaller families might be sufficient to alter behavior (Westoff and Koffman 2011). Social norms spread mainly through social networks and can reduce fertility through the mechanisms of social learning through peers and social influence. Social norms typically take longer to spread in heterogeneous societies than in homogeneous ones.

Gender inequality is important in determining fertility behavior. Men and women in Africa often have different fertility preferences, with women's desired fertility generally lower than that of men (Voas 2003). This is likely the case because women bear more of the costs associated with childbearing and child-rearing. The amount of care time invested, the exposure to health risks, and the opportunities forgone are greater for women than for men. There is also evidence that women are more directly attached to the welfare of their children than men. When given similar financial resources, women spent more on child health, education, and nutrition than men (Thomas 1990, 1994).

As a result of these factors, the number of children a couple has depends directly on a woman's position in the household and her bargaining power relative to that of her husband. Larger gaps between a husband and wife in age, education, and earnings are associated with more distorted bargaining power and higher household position for men, who tend to be older, more educated, and higher earners than their wives. This imbalance in bargaining power and household status allows men's preferences to dominate household decision making regarding work, resource allocation, and ideal family size. Increasing female education and improving labor market opportunities for women to put them on a par with men thus affects a range of decisions, including those that determine fertility.

Delaying the Age of Marriage and Planning Families

Reducing child mortality, improving women's education, influencing social norms, and promoting gender equality are factors that determine desired fertility. In contrast, the proximate determinants of fertility are the biological processes or behavioral mechanisms for women and couples to regulate their fertility directly. The following are the key proximate determinants of fertility:

- Postpartum insusceptibility to pregnancy due to extended periods of exclusive breastfeeding (postpartum lactational amenorrhea) and sexual abstinence after birth
- Nonmarriage and lack of sexual activity, usually by delays in the age of marriage, cohabitation, or sexual debut
- Use of contraception
- Abortion.

It is estimated that without any control of fertility through one of these four proximate channels, women would have an average of just over 15 children during their reproductive lives (Bongaarts 1978). Actual fertility rates in a population are generally much lower than this theoretical limit. The highest fertility rate is around 7 children per woman in rural areas of the Democratic Republic of Congo. Total fertility rates are much lower in Ethiopia and Ghana, particularly in the capital cities and other urban areas. In Accra and Addis Ababa, for example, fertility is close to around 2 children—the replacement level of fertility.

Different proximate determinants of fertility play varying roles in determining realized fertility (figure O.10). A major factor in reducing fertility below the theoretical limit is postpartum insusceptibility, with a smaller contribution from a

Figure O.10 Proximate Determinants of Fertility in the Democratic Republic of Congo, Ethiopia, and Ghana, Various Years

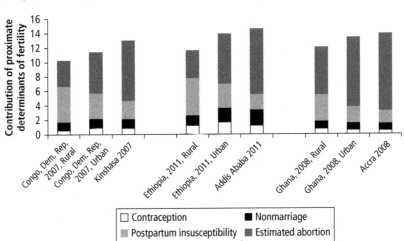

Source: Madhavan and Guengant 2013.

lack of or delay in marriage and very small effects of contraception and estimated abortion (Rossier 2003).[2] As fertility rates fall, the role of postpartum insusceptibility declines because fewer births imply fewer periods of insusceptibility. A major explanation for the difference in fertility between capital cities and rural areas is the higher age of marriage in capital cities, with smaller effects from contraceptive use and abortion. A study in Ethiopia finds that education reform had significant effects on the educational attainment of girls and the fertility of young women—mostly due to delay in the age of marriage (Pradhan and Canning 2013).

Contraception plays an important role in determining fertility, although the precise effect of family planning programs has been debated in the literature (Bongaarts 1994; Pritchett 1994). Recent analysis over a wide set of countries suggests that, although the gap between actual and desired fertility is less than 0.5 child per woman in most countries, the average gap is much higher in Sub-Saharan Africa, where it is more than 2 children per woman (Canning et al. 2013). These findings imply that family planning and other supply-side factors could potentially have a much bigger role in lowering fertility in Sub-Saharan Africa. Family planning is also highly cost-effective. Reproductive health, child health, and family planning interventions were carried out in Matlab, Bangladesh, in the 1980s and in Navrongo, Ghana, in the 1990s, with some areas receiving the treatment in each site and other areas acting as controls. In both countries there was a reduction in total fertility of about 1 to 1.5 children per woman in the treatment areas relative to the control areas (Debpuur et al. 2002; Schultz 2009a).

While the high desired fertility in Sub-Saharan Africa means that large reductions in fertility will likely require prior reductions in child mortality and female education, the gap between actual and desired fertility means that family planning can play a substantial role. Family planning allows women and families to achieve their desired family size through better timing and spacing of births and reduces the total number of births; these effects can bring large welfare benefits. In addition, the effects of family planning interventions are very quick, while the effects of the more distal determinants of desired fertility are slower; mortality expectations may lag behind reductions in child mortality and the fertility effects of girls' education only occur when these girls reach reproductive age. For these reasons, family planning interventions have the best prospects of speeding up the fertility transition in the near term, which may make them an attractive option for policy makers.

Human Development Payoffs

The concept of the demographic dividend was originally constructed to explain the link between the demographic transition, changes in age structure, and economic growth. While the main focus of the literature has been on economic outcomes, the demographic transition has also had profound impacts on human development, regardless of the economic return.

Better Child and Maternal Health

The transition from high fertility to low fertility can do much to improve maternal and child health in Sub-Saharan Africa. Smaller family size allows for increased investment per child in health, nutrition, and education. While it is well understood that improvements in education can lead to better economic outcomes, investments in health and nutrition in early childhood can have large effects on educational outcomes and incomes in adulthood. Early childhood health and nutrition affect children's physical and cognitive development, which in turn contributes to long-term health and economic well-being (Bleakley 2010). Moreover, improvements in child health have long-lasting effects on adult health and longevity (Barker 1992). Better adult health can further reinforce the incentive to continue investing in education and human capital development, given that a longer, healthy life span increases the time for recouping the returns to educational investments (Kalemli-Ozcan 2003).

Lower fertility rates are usually associated with increases in the mother's age at first birth and in the time interval between births (Finlay and Canning 2013). Delaying the age at first birth can reduce the pregnancy and childbirth risks facing adolescent girls. In Sub-Saharan Africa, teenage births are associated with a significantly higher risk of child mortality, child stunting, and maternal anemia (Finlay, Özaltin, and Canning 2011). Very short birth intervals do not allow the mother to recover from the physical stress of childbearing, increasing the risk of pregnancy-related and postpartum obstetric complications. Birth gaps of less than 18 months are associated with a doubling of the relative risk of child mortality (figure O.11). Birth spacing of at least 18 months between children contributes to substantial improvements in child and maternal health outcomes. Reducing high-risk early fertility and lengthening the interval between births can substantially improve the health and well-being of women and their children by decreasing the risk of maternal and child mortality (Ahmed et al. 2012; Jain 2011). These impacts point to the human development payoffs of supporting family planning for timing and spacing births, independent of any effect on total family size.

Investments in Girls' Education

Lowering fertility can increase educational investments through several mechanisms. Perhaps most well-known is the quantity-quality trade-off described earlier, through which fertility decisions and the allocation of investments in human capital are determined jointly. The demographic-economic relationship between fertility and education implies that lower fertility is both a cause and a consequence of increased educational investments; in particular, both fertility

Figure O.11 Adjusted Relative Risk of Infant Mortality in Sub-Saharan Africa, by Birth Interval, 1987–2011

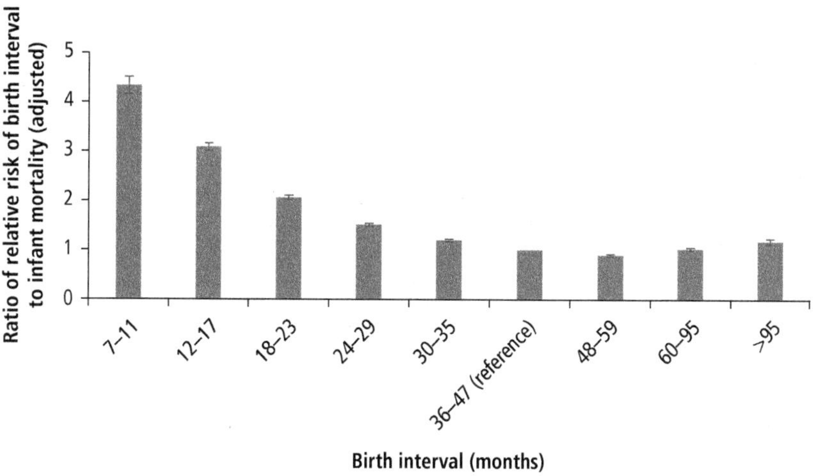

Birth interval (months)

Source: Finlay and Canning 2013.
Note: Depicts the relative risk of infant mortality in Sub-Saharan Africa from the time since the previous birth, adjusting for other household characteristics.

and child schooling are determined by a common set of factors that affect families' incentives and preferences.

The provision of family planning services to people who desire smaller families can both reduce fertility and increase schooling. This effect may be particularly pronounced for girls' schooling because girls in high-fertility households are frequently kept out of school to care for their younger siblings. The Matlab study[3] finds strong effects of lower fertility where family planning interventions helped to lower fertility rates and improve child health and educational outcomes (Schultz 2009b). In addition to the results from Matlab, a study in Sub-Saharan Africa finds that unplanned births reduced the enrollment of young children and increased the dropout rate of older children, suggesting that additional births could tighten the resource constraints facing families (Eloundou-Enyegue and Williams 2006; Koissy-Kpein, Kuepie, and Tenikue 2012).

Aggregate spending on children is a fairly constant share of national resources in many countries and is independent of the size of the youth cohort, which implies that lower fertility can increase the resources potentially available to each child (Mason et al. 2009). Countries with the largest gains in spending per student tend to be those with lower rates of fertility and youth dependency (map O.1). However, the link is not guaranteed. Zimbabwe, for example, has seen large reductions in fertility, but even faster reductions in overall spending on education, reducing the amount of spending per child.

Map 0.1 Contribution of Age Structure to Recent Changes in Resources per Child in Sub-Saharan Africa, 1990–2050

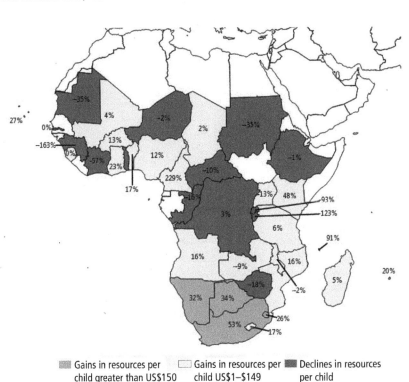

Gains in resources per child greater than US$150   Gains in resources per child US$1–$149   Declines in resources per child

Source: Eloundou-Enyegue 2013.
Note: Country values indicate percentage change in resources per child.

Investments in education can have substantial effects on earnings as an adult: each additional year of schooling is associated with a 10 percent increase in wages (Psacharopoulos 1994). Smaller youth cohorts can therefore increase the availability of educational funding per child and can lead to an expansion in school enrollment as well as an improvement in educational quality (Eloundou-Enyegue and Giroux 2013).

Jobs Payoffs

Economic growth is driven by increasing the amount of inputs used for production or by increasing the productivity of those inputs. One of the most important inputs for production is labor, which accounts for about two-thirds of all output produced (Hall and Jones 1999). Yet most models of economic growth do not focus on labor supply. Instead, they assume a fixed number of workers per capita. But substantial variations in the number of workers per capita over time can have significant impacts on GDP growth. For example, in East Asia the number of workers per capita has risen sharply over the last 40 years. This increase in labor supply, together with increases in physical and human capital inputs as opposed to increases in total factor productivity (TFP), accounts for most of the economic growth and development associated with the Asian economic miracle (Young 1995).

Increases in the workforce per capita stem primarily from two sources. One is the age structure of the population, which determines the ratio of working-age people to the total population. Labor force participation rates vary by age, with the highest rates between ages 25 and 60. So, a change in the population age structure can affect the labor supply per capita. The second source is a change in gender-specific labor force participation rates. While participation rates for men of working age tend to be uniformly high over time, those for women can fluctuate dramatically, which can rapidly change the total number of workers and thus output per capita.

Aggregate demographic forces can also affect the productivity of workers. An increase in the labor force can reduce the amount of available land and capital stock per worker, lowering productivity. In the long run, a shortage of capital can be corrected by investment, but not for the availability of land. In addition, a larger youth cohort may receive fewer resources and less schooling, which could reduce their educational attainment and their productivity when they enter the labor force.

Changing Age Structure

The most direct effect of demographic change on the labor force is through the age structure (figure O.12). The working-age range is conventionally defined as the population between ages 16 and 64, although the actual working-age range can be narrower or wider in practice, with children either working before age 16 or remaining in school after age 16 and older persons either taking early retirement or working longer into old age. In countries with high fertility rates, the rate of youth dependency is also high—the ratio of working-age people to dependents is around 1. As fertility falls, the youth dependency rate declines and the ratio of working-age people to dependents rises. When fertility falls to the replacement level of 2 children per woman, there are 2.5 workers per dependent. If output per worker stays constant, a rise in the working-age share of the population from 1 worker per dependent to 2.5 workers per dependent would lead to a 43 percent rise in income per capita. A few countries in Southern Africa have fertility rates comparable to those of North Africa and

Figure 0.12 Ratio of Working-Age Population 16–64 Years of Age to Dependents and Total Fertility Rate in Africa, 2010

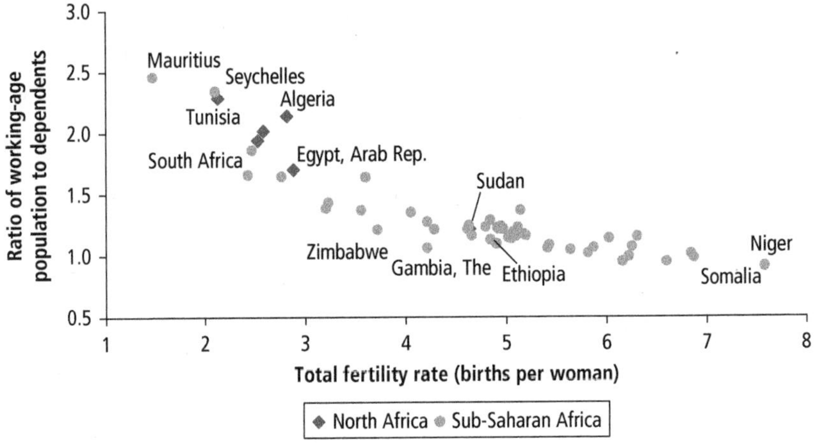

Source: Pradhan and Canning 2013.

a high ratio of working-age to dependent population, but most Sub-Saharan African countries still have high fertility rates.

More Women in the Workforce

The rapid economic growth of the Asian Tigers was fueled in large part by a rise in inputs associated with labor per capita, in part by an increase in the working-age share of the population, and in part by an increase in female labor force participation. Childrearing takes time and money, and the time required for child care may reduce the supply of labor. Fertility and female labor supply are decisions made in tandem. Women who have fewer children may decide to work more, and women who have good jobs and earn high wages may decide to have fewer children. In developed countries, the introduction of the contraceptive pill and legalization of abortion had significant impacts on fertility and led to increases in female participation in the labor force (Bailey 2006). Similarly, in Latin American countries, family planning services led to reductions in fertility and subsequent increases in female labor supply (Miller 2010).

But fertility reductions may have little effect on the female labor supply in the poorest developing countries, since almost all women in these countries work, independent of the number of children they have (Goldin 1994). In rural areas, women often work in the home and are usually either self-employed or unpaid workers in a family enterprise. In such settings, the household is a production unit as well as a consumption unit, and it is possible to combine child care with work.

This dual home-work environment may account for the small impact of family planning programs on female labor market participation in Matlab in rural Bangladesh; most of the labor market effect of the program was on female earnings (Schultz 2009b). In contrast, the workplace and home are often separated in urban environments in middle- and higher-income countries, making it more difficult to combine work and child care. But even in these settings, labor supply is not a simple binary choice. Women with low schooling and young children may undertake more flexible, less formal work rather than leave the labor market completely (Radhakrishnan 2010; Schultz 1990). This suggests that the effects of lower fertility on female labor supply may be seen primarily in more highly educated women in urban areas, who have the possibility of formal employment outside the home.

The demographic dividend resulting from a large supply of labor per capita due to favorable age structure and increased supply of female labor is not automatic (Bloom, Canning, and Sevilla 2003). Reductions in fertility do increase the working-age share of the population, but until fertility falls below the replacement level, future cohorts of working age are still larger than their predecessors. While the potential labor force per capita grows, the increase in labor supply must be matched by an increase in demand for labor to produce economic growth effectively. Countries with better governance and market-oriented economic polices experience substantial economic benefits when the fertility and youth dependency rates decline. But in the absence of good governance and appropriate economic policies, the labor supply effects may be wasted, and countries may miss their window of opportunity to attain a demographic dividend (Bloom, Canning, and Malaney 1999).

Economic Growth in Africa

The demographic transition generates a large supply-side shock to the economy, potentially increasing the number of workers, the human capital of the workforce, and the level of saving. But if the demographic dividend is to produce economic growth, this supply has to be matched by an increase in demand (box O.1). While many Asian countries benefited from the demographic dividend, Latin America and North Africa have seen much smaller economic gains from their changing age structure. The demographic transition raises the stakes for economic policy: the potential dividend magnifies the effects of good, or bad, policy choices.

One reason for being optimistic about the prospects for a demographic dividend in Africa is that, after a period of slow economic growth, the economic performance of the region has taken off in the last decade. Is this a short-run blip or a fundamental change? If the latter, it could be the start of a long-run

BOX 0.1

Cohort Size and Youth Unemployment

The demographic dividend occurs when the ratio of working-age to dependent population starts to rise. But the absolute number of young workers entering the labor force is also rising, and a large youth cohort can have negative effects on productivity. Being born into a large cohort, known as generational crowding, may reduce cohort wages and curtail individual labor supply (Korenman and Neumark 2000). The presence of a large youth cohort may also lead to large-scale youth unemployment. In Sub-Saharan Africa, it is more likely that large numbers of young workers will be forced to work in low-productivity sectors such as agriculture and informal household enterprises. Large inflows of youth into the labor market also make it difficult to generate enough jobs to ensure that youth are productively employed. The key challenge in realizing the demographic dividend is to employ the working-age share of the population productively, which will increase output per capita and economic growth.

---

improvement in economic performance and growth that can provide jobs for the large working-age cohorts that are coming.

GDP growth rates in Africa were more than 4 percent a year in the 1960s and then fell between 1970 and 1995 before returning to levels above 4 percent a year after 2005 (figure O.13). But population growth in the region has been steady at just below 2.5 percent a year. This steady rise in population implies that GDP growth is much lower in per capita terms; indeed, GDP per capita fell in Sub-Saharan Africa between 1980 and 1995.

Increased economic growth creates the fiscal space needed to sustain investments in maternal and child health and in quality education, especially for girls. Moreover, economic growth can create the jobs needed to harness workforce expansion and achieve even faster economic growth.

How the Age Structure Can Drive Growth

Four features are favorable to growth: a rising share of the working-age population, increasing physical capital per worker (Zelleke et al. 2013), rising TFP (Tahari et al. 2004), and rising human capital in the form of rising education (figure O.14). Employment growth in the form of higher participation rates for the working-age population has played a very minor role in the past, but current trends suggest that the continent is ready for transformational economic growth beyond natural resources.

Swings in TFP drive the results for most of the 50 years to 2010, with a sharp decline between 1970 and 1995 linked to poor economic performance. The declines in productivity in Sub-Saharan Africa during this period may be

Figure O.13 Growth of GDP and GDP per Capita in Sub-Saharan Africa, 1965–2010

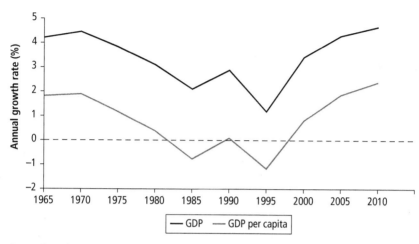

Source: Cho and Tien 2013.
Note: Data compiled from a sample of 32 balanced Sub-Saharan African countries.

Figure O.14 Growth of Income per Capita in Sub-Saharan Africa, by Source, 1960–2010

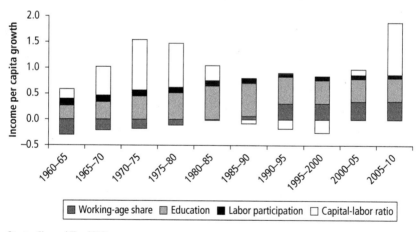

Source: Cho and Tien 2013.
Note: Data compiled from 32 Sub-Saharan African countries.

due in part to unfavorable geography (Bloom et al. 1998), political instability (Collier and Gunning 1999), poor economic policies (Easterly and Levine 1997), and rent seeking induced by natural resource exploitation (Sachs and Warner 2001). In particular, debt overhang following a decline in resource prices may reduce productivity (Deaton 1999). These overhangs are likely the result of large price movements, such as changes in the price of oil and raw materials, as well as competition from other countries.

Since the mid-1990s, the contribution of agriculture to GDP has fallen and that of industry has risen. Simultaneously, the workforce has shifted away from agriculture and into higher-productivity jobs in industry and services; productivity is usually quite low in agriculture relative to other sectors. This sectoral shift is usually associated with rapid economic growth (Bloom et al. 2010). In Africa, the relative share of industry in GDP remained fairly steady at around 25 percent between 1970 and 2000. Since 2000, it has risen to about 30 percent. In contrast to wide swings in some other variables, increasing levels of education made a steady contribution to economic growth in Africa over the whole period.

As some African countries, particularly those in Southern Africa, began moving through the demographic transition in the 1990s, the youth dependency rate fell and the working-age share of the population rose, indicating an increase in the number of workers and in income per capita (figure O.15). This positive effect of a changing age structure contrasts with the situation before 1985, when youth dependency was rising and the working-age population share was declining, slowing economic growth. A rise in labor force participation rates also contributed to economic growth, but the effect was very small.

The decomposition described here is at the regional level, which can hide amazing heterogeneity in all of the variables driving these changes. For example, some countries are growing much faster than others, likely for different reasons.

Figure O.15 Labor Income and Consumption per Capita in Kenya, by Age, 1994

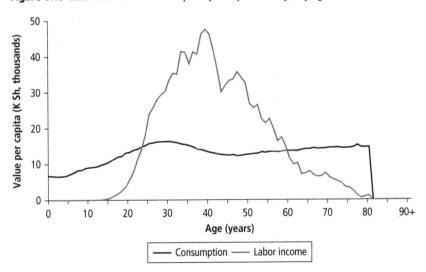

Source: National Transfer Accounts (http://www.ntaccounts.org/web/nta/show).

And fertility rates—which directly determine the working-age structure of the population and therefore contribute differently to slowing growth (for countries with high dependency ratios) or driving growth (for countries with low dependency ratios)—vary from country to country.

Savings Payoffs

Rapid economic growth in East Asia was mainly due to increases in factor inputs—most notably labor, capital, and education (Young 1995). Improvements in TFP played a minor role. All of the Asian Tigers enjoyed a surge in labor force per capita due to changes in the working-age share of the population and female labor force participation as well as increased savings and investment. The private saving rate in Taiwan, China, rose from around 5 percent in the 1950s to well over 20 percent in the 1980s and 1990s. Saving rates vary by age and are highest for Taiwanese households with heads who are between 50 and 60 years old. The rise in saving in Taiwan, China, and the other Asian Tigers can be explained in part by changes in the population age structure and in part by increases in life expectancy, which increase the incentive to save for retirement.

The life-cycle pattern of labor income is considerably different from that of consumption (Mwabu, Muriithi, and Mutegi 2011). Consumption by age is fairly flat, though somewhat lower for children than for adults, but labor income is concentrated in the working-age years and peaks at around age 40 (figure O.15). In Kenya, consumption exceeds labor income before age 23 and after age 60. This deficit of labor income to consumption can be financed by public or private transfers, by borrowing, or by accumulated assets.

In most countries, the young rely mainly on private transfers from other household members for their consumption and receive some public transfers for health and education. For the elderly, a wide range of approaches are used to finance consumption across the world, with some countries relying on private savings, others on government transfers, and others on private or family transfers. Family transfers to fund the consumption of the elderly are significant in East Asia. In most countries and regions of the world, however, funds tend to flow in the opposite direction, as the elderly make transfers to younger family members. In Sub-Saharan Africa, there are few data on age-specific income and consumption. In South Africa, despite a government-provided old-age pension, the major source of financing for old-age consumption is private savings (Oosthuizen 2013). It seems likely that people in most poor African countries rely on family transfers and, to some extent, private savings.

The need for income in old age implies that working-age adults, and especially older working-age adults, typically save for retirement, although this depends heavily on the incentives in the public pension system (Bloom et al. 2007). In Asia, rising working-age shares in the population were associated with a boom in savings and investment. The effect is expected to be less dramatic in

Africa, at least in the short run. In aggregate data, savings are higher when the working-age share of the population is larger. But there is also a strong income effect, because national saving rates are very low in low-income countries. In household data for very poor African countries, there is little evidence of life-cycle saving. For the poor, most savings are precautionary, in the event of health or income shocks in the near future, and are accrued in physical rather than financial assets (Aryeetey and Udry 2000). In higher-income countries, such as South Africa, there is substantial saving for retirement among workers in the formal sector. This mechanism may become more important for poorer countries over time as workers transition from informal to formal employment. In the short run, however, most of the poorer countries in the region need to maintain inflows of foreign borrowing and foreign direct investment to finance investment and to maintain or increase the capital-labor ratio.

Investment Payoffs

Investment and capital formation have been drivers of economic growth in Sub-Saharan Africa over the last decade (figure O.16). Between 1985 and 2000, capital per worker declined because of low investment rates and large increases in the workforce. From 2005 to 2010, investment escalated tremendously, caus-ing Sub-Saharan Africa to witness the highest rate of growth of capital per worker it has ever seen. There is a large gap between investment and savings in Sub-Saharan Africa, with about half of investment funded by the public sector, by borrowing abroad, or by FDI. In particular, FDI has risen sharply, from an annual rate of about 1 percent of GDP in 1995 to around 6 percent of GDP today. This boom in FDI explains a large part of the region's recent economic growth.

As with most of the other variables in this decomposition of regional eco-nomic growth, the level and nature of FDI hide considerable heterogeneity among countries, and these differences are important because the nature of FDI may have different impacts on expanding employment in different coun-tries. Resource-rich countries (mainly oil-producing) are likely to benefit from rising commodity (oil) prices. Countries with greater political stability (such as reduced conflict) are likely to attract FDI and induce TFP growth. Countries with better human capital are likely to create an economic environment condu-cive to research and development and innovation, which can drive TFP growth. Countries with more openness (such as members of a customs union) are also a better environment for TFP growth.

Countries in Sub-Saharan Africa fall into three categories: oil-producing, non-oil resource-rich, and resource-poor countries. FDI has grown in all three, but at different rates (figure O.16). There has been a large increase in the share of FDI in GDP among resource-rich countries (both oil and nonoil), particularly in the late 2000s. But there has also been a substantial increase among resource-poor countries. The nature of FDI is important because it will affect the likelihood of

Figure O.16 FDI as a Share of GDP in Sub-Saharan African Countries, by Resource Status, 1980–2010

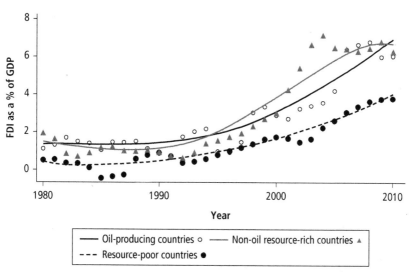

Source: Cho and Tien 2013.

investments that will produce jobs: generating high-paying jobs for the youth bulge moving into working age is essential to capturing the economic payoffs.

The growth story for Africa is promising, with three notable contributors to the regional growth spurt: the potential for a favorable demographic structure if the demographic transition is accelerated in lagging countries, the increase in physical capital through investment, and the progress in total factor productivity.

What the Demographic Dividend Could Deliver

Growth decompositions can serve as the basis for modeling how changes in fertility can affect economic growth. Using mortality projections as the constant, various fertility scenarios were constructed for Nigeria tracing the economic consequences associated with each of them. Based on the model of Ashraf, Weil, and Wilde (2013), this decomposition takes into account the effects of fertility on age structure, female labor market participation, educational investments, changes in the capital-labor ratio, and industrialization. Figure O.17 presents projections for income per capita (adjusted for real purchasing power parity) for Nigeria using data from the United Nations population projections as a baseline (UN Population Division 2013). The low-, medium-, and high-fertility scenarios diverge slowly and eventually differ by about half a child so that the TFR under the low-fertility scenario is eventually about 1 child per woman lower than the total fertility rate in the high-fertility scenario. Under these scenarios, income per capita in the high-fertility scenario is projected to be just over

Figure 0.17 Income per Capita under High-, Medium- and Low-Variant Scenarios in Nigeria, 2010–2100

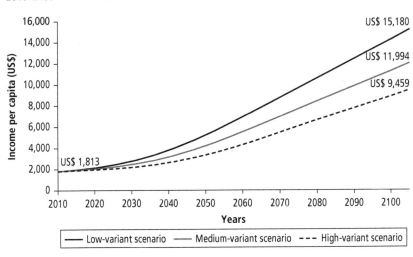

Source: Canning, Karra, and Wilde 2013.

US$9,000 by 2060 (compared with just under US$2,000 today), while income per capita in the low-fertility scenario is projected to be more than US$13,000 by 2060. The low-fertility scenario raises the growth of income per capita by about 0.7 percentage point per year.

Policies to Speed up the Demographic Transition

To reap a large demographic dividend in the near term, Africa requires polices that accelerate the reduction in child mortality and help couples to achieve a smaller family size. A faster demographic transition will make the short-term benefits of the demographic transition much larger. A second set of policies takes advantage of the supply-side potential released by the demographic transition.

Policies in three key areas would help to accelerate the fertility transition and increase the demographic dividend: reductions in child mortality, increases in female education, and improved access to comprehensive family planning services. Improvements in these three areas are desirable regardless of the potential economic payoffs, but they should receive even higher priority than they do today.

The first set of policies is intended to reduce child (under-five) mortality. Independent of its intrinsic value, reducing child mortality will also reduce desired fertility. While many Sub-Saharan countries have made large improvements over the last decade, child mortality remains high (Lozano et al. 2011). The leading causes of child mortality are complications during pregnancy and childbirth, newborn illness, childhood infections, malnutrition, and HIV/AIDS (Kinney et al. 2010). Cost-effective preventive interventions that can substantially reduce childhood mortality include maternal tetanus toxoid vaccination, exclusive breastfeeding, clean cord care, immunizations, vitamin A supplementation, prevention of mother-to-child transmission of HIV, and expansion of the use of insecticide-treated mosquito nets (Friberg et al. 2010). Neonatal resuscitation and case management of childhood illnesses such as diarrhea, pneumonia, malaria, and measles are also highly effective.

The second set of policies focuses on increasing female education. Educating women increases their ability to make decisions about their own and their children's health, their ability to access and use family planning methods, their bargaining position within the household, and their incentive to work. While school enrollment has been increasing in Africa, female enrollment has tended to lag behind male enrollment, particularly in some subregions. Enrollment is likely to be lower for girls than for boys when the household is poor or the girls have young siblings (Glick and Sahn 2000). Policies that can increase girls' enrollment in school include general increases in educational access, especially at the secondary level (Birdthistle et al. 2011). Conditional cash transfer programs requiring school attendance for cash disbursement have been shown to increase girls' school attendance substantially. In Bangladesh, the school stipend improved girls' achievement scores and led to a delay in their age of marriage. There is also evidence that unconditional transfers produced results, suggesting that reducing the pressure on household consumption marginally alleviated household poverty and allowed parents to send their girls to schools (Baird, McIntosh, and Özler 2009).

The third set of policies focuses on comprehensive family planning services. While the willingness to pay for contraception varies, women are more likely to buy contraception if the prices are highly subsidized, particularly those women who do not work and want fewer children than their husband (Prata et al. 2013). Reducing the cost of access to family planning services for low-income women and women whose bargaining position within the household is weak is therefore desirable. The quality and cost of services offered alongside contraceptives affects the uptake of contraception. While most women in Sub-Saharan Africa know about contraception, many do not consider contraceptives safe and a substantial number of users report side effects (Aryeetey, Kotoh, and Hindin 2011). While some women who stop using injectable contraceptives cite costs and stockouts as reasons for discontinuing their use, most report side effects as the principal reason (Burke and Ambasa-Shisanya 2011). Counseling and treatment services to address the effects of contraceptive use and opportunities to switch between contraceptive methods to minimize side effects are important aspects of high-quality family planning. When high-quality services are provided in Sub-Saharan Africa, families use contraceptives mainly for timing and spacing births rather than for limiting them (Phillips et al. 2012). This suggests that family planning programs should emphasize reversible methods. It is also important to include other aspects of family planning such as information not only about the pros and cons of different methods but also about the benefits of delaying, spacing, and limiting births.

Policies to Reap the Demographic Dividend

To harness the demographic dividend, policies are required that both hasten the transition to smaller cohorts and enable cohorts to be productive. The number of policies and their prioritization will need to be nuanced for each country, depending on the state of its transition and its economic environment.

During the initial part of the demographic transition, the rise in the ratio of working-age to dependent population produces an automatic demographic dividend, but the dividend is even greater if young workers are employed productively. This may be difficult in the early part of the transition, when the absolute numbers of youth are rising and the economy might not be able to absorb the cohort into productive employment. However, there is scope for higher productivity in the formal sector, the agriculture sector, and the nonfarm informal sector.

The East Asian model focused on export-led growth. Africa could replace East Asia as the world's source of labor-intensive manufacturing due to rising wage rates in East Asia. In the past, political uncertainty deterred multinationals from setting up manufacturing bases in Africa. Despite low wages overall, Africa is a high-cost location because of the high cost of infrastructure and nonlabor inputs and the payment of high wages for workers with key skills. Trade barriers also add to costs (Iwanow and Kirkpatrick 2009). But the recent rise of FDI into Africa reflects a growing confidence in the region's manufacturing sector. In addition, expanding manufacturing increases the network of suppliers, which can encourage new investors to set up in Africa, generating the possibility of a rapid economic takeoff (Samir et al. 2010).

The challenge in most of Sub-Saharan Africa lies in engaging the large youth cohort in high-productivity formal sector jobs rather than in informal, low-productivity, low-wage jobs in agriculture or household-based enterprises. In higher-income countries such as South Africa, a large youth cohort can mean high youth unemployment. But in most Sub-Saharan countries, the large informal sector results in low unemployment rates, but with youth employed in low-productivity jobs.

One approach to harnessing the youth dividend is to increase the competitiveness of production in African countries and to expand exports and jobs in the formal sector. Despite low wages, much of Africa is not highly competitive in international markets due to government failures, high barriers to trade, lack of infrastructure, and lack of skilled manpower. Since most jobs are in the informal sector, policies can seek to raise the productivity of the informal sector. At the same time, policies can seek to increase the competitiveness of exports, which will expand the formal sector (World Bank 2013).

Raising agricultural productivity requires land policies that improve land titles and increase productivity—for example, policies that make credit available for investment in new farming techniques. It also requires policies that improve the skills needed to adopt high-productivity methods of farming and the infrastructure needed to connect farms to markets. Large numbers of informal household enterprises provide consumer services and consumables. Since these enterprises are outside the usual system of regulation, they may face harassment from the authorities. But they can also offer potential growth opportunities. By providing household enterprises with operating security and official recognition, governments can enable them to enter the formal sector eventually and to abide by formal regulations. This process may involve allotting official spaces to informal enterprises operating in cities and providing legal access to public infrastructure services such as water and electricity. As in the agriculture sector, the provision of financial services and skills can help informal enterprises to grow.

Prominent features of the Sub-Saharan African demographic transition will be the youth bulge and the higher labor force participation of women. Both can be addressed in part by employment policies ensuring that youth and particularly young women have appropriate labor skills. But the sheer size of the growing labor force means that youth and female employment policies will in themselves be inadequate. What is needed is a large increase in labor demand resulting from a substantial rise in economic growth. The demographic transition ensures the labor supply side of growth, but labor demand is needed to turn the transition into a demographic dividend.

In addition to increasing the opportunities for employment, Sub-Saharan Africa needs to prepare for the second demographic dividend by increasing savings for retirement. This effort requires setting up low-cost savings schemes accessible to workers in the informal and formal sectors and directing the boost in savings toward productive investment, eventually replacing foreign funds as the main source of investment financing.

There is a natural order of timing for the recommended policies, depending on a country's location in the demographic transition (table O.3). In countries with high fertility, policy makers should focus on the pace of the demographic transition. For high-fertility countries with high child mortality, reducing child mortality should be the highest priority. For countries with high fertility despite low child mortality, such as Tanzania, action on the other determinants of desired fertility, such as female education, is indicated. Family planning activities should be directed to countries with a high unmet need for family planning (Casterline and El-Zeini 2014).

In countries where fertility is falling and the working-age share is rising, the focus should be on creating high-productivity employment for the large working-age cohort and encouraging investments in the health and education of the smaller youth cohort. In more mature economies, with larger formal sectors, which are near the high point of their dividend, the focus should be on generating domestic saving and female labor force participation outside the home. Ensuring sufficient savings for retirement will also address the issue of an aging population that will emerge as the transition comes to an end.

These policy recommendations may be difficult to implement in fragile states and countries where some areas are not under the government's control. In such cases, lack of security may make any interventions difficult and economic development nearly impossible. Therefore, emphasis should be placed on maintaining child health, access to health care, and family planning, where possible, to develop the preconditions for a demographic dividend.

The growth in Africa's working-age population will be relentless and inevitable. Will that growth produce a demographic dividend or a demographic disaster? The answer is up to Africa's policy makers—today. With the right policies, Africa's transition to smaller families can be accelerated. With the right policies, Africa's labor markets can provide productive work for a rapidly growing workforce. With the right policies, Africa can reap a tremendous demographic dividend to propel its economic takeoff.

Table O.3 Policies to Reap the Demographic Dividend

Purpose	Policies
Accelerate the fertility decline	Reduce child mortality, morbidity, malnutrition
	Increase female education and gender equity
	Address social norms on fertility
	Reduce child marriage
	Expand comprehensive family planning programs
Reap the first economic dividend	Improve education and human capital
	Attract foreign direct investments
	Improve business environment to build demand for labor
	Reduce trade barriers
	Encourage female employment outside the home
Reap the second economic dividend	Improve policies and institutions for domestic savings and investment

Notes

1. The *World Development Report 2012* on gender equality and development identifies the following areas as key priorities for addressing gender disparities: lowering the deaths of girls and women, eliminating gender disadvantage in education, increasing economic opportunities and lowering the earning and productivity gaps between women and men, shrinking the gender difference in voice in households and societies, and limiting the reproduction of gender inequality across generations (World Bank 2011). This book encompasses the recommendations of the *World Development Report 2012* regarding gender empowerment and specifically regarding the health of women and girls, educational opportunity, and labor participation in the formal sector.
2. Abortion rates are difficult to estimate from survey data due to stigma and underreporting. They are therefore modeled using a regression framework proposed by the Guttmacher Institute.
3. The Matlab and Navrongo studies are cited because they were designed to capture the causal impact of family planning on lowering fertility. Many other studies capture only correlations.

References

Ahmed, S., Q. Li, L. Liu, and AO Tsui. 2012. "Maternal Deaths Averted by Contraceptive Use: An Analysis of 172 Countries." *The Lancet* 380 (9837): 111–25.

Aryeetey, E., and C. Udry. 2000. "Saving in Sub-Saharan Africa." CID Working Paper 38, Harvard University, Center for International Development, Cambridge, MA.

Aryeetey, R., A. Kotoh, and M. Hindin. 2011. "Knowledge, Perceptions, and Ever Use of Modern Contraception among Women in the Ga East District, Ghana." *African Journal of Reproductive Health* 14 (4): 2335–45.

Ashraf, Q. H., D. N. Weil, and J. Wilde. 2013. "The Effect of Fertility Reduction on Economic Growth." *Population and Development Review* 39 (1): 97–130.

Bailey, M. J. 2006. "More Power to the Pill: The Impact of Contraceptive Freedom on Women's Life Cycle Labor Supply." *Quarterly Journal of Economics* 121 (1): 289–320.

Baird, S., C. McIntosh, and B. Özler. 2009. "Designing Cost-Effective Cash Transfer Programs to Boost Schooling among Young Women in Sub-Saharan Africa." Policy Research Working Paper 5090, World Bank, Development Research Group, Washington, DC.

Barker, D. J. P. 1992. *The Fetal and Infant Origins of Adult Disease.* London: BMJ Books.

Becker, G. S. 1981. *A Treatise on the Family.* Cambridge, MA: Harvard University Press.

Ben-Porath, Y. 1976. "Fertility Response to Child Mortality: Micro Data from Israel." *Journal of Political Economy* 84 (4): S163–78.

Birdthistle, I., K. Dickson, M. Freeman, and L. Javidi. 2011. "What Impact Does the Provision of Separate Toilets for Girls at Schools Have on Their Primary and Secondary School Enrolment, Attendance, and Completion? A Systematic Review of the

Evidence." University of London, Institute of Education, Social Science Research Unit, EPPI-Centre.

Bleakley, H. 2010. "Health, Human Capital, and Development." *Annual Review of Economics* 2: 283–310.

Bloom, D. E., and D. Canning. 2003. "From Demographic Lift to Economic Liftoff: The Case of Egypt." *Applied Population and Policy* 1 (1): 15–24.

Bloom, D. E., D. Canning, G. Fink, and J. E. Finlay. 2009. "Fertility, Female Labor Force Participation, and the Demographic Dividend." *Journal of Economic Growth* 14 (2): 79–101.

———. 2012. "Microeconomic Foundations of the Demographic Dividend." PGDA Working Paper 93, Harvard University, Program on the Global Demography of Aging, Cambridge, MA.

Bloom, D. E., D. Canning, L. Hu, Y. Liu, A. Mahal, and W. Yip. 2010. "The Contribution of Population Health and Demographic Change to Economic Growth in China and India." *Journal of Comparative Economics* 38 (1): 17–33.

Bloom, D. E., D. Canning, and P. Malaney. 1999. "Population Dynamics and Economic Growth in Asia." CID Working Paper 15, Harvard University, Center for International Development, Cambridge, MA.

———. 2000. "Demographic Change and Economic Growth in Asia." *Population and Development Review* 26 (supplement): 257–90.

Bloom, D. E., D. Canning, R. K. Mansfield, and M. Moore. 2007. "Demographic Change, Social Security Systems, and Savings." *Journal of Monetary Economics* 54 (1): 92–114.

Bloom, D. E., D. Canning, and J. Sevilla. 2003. *The Demographic Dividend: A New Perspective on the Economic Consequences of Population Change.* Population Matters Monograph MR-1274. Santa Monica, CA: RAND Corporation.

Bloom, D. E., J. D. Sachs, P. Collier, and C. Udry. 1998. "Geography, Demography, and Economic Grown." *Brookings Papers on Economic Activity* 2: 207–95.

Bloom, D. E., and J. G. Williamson. 1998. "Demographic Transitions and Economic Miracles in Emerging Asia." *World Bank Economic Review* 12 (3): 419–55.

Bongaarts, J. 1978. "A Framework for Analyzing the Proximate Determinants of Fertility." *Population and Development Review* 4 (1): 105–32.

———. 1994. "The Impact of Population Policies: Comment." *Population and Development Review* 20 (3): 616–20.

Bongaarts, J., and J. Casterline. 2013. "Fertility Transition: Is Sub-Saharan Africa Different?" *Population and Development Review* 38 (1): 153–68.

Bongaarts, J., and S. C. Watkins. 1996. "Social Interactions and Contemporary Fertility Transitions." *Population and Development Review* 22 (4): 639–82.

Burke, H., and C. Ambasa-Shisanya. 2011. "Qualitative Study of Reasons for Discontinuation of Injectable Contraceptives among Users and Salient Reference Groups in Kenya." *African Journal of Reproductive Health* 15 (2): 67–78.

Canning, D., I. Günther, S. Linnemayr, and D. Bloom. 2013. "Fertility Choice, Mortality Expectations, and Interdependent Preferences: An Empirical Analysis." *European Economic Review* 63 (C): 273–89.

Canning, D., M. Karra, and J. Wilde. 2013. "A Macrosimulation Model of the Effect of Fertility on Economic Growth: Evidence from Nigeria." Working Paper, Harvard University, Cambridge, MA.

Casterline, J. B., and L. O. El-Zeini. 2014. "Unmet Need and Fertility Decline: A Comparative Perspective on Prospects in Sub-Saharan Africa." *Studies in Family Planning* 45 (2): 227–45.

Chicoine, L. E. 2012. "Education and Fertility: Evidence from a Policy Change in Kenya." Institute for the Study of Labor (IZA), Bonn. http://econpapers.repec.org/paper/izaizadps/dp6778.htm.

Cho, Y., and B. Tien. 2013. "Compilation of 32 SSA Countries." Background paper for this book, World Bank, Washington, DC.

Collier, P., and J. W. Gunning. 1999. "Why Has Africa Grown Slowly?" *Journal of Economic Perspectives* 13 (3): 3–22.

Deaton, A. 1999. "Commodity Prices and Growth in Africa." *Journal of Economic Perspectives* 13 (3): 23–40.

Debpuur, C., J. F. Phillips, E. F. Jackson, A. Nazzar, P. Ngom, and F. N. Binka. 2002. "The Impact of the Navrongo Project on Contraceptive Knowledge and Use, Reproductive Preferences, and Fertility." *Studies in Family Planning* 33 (2): 141–64.

Duflo, E., P. Dupas, M. Kremer, and S. Sinei. 2006. "Education and HIV/AIDS Prevention: Evidence from a Randomized Evaluation in Western Kenya." Working Paper 4024, World Bank, Washington, DC. http://ideas.repec.org/p/wbk/wbrwps/4024.html.

Easterly, W., and R. Levine. 1997. "Africa's Growth Tragedy: Policies and Ethnic Divisions." *Quarterly Journal of Economics* 112 (4): 1203–50.

Eloundou-Enyegue, P. M. 2013. "Demographic Dividend for Africa Schooling? Theory and Early Evidence." Background paper for this book, World Bank, Washington, DC.

Eloundou-Enyegue, P. M., and S. C. Giroux. 2013. "The Role of Fertility in Achieving Africa's Schooling MDGs: Early Evidence for Sub-Saharan Africa." *Journal of Children and Poverty* 19 (1): 21–44.

Eloundou-Enyegue, P. M., and L. Williams. 2006. "Family Size and Schooling in Sub-Saharan African Settings: A Reexamination." *Demography* 43 (1): 25–52.

Finlay, J. E., and D. Canning. 2013. "The Association of Fertility Spacing, Timing, and Parity with Child Health." Background paper for this book, World Bank, Washington, DC.

Finlay, J. E., E. Özaltin, and D. Canning. 2011. "The Association of Maternal Age with Infant Mortality, Child Anthropometric Failure, Diarrhoea, and Anaemia for First Births: Evidence from 55 Low- and Middle-Income Countries." *BMJ Open* 1 (2): n.p.

Friberg, I. K., M. V. Kinney, J. E. Lawn, K. J. Kerber, M. O. Odubanjo, et al. 2010. "Sub-Saharan Africa's Mothers, Newborns, and Children: How Many Lives Could Be Saved with Targeted Health Interventions?" *PLoS Medicine* 7 (6): e1000295.

Glick, P., and D. E. Sahn. 2000. "Schooling of Girls and Boys in a West African Country: The Effects of Parental Education, Income, and Household Structure." *Economics of Education Review* 19 (1): 63–87.

Goldin, C. 1994. "The U-Shaped Female Labor Force Function in Economic Development and Economic History." National Bureau of Economic Research, Cambridge, MA.

Hall, R. E., and C. I. Jones. 1999. "Why Do Some Countries Produce So Much More Output per Worker Than Others?" *Quarterly Journal of Economics* 114 (1): 83–116.

Hanushek, E. A. 1992. "The Trade-Off between Child Quantity and Quality." *Journal of Political Economy* 100 (1): 84–117.

Hossain, M. B., J. F. Phillips, and T. K. LeGrand. 2007. "The Impact of Childhood Mortality on Fertility in Six Rural Thanas of Bangladesh." *Demography* 44 (4): 771–84.

Iwanow, T., and C. Kirkpatrick. 2009. "Trade Facilitation and Manufactured Exports: Is Africa Different?" *World Development* 37 (6): 1039–50.

Jain, A. K. 2011. "Measuring the Effect of Fertility Decline on the Maternal Mortality Ratio." *Studies in Family Planning* 42 (4): 247–60.

Kalemli-Ozcan, S. 2003. "A Stochastic Model of Mortality, Fertility, and Human Capital Investment." *Journal of Development Economics* 70 (1): 103–18.

Kalemli-Ozcan, S., H. E. Ryder, and D. N. Weil. 2000. "Mortality Decline, Human Capital Investment, and Economic Growth." *Journal of Development Economics* 62 (1): 1–23.

Kinney, M. V., K.J. Kerber, R. E. Black, B. Cohen, F. Nkrumah, H. Coovadia, P.M. Nampala, and J. E. Lawn. 2010. "Sub-Saharan Africa's Mothers, Newborns, and Children: Where and Why Do They Die?" *PLoS Medicine* 7 (6): e1000294.

Koissy-Kpein S., M. Kuepie, and M. Tenikue. 2012. "Fertility Shock and Schooling." CEPS/INSTEAD Working Paper 2012-12, Centre for Population, Poverty, and Public Policy Studies, Luxembourg.

Korenman, S., and D. Neumark. 2000. "Cohort Crowding and Youth Labor Markets (A Cross-National Analysis)." In *Youth Employment and Joblessness in Advanced Countries*, edited by D. G. Blanchflower and R. B. Freeman, 57–106. Chicago: University of Chicago Press and National Bureau of Economic Research.

Lee, R. D. 2000. "Intergenerational Transfers and the Economic Life Cycle: A Cross-Cultural Perspective." In *Sharing the Wealth: Demographic Change and Economic Transfers between Generations*, edited by A. Mason and G. Tapinos, 17–56. Oxford: Oxford University Press.

Lee, R. D., and K. L. Kramer. 2002. "Children's Economic Roles in the Maya Family Life Cycle: Cain, Caldwell, and Chayanov Revisited." *Population and Development Review* 28 (3): 475–99.

LeGrand, T. K., T. Koppenhaver, N. Mondain, and S. Randall. 2003. "Reassessing the Insurance Effect: A Qualitative Analysis of Fertility Behavior in Senegal and Zimbabwe." *Population and Development Review* 29 (3): 375–403.

LeGrand, T. K., and J. F. Phillips. 1996. "The Effect of Fertility Reductions on Infant and Child Mortality: Evidence from Matlab in Rural Bangladesh." *Population Studies* 50 (1): 51–68.

Lozano, R., H. Wang, K. J. Foreman, J. K. Rajaratnam, M. Naghavi, J. R Marcus, L. Dwyer-Lindgren, K. T Lofgren, D. Phillips, C. Atkinson, A. D. Lopez, and C. J. L. Murray. 2011. "Progress towards Millennium Development Goals 4 and 5 on Maternal and Child Mortality: An Updated Systematic Analysis." *The Lancet* 378 (9797): 1139–65.

Madhavan, S., and J. P. Guengant. 2013. "Proximate Determinants of Fertility." Background paper for this book. Washington, DC, March.

Mason, A., R. Lee, A-C Tung, M-S Lai, and T. Miller. 2009. "Population Aging and Intergenerational Transfers: Introducing Age into National Accounts." In *Developments in the Economics of Aging*, edited by D. A. Wise. Chicago: University of Chicago Press.

Miller, G. 2010. "Contraception as Development? New Evidence from Family Planning in Colombia." *Economic Journal* 120 (545): 709–36.

Mwabu, G., M. K. Muriithi, and R. G. Mutegi. 2011. "National Transfer Accounts for Kenya: The Economic Lifecycle in 1994." In *Population Aging and the Generational Economy: A Global Perspective*, edited by R. Lee and A. Mason. Cheltenham: Edward Elgar, International Development Research Centre.

Oosthuizen, M. 2013. "South African National Transfer Accounts 2005: Version 1." National Transfer Accounts Project. http://www.ntaccounts.org.

Osili, U. O., and B. T. Long. 2008. "Does Female Schooling Reduce Fertility? Evidence from Nigeria." *Journal of Development Economics* 87 (1): 57–75.

Phillips, J. F., E. F. Jackson, A. A. Bawah, B. MacLeod, P. Adongo, C. Baynes, and J. Williams. 2012. "The Long-Term Fertility Impact of the Navrongo Project in Northern Ghana." *Studies in Family Planning* 43 (3): 175–90.

Pradhan, E., and D. Canning. 2013. "Socioeconomic Determinants of Fertility." Background paper for this book, World Bank, Washington, DC, March.

Prata, N., S. Bell S, K. Weidert K, and A. Gessessew. 2013. "Potential for Cost Recovery: Women's Willingness to Pay for Injectable Contraceptives in Tigray, Ethiopia." *PloS One* 8 (5): e64032.

Pritchett, L. 1994. "Desired Fertility and the Impact of Population Policies." *Population and Development Review* 20 (1): 1–55.

Psacharopoulos, G. 1994. "Returns to Investment in Education: A Global Update." *World Development* 22 (9): 1325–43.

Radhakrishnan, U. 2010. "A Dynamic Structural Model of Contraceptive Use and Employment Sector Choice for Women in Indonesia." Center for Economic Studies Paper CES-WP-10-28, U.S. Census Bureau, Washington, DC.

Rossier, C. 2003. "Estimating Induced Abortion Rates: A Review." *Studies in Family Planning* 34 (2): 87–102.

Sachs, J. D., and A. M. Warner. 2001. "The Curse of Natural Resources." *European Economic Review* 45 (4): 827–38.

Sah, R. K. 1991. "The Effects of Child Mortality Changes on Fertility Choice and Parental Welfare." *Journal of Political Economy* 99 (3): 582–606.

Samir, K., B. Barakat, A. Goujon, V. Skirbekk, W. Sanderson, and W. Lutz. 2010. "Projection of Populations by Level of Educational Attainment, Age, and Sex for 120 Countries for 2005–2050." *Demographic Research* 22 (15): 383–472.

Schultz, T. P. 1969. "An Economic Model of Family Planning and Fertility." *Journal of Political Economy* 77 (2): 153–80.

———. 1976. "Interrelationships between Mortality and Fertility." *Population and Development Review* 24 (2): 239–89.

———. 1990. "Women's Changing Participation in the Labor Force." *Economic Development and Cultural Change* 38 (3): 451–88.

———. 1997. "Demand for Children in Low-Income Countries." In *Handbook of Population and Family Economics*, edited by M. R. Rosenzweig and O. Stark. Amsterdam: North-Holland.

———. 2005. "Productive Benefits of Health: Evidence from Low-Income Countries." In *Health and Economic Growth: Findings and Policy Implications*, edited by G. Lopez-Casasnovas, B. Riveras, and L. Currais. Cambridge, MA: MIT Press.

———. 2009a. "The Gender and Intergenerational Consequences of the Demographic Dividend: An Assessment of the Micro- and Macro- Linkages between the Demographic Transition and Economic Development." *World Bank Economic Review* 23 (3): 427–42.

———. 2009b. "How Does Family Planning Promote Development? Evidence from a Social Experiment in Matlab, Bangladesh: 1977–1996." Yale University, Economic Growth Center, New Haven, CT.

Tahari, A., D. Ghura, B. Akitoby, and E. B. Aka. 2004. "Sources of Growth in Sub-Saharan Africa." IMF Working Paper WP/04/176, International Monetary Fund, Washington, DC.

Thomas, D. 1990. "Intra-Household Resource Allocation: An Inferential Approach." *Journal of Human Resources* 25 (4): 635–64.

———. 1994. "Like Father, Like Son; Like Mother, Like Daughter: Parental Resources and Child Height." *Journal of Human Resources* 10 (1): 950–88.

UN (United Nations) Population Division. 2013. *World Population Prospects: The 2012 Revision*. New York: United Nations, Population Division, Department of Economic and Social Affairs.

Urdal, H. 2006. "A Clash of Generations? Youth Bulges and Political Violence." *International Studies Quarterly* 50 (3): 607–29.

Voas, D. 2003. "Conflicting Preferences: A Reason Fertility Tends to Be Too High or Too Low." *Population and Development Review* 29 (4): 627–46.

Westoff, C. F., and D. A. Koffman. 2011. "The Association of Television and Radio with Reproductive Behavior." *Population and Development Review* 37 (4): 749–59.

World Bank. 2011. *World Development Report 2012: Gender Equality and Development*. New York: Oxford University Press.

———. 2012. World Development Indicators. Washington, DC: World Bank.

———. 2013. *Youth Employment in Sub-Saharan Africa*. Africa Region Regional Study. Washington, DC: World Bank.

Young, A. 1995. "The Tyranny of Numbers: Confronting the Statistical Realities of the East Asian Growth Experience." *Quarterly Journal of Economics* 110 (3): 641–80.

Zelleke, G., A. Sraiheen, and K. Gupta. 2013. "Human Capital, Productivity, and Economic Growth in 31 Sub-Saharan African Countries for the Period 1975–2008." *International Journal of Economics and Finance* 5 (10): 1–17.

Chapter 1

The State of Demographics in Sub-Saharan Africa

Introduction

Demography is the story of people. Understanding that story is important because it provides a powerful lens for viewing future trends, explaining changes a country is likely to face, and providing an opportunity to create a policy environment that takes maximum advantage of a country's demographic potential. Taking advantage of demographic potential is crucial, as the world is likely to see continuing population growth, from 2 billion in 1950 to 6.9 billion in 2010 and to 10.9 billion by 2100 (UN Population Division 2013). The impact of population growth on economic development has generated many theories, most of which fall into three categories suggesting that population growth could *restrict, promote,* or *be neutral to* economic growth.

At the end of the eighteenth century, Thomas Malthus hypothesized that populations would inevitably grow due to the innate human desire to procreate, but that the supply of land, physical capital, and knowledge would remain fixed or would increase at a slower pace than the population. This would inevitably put additional pressure on scarce resources, particularly on the availability of food, leading to increased hunger, high mortality, and lower living standards to the point of bare subsistence. At bare subsistence, the death rate would be high enough to check population growth (Malthus 1888).

Malthus's doomsday scenario has not played out—due in part to technical progress in farming and the industrialization of agriculture, which have increased the production of food (Bloom, Canning, and Sevilla 2003; see box 1.1). This outcome has generated a more optimistic view of population growth based largely on the theory that a greater population stimulates technological change and innovation.

BOX 1.1

The Challenges of Fixed Global Resources and Environmental Degradation

Up to now, there has been little evidence of a strong Malthusian effect as a result of large population size. However, given fixed global resources, several significant Malthusian challenges beyond the historical problems of limited land and agriculture may emerge in the future.

One particular concern involves the depletion of traded commodities such as fossil fuels. As the supply of these goods declines, prices are expected to rise, although potential shortages are spurring innovations that increase the efficiency of use and the development of substitutes.

Widespread environmental degradation and global warming are more worrying developments because the lack of formal price mechanisms as a means of regulating supply implies that there is no automatic market incentive to respond to these concerns. Changing demography worldwide may lead to lower fertility and slower population growth, which may alleviate some of the burden on the environment (O'Neilla et al. 2010). However, rising per capita incomes that accompany lower fertility may well generate their own environmental pressures.

Empirical studies in the 1980s led to a view of "population neutralism," which held that the rate of population growth had no significant effect on a country's economic prospects either way. As a result, many developing countries and international development agencies came to regard population issues as less urgent than before, and population matters became less evident in the literature on economic development (Bloom, Canning, and Sevilla 2003).

The population debate was thus primarily about whether population growth affects aggregate economic performance. More recent economic studies have focused on the idea that population growth can have different sources and that different sources can have different effects on economic growth (Bloom, Canning, and Malaney 2000; Bloom, Canning, and Sevilla 2003; Bloom and Williamson 1998). Population growth through improved health and longer life spans, for example, can have very different economic consequences than population growth through high fertility or immigration. Better health and longer life spans tend to be beneficial for the economy, while high fertility tends to increase population without increasing output in the short run, lowering income per capita. High fertility also leads to high youth dependency rates, reducing the availability of resources per child to invest in health and education.

This modern literature once again gives demography a central place in thinking about economic growth and development. In addition, future demographic changes are much more predictable than many factors affecting economic performance; demography allows us to see far into the future and helps us to predict where countries are heading.

Population and Economic Development

The recent literature considers the sources of population growth as having important consequences for a country's economic development. Historically, the world had high mortality, high fertility, and little population growth. The "demographic transition" is the process by which a population moves from this high-mortality, high-fertility state to a low-mortality, low-fertility state (figure 1.1).

Starting from high levels of mortality and fertility in stage 1, the reductions in mortality in stage 2 are due to improvements in nutrition; to public health measures such as improved water, sanitation, and vaccinations; and to medical advances. In the early phases of stage 2, lower mortality is mainly among children, which means that couples have larger families than desired and societies face scarcer resources per capita. The reduction in child mortality, which results in large families, usually leads to a decline in fertility in stage 3. In stage 4, fertility falls far enough to balance the new death rate, and the population stabilizes.

Figure 1.1 Stages of the Demographic Transition

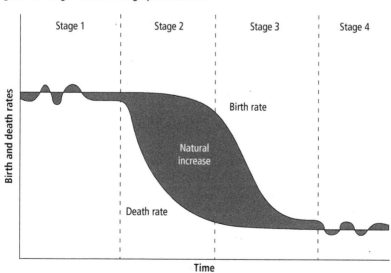

Source: Population Reference Bureau (www.prb.org).

In stages 2 and 3, the death rate is lower than the birth rate, and the population grows rapidly. Differences in the timing of the changes in death and birth rates also lead to large shifts in population age structure. At the beginning of the transition, low mortality among children creates a large youth cohort that works its way through the age structure; later in the transition, a fall in fertility means that subsequent youth cohorts are smaller. When it is young, this large cohort raises the youth dependency rate and lowers the working-age share of the population; when it reaches working age, it raises the working-age share of the population. As it ages, the cohort eventually increases the old-age dependency rate and lowers the working-age share.

East Asia exemplifies the transition well (figure 1.2). Due to rapidly declining fertility after 1960, the region saw a rapid increase in the working-age share of its population. This increased share, which is now peaking, has been linked to the region's economic takeoff. However, as this large cohort ages, the working-age share will shrink and old-age dependency will rise.

Research confirms that the source of population growth rates is vital. In particular, the economic effects of population growth depend fundamentally

Figure 1.2 Actual and Projected Demographic Changes in East Asia, 1950–2060

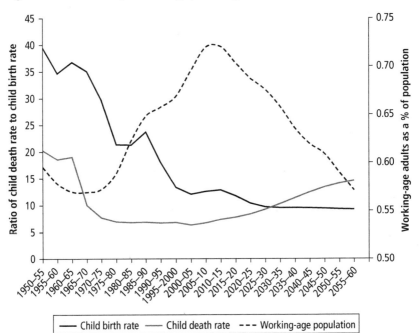

Source: UN Population Division 2012.
Note: Data after 2010 are projections based on medium-variant fertility. The period covers July 1 of the first year to June 30 of the second year.

Figure 1.3 Crude Birth Rates and Economic Growth in a Sample of Countries, 1980–2000

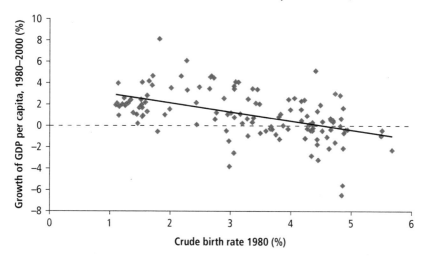

Source: Based on data for 127 countries from the World Bank's World Development Indicators (World Bank 2011).
Note: Gross domestic product (GDP) per capita is measured at purchasing power parity. Growth is the annual average for the period.

on whether the growth is due to a high birth rate or a low death rate (Kelley and Schmidt 1995). Moreover, simply combining these two sources of population growth will not reflect the cumulative effects of population growth on economic performance. For example, if population growth has negative consequences for economic growth, one would expect to see a negative association between the birth rate and economic growth, and figure 1.3 shows just that.

A positive relationship between the death rate and economic growth would also be expected, as high death rates ease population pressure, but here the association shown in figure 1.4 for the same sample is *negative*, indicating that countries with higher death rates have *lower* rates of economic growth. The effects of birth and death rates therefore are not equal and indeed are opposite, as is required for population growth to be a meaningful summary statistic.

There are several reasons why the consequences of reducing the rate of population growth by increasing the rate of deaths rather than decreasing the rate of fertility are quite different. Lower death rates increase population numbers, but they also reflect gains in life expectancy, which, in developing countries, are driven by improved childhood health. Moreover, declining mortality is usually accompanied by declining morbidity. Some recent literature shows that early childhood health and nutrition, both in utero and during the first few years of life, have a significant impact on physical and cognitive development,

Figure 1.4 Crude Death Rates and Economic Growth in a Sample of Countries, 1980–2000

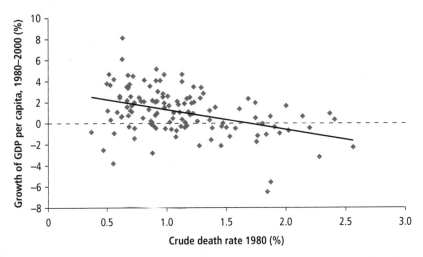

Source: Based on data for 127 countries from the World Bank's World Development Indicators (World Bank 2011).
Note: GDP per capita is measured at purchasing power parity. Growth is the annual average for the period.

educational outcomes, and, eventually, earnings as an adult (Bleakley 2003, 2010). In addition, a decline in death rates leads to expectations of a longer life span, which can increase the incentive to invest further in human capital (Bloom et al. 2007).

Low death rates can, therefore, go hand in hand with a healthy population and a highly productive workforce. At the aggregate level, countries that have high life expectancy subsequently have higher economic growth (Bloom, Canning, and Sevilla 2004). Inference using aggregate data is difficult due to the long lag between better health in early childhood and its economic consequences and the fact that better health affects population size as well as worker productivity. And there has been much debate on whether this observed relationship can be considered causal (Acemoglu and Johnson 2007; Bloom, Canning, and Fink 2009).

The age structure of the population matters because people at different ages interact with the economy differently, altering its performance. Young people require heavy investment in health and education, working-age persons provide the majority of labor, producing far more than they consume, and the elderly require specialized access to health care and retirement income. As the share of working-age population rises, labor supply expands. If aligned with prudent social and economic policies, this increasing labor supply can boost the economy and create a virtuous circle.

In short, the demographic dividend is a potential economic opportunity created by changes in the population age structure due to a decline in mortality and fertility and an increase in the ratio of working-age population to dependents. Harnessing that dividend requires investments in health and education and economic policies that absorb the increasing labor supply into the economy, allowing people to save and invest in future retirement.

There are two types of demographic dividend: a labor force dividend and a savings dividend. The labor force dividend focuses on the labor supply effects of changes in age structure. This first dividend arises mechanically because of increases in the ratio of working-age adults to dependents. The dividend for the economy is transitory, however, and per capita production will only rise if the labor market can absorb the increasing number of working adults. With lower fertility, women may be more likely to enter the labor force. Policies that encourage women to participate in the formal labor force can magnify the labor dividend. Depending on the type of labor activity available, early investments in education may enable higher production per capita (Bloom, Canning, and Sevilla 2003; Mason 2005).

The second demographic dividend can be reaped if national economic policies facilitate and encourage savings. Saving for retirement comes mainly from older workers who believe that they still have a long life ahead of them. Formal retirement or pension plans, as well as savings institutions, can help to channel these savings to productive investments. Domestic investments increase the amount of capital available to the economy and lift output per worker; foreign investment improves current account balances and increases national income. Unlike the effect of the first dividend, these gains in income per capita can be permanent. However, they are not automatically so; for the gains to become permanent, governments must align their economic and social policies.

The Demographic Transition in East Asia and Latin America

Different regions experience the demographic transition in different ways. In East Asia and Latin America, declines in mortality began in the mid-1940s and were followed within two decades by declines in fertility, resulting in the working-age population growing four times faster than the dependent population (youth and elderly) in 1965–90. This section discusses the transitions in these two regions.

Purposeful Steps: East Asia
Several East Asian governments promulgated far-sighted education, health, labor, and economic policies that allowed them to reap the demographic dividend. Economies such as Indonesia; Japan; the Republic of Korea; Singapore;

Taiwan, China; and Thailand experienced a relatively quick demographic transition: the region's infant mortality rate, for example, fell from 181 per 1,000 live births in 1950 to 34 by 2000 (figure 1.5). In the 1950s, these East Asian countries had launched voluntary population policies that incentivized families to have fewer children, accelerating the fertility decline (Mason 2001). Of all the economies in the world with high fertility in 1960, six had achieved replacement fertility by 1990, all six of them in East Asia—China; Hong Kong SAR, China; Korea; Singapore; Taiwan, China; and Thailand (Mason 2003).

Youth dependency rates also declined quickly, and the increase in labor supply per capita was fueled further by the increase in female labor force participation. Even though the fertility decline was rapid, the population grew during the transition because death rates fell ahead of birth rates, lifting both the share and the size of the working-age population. Governments responded by expanding their manufacturing and service sectors, but the success of East Asian countries in reaping the labor dividend was not automatic: governments were in a position to adjust the political and economic institutions and to change policies and markets to absorb the increased labor supply. Enhanced research capacities, infrastructure (for labor-intensive manufacturing and services), incentives, subsidies, and access to credit were all elements of the response (Hayami 1997; Mason 2003). The savings dividend of these East Asian economies was even larger than the labor dividend, facilitated by policies that promoted savings and investments (World Bank 2001).

Missed Opportunities: Latin America

Similar to the trends in Southeast Asia and to an extent in East Asia, under-five mortality in Latin America tumbled from 131 per 1,000 live births in 1965 to 32 in 2000, followed by a decline in fertility from 5.0 in 1975 to 2.5 in 2000. Latin America's total dependency rate (ratio of dependents to working-age population) closely followed that of Southeast Asia (figure 1.5, panel a).

In the region, Brazil experienced very rapid demographic change. Its total fertility rate (TFR) fell from 6.2 in 1965 to 2.7 in 1990; the current TFR is estimated at 1.8 (Rodriguez-Wong and de Carvalho 2004), a change that took almost a century in most European nations. The lower youth dependency rate created an opportunity for stronger economic growth. The demographic bonus was expected to appear in the 1990s, but fast-growing international and domestic debt led to economic stagnation and high inflation. Brazil attempted to move in the right direction by liberalizing trade, privatizing corporations, and shifting the currency to a floating exchange rate regime, and these policies attracted strong inflows of foreign direct investment (FDI). However, the country was unable to meet the demand for jobs, and the economy was unable to harness the potential of the changed age structure (Müller and Woellert 2013).

Figure 1.5 Demographic Trends in Latin America, Southeast Asia, and East Asia, 1950–2010

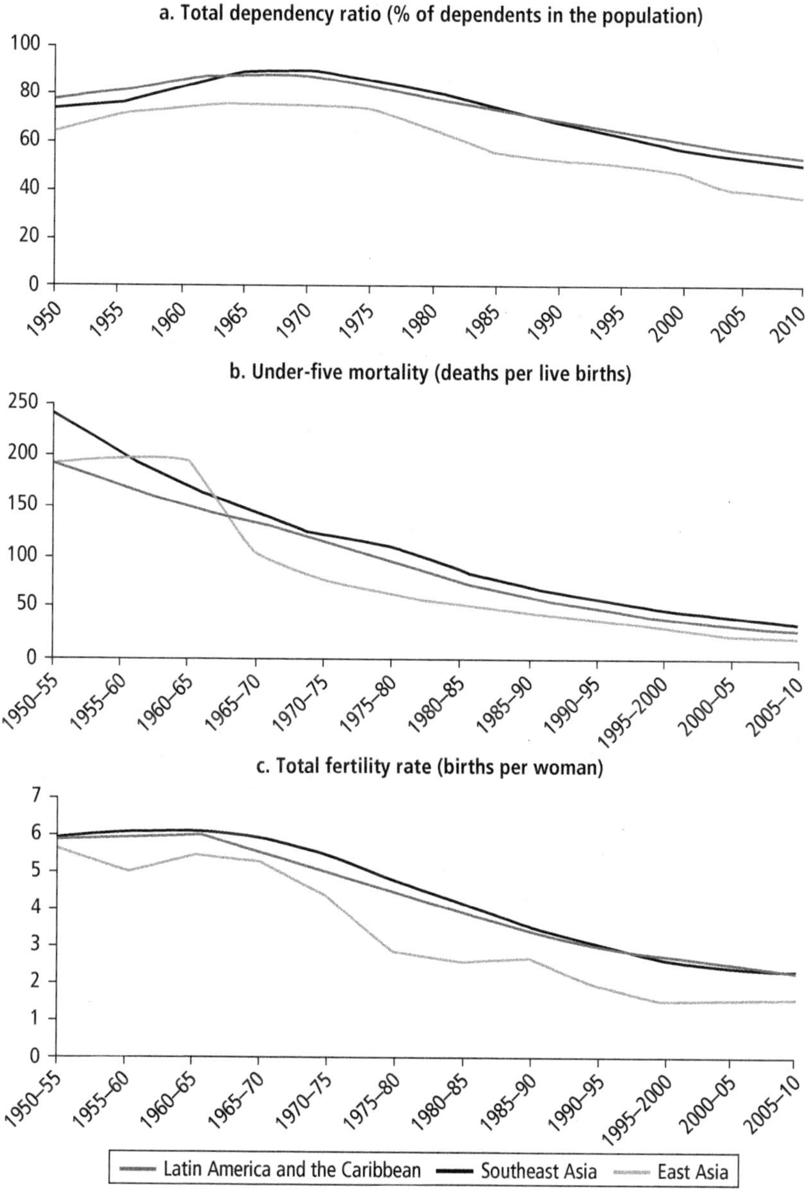

a. Total dependency ratio (% of dependents in the population)

b. Under-five mortality (deaths per live births)

c. Total fertility rate (births per woman)

Latin America and the Caribbean   Southeast Asia   East Asia

Source: Bakilana 2013.
Note: The total dependency ratio is defined as the ratio of population ages 0–14 and 65+ per 100 population ages 15–64. The period covers July 1 of the first year to June 30 of the second year.

Latin America's failure had stark results: in 1975–95, the region's annual growth of gross domestic product (GDP) per capita was *an eighth* of East Asia's (0.7 and 6.8 percent, respectively). Although Brazil—and indeed many other Latin American countries—have reversed the trend with the rise in worldwide commodity prices and a change in social policies, the window of opportunity for economic growth fueled by demographics will be relatively small.

Population Trends in Sub-Saharan Africa

Sub-Saharan Africa has undergone—and is set to continue undergoing— profound demographic changes:

- A rapid decline in death rates, particularly among children
- A more than tripling of its population, from 186 million in 1950 to 670 million in 2000
- A forecast further doubling of the population by 2060.[1]

Considerable uncertainty surrounds past—even current—data, however. Vital registration of births and deaths is patchy in many countries. Until the World Fertility Survey in the 1970s and demographic and health surveys (DHSs) beginning in the 1980s, child mortality and fertility rates had very few supporting data. The DHSs now provide generally good data, but they are based on samples of the population and suffer from considerable statistical "noise." For this reason, the national figures for child mortality and fertility based on DHS data are usually smoothed over time in an attempt to remove sampling variations. But data on adult—particularly old-age—mortality are missing in many countries and are often constructed from life tables, which assume a stable relationship between child and adult mortality rates or infer mortality rates from changes in cohort size in successive censuses.

The United Nations (UN) produces population projections for Sub-Saharan Africa to 2100 based on assumed (that is, as in other regions) time paths of fertility. It has three projections: median (baseline), low (total fertility rate of 0.5 child per woman lower than the baseline), or high (0.5 child higher).

As shown on map 1.1, Africa's share of the global population is projected to rise from 17 percent (1.0 billion) in 2010 to 24 percent (2.2 billion) by 2050 and to 35 percent (3.6 billion) by 2100, alongside changes in the share of other regions (UN Population Division 2012).

Sub-Saharan Africa's population growth rose to a peak of 2.8 percent a year in 1980 and, although it has slowed, remains high relative to that of other regions (figure 1.6). Latin America's population growth peaked in the 1960s at 2.7 percent a year but has declined steadily since and is now at 1.2 percent.

Map 1.1 Share of the World's Population Living in Sub-Saharan Africa, 2010–2100

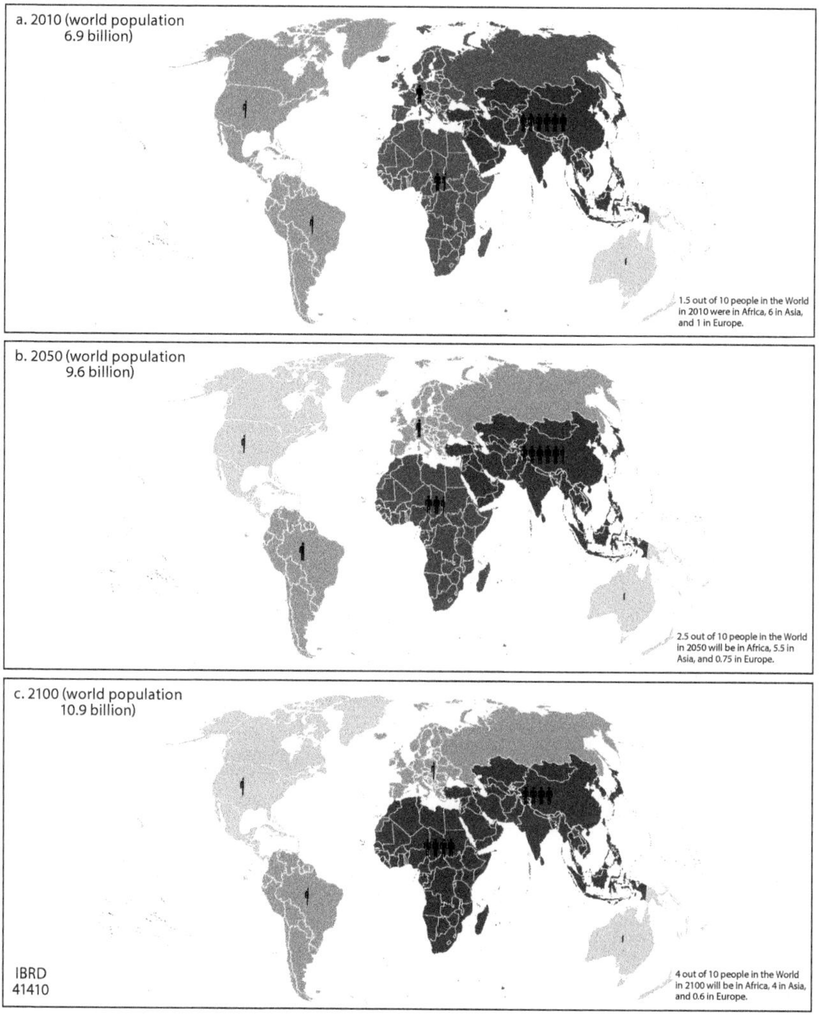

a. 2010 (world population 6.9 billion)

1.5 out of 10 people in the World in 2010 were in Africa, 6 in Asia, and 1 in Europe.

b. 2050 (world population 9.6 billion)

2.5 out of 10 people in the World in 2050 will be in Africa, 5.5 in Asia, and 0.75 in Europe.

c. 2100 (world population 10.9 billion)

IBRD
41410

4 out of 10 people in the World in 2100 will be in Africa, 4 in Asia, and 0.6 in Europe.

Source: Analysis of data from UN Population Division 2012.

UN medium-variant fertility projections have Africa's population growth continuing to slow, but still staying higher than growth in other regions until at least 2050. According to these projections, Europe's population will start to decline in 2020–25, as Latin American and Asian growth falls toward zero.

The rest of this section looks at demographic change in Sub-Saharan Africa in more detail.

Figure 1.6 Actual and Projected Population Growth Rates in Select World Regions, 1950–2060

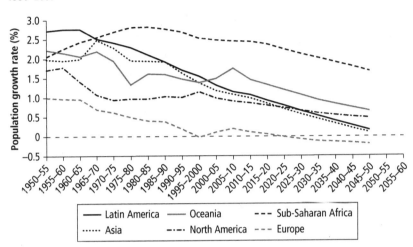

Source: UN Population Division 2012.
Note: Data after 2010 are projections based on medium-variant fertility. The period covers July 1 of the first year to June 30 of the second year.

Life Expectancy and Under-Five Mortality

In the 1950s Sub-Saharan Africa's life expectancy was barely 40 years, while Europe's was above 65. Even today, Africa has yet to match the Europe of six decades ago: its life expectancy is about 55 and is only set to exceed 65 after 2045 (figure 1.7). Life expectancy in Africa is still so low in part because of the dire effects of the human immunodeficiency virus (HIV) and acquired immunodeficiency syndrome (AIDS) epidemic in the hardest-hit countries.[2]

Life expectancy at birth has been on the rise in most African countries since the 1960s, but progress has been slow overall and even thwarted in some countries. During 1950–55, 307 out of every 1,000 African children born did not survive to see their fifth birthday, and despite rapid declines during the last few decades, the burden of childhood mortality remains very high. During 2005–10, under-five mortality was estimated at 136 deaths per 1,000 live births, compared with around 9 in Europe, 54 in Asia, and 38 in Latin America. Child mortality in Sub-Saharan Africa today is on a par with that of North Africa and South Asia in the 1980s. It is projected to fall to about 50 after 2045 (figure 1.8).

Fertility

Although fertility has declined in Sub-Saharan Africa, the rate of decline has generally been slower and the level remains far higher than in the rest of the

Figure 1.7 Actual and Projected Life Expectancy at Birth in Select World Regions, 1950–2050

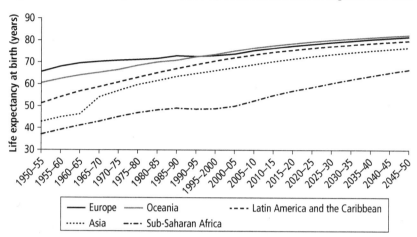

Source: UN Population Division 2012.
Note: Data after 2010 are projections based on medium-variant fertility. The period covers July 1 of the first year to June 30 of the second year.

Figure 1.8 Actual and Projected Under-Five Mortality Rate in Select World Regions, 1995–2050

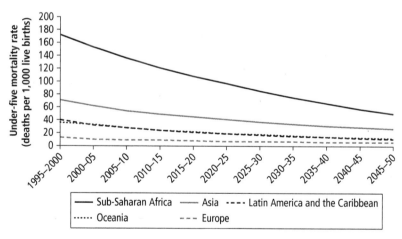

Source: UN Population Division 2012.
Note: Data after 2010 are projections based on medium-variant fertility. The period covers July 1 of the first year to June 30 of the second year.

world (figure 1.9). The total fertility rate in Africa declined from 6.5 children per woman in 1950–55 to 5.4 in 2005–10, a time in which the TFR in East Asia declined from 5.6 to 1.6. In the 1960s, fertility began to drop in Asia and Latin America, while rates in Sub-Saharan Africa stagnated, quickly widening the gap between regions. By the 1980s the gap between world regions had widened

Figure 1.9 Total Fertility Rate in Select World Regions, 1960–2010

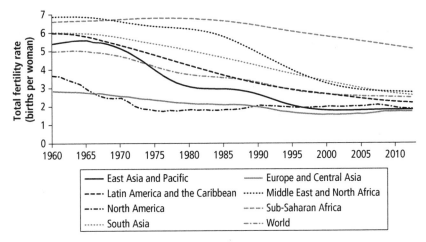

Source: World Bank 2013.

to around 2.5 and persisted largely due to the slow decline in TFR in most Sub-Saharan African countries.

Fertility is projected to be at replacement level in Asia and Latin America by 2045, but still at around 3 children per woman in Sub-Saharan Africa. However, there will be sharp differences within and across countries, as discussed below.

Age Structure

Much of Africa's population is young, but the size of population groups and their share of total population have changed significantly in recent decades. Projections suggest further changes: UN medium-variant projections suggest that, as fertility continues to decline, the proportion of the population in the 0–14 years of age will also decline. By 2050, the portion of youth in the population is projected to reach 32 percent, a decline of some 12 percentage points from 2010.

In 2010, 53 percent of Africa's population was between the ages of 15 and 64. For the region as a whole, this share has hardly changed since 1950. In the early to mid-1980s, the percentage of the working-age population reached a low of about 50 percent, before rising slightly to current levels. In 1950, about 98 million people were in this age range for the whole region. By 2010, although the changes in percentage terms were small, the size of this age group had grown to about 450 million people. The working-age share is projected to grow

Figure 1.10 Population Pyramid for Sub-Saharan Africa, 2010 and 2060

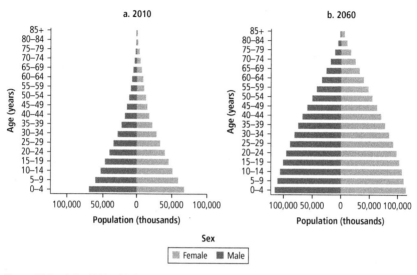

Source: UN Population Division 2012.
Note: Data after 2010 are projections based on medium-variant fertility.

in size over the next decades to reach, depending on projection assumptions, between 843 million and 885 million people by 2035. According to the low- and high-variant projections, the working-age population could be as large as 1.2 billion–1.6 billion by 2060. The medium-variant projection is shown in figure 1.10.

Sub-Saharan Africa has about 43 million people ages 60 and older, compared with 414 million in Asia, 161 million in Europe, and 64 million in North America. The proportion of elderly in Sub-Saharan Africa was about 5 percent in 2010, hardly changed from 5.2 percent in 1950. While the absolute number of old people increased between 1950 and 2010, the proportion of elderly decreased slightly. Projections suggest that the share of elderly in Sub-Saharan Africa will rise to about 8 percent by 2050, but, compared to other regions of the world, this share is very low: the elderly constitute almost 10 percent of the population in Asia and 22 percent in Europe.

Though rising, the median age is much lower in Africa than in other regions. Higher fertility in the 1950s led the median age in Africa to decline from 19 years in 1950 to 17.3 years in 1985–90. The median age is now about 18.6 years and is projected to increase to about 25 years by 2050. This compares with 40.1 in

Europe, 38.4 in North America, and 29.0 in Asia. Projections suggest that the wide gap in median age between Sub-Saharan Africa and other regions will persist in the next decades, despite some narrowing.

Dependency Rate

The total dependency rate is higher in Sub-Saharan Africa than in other regions due to the young population age structure and high youth dependency. In 1950 the total dependency rate was around 80 dependents per 100 persons of working age, compared with about 50 in Europe and 55 in North America. In Sub-Saharan Africa, the increase stemmed from large increases in the number of children. While the total dependency rate (including both children and elderly) started to decline in Asia and in Latin America and the Caribbean sometime after the mid-1960s, it continued to rise in Africa, reaching a peak in the mid-1980s of about 95 dependents per 100 people of working age.

Since the early to mid-1980s, the child dependency ratio has dropped slowly in Africa, from a peak of 88 children per 100 adults. At that time, there were 56 more children per 100 working-age adults in Sub-Saharan Africa than in Europe or North America (UN Population Division 2013). As the ratio has plummeted in other regions, the gap between Africa and other regions has persisted, although it is expected to narrow as child dependency declines in Sub-Saharan Africa.

Demographic Trends within Sub-Saharan Africa

The trends in Sub-Saharan Africa as a whole mask the wide variation within Africa by region, country, and place of residence (urban or rural). Much of the population growth in Sub-Saharan Africa will occur in East and West Africa. In 2010, about 38 percent of the population lived in East Africa, 36 percent in the West, and about 14 percent in Middle Africa. UN projections suggest that by 2060, 40 percent of the population will live in East Africa, 38 percent will live in West Africa, and about 14 percent will live in Middle Africa.

Sub-Saharan Africa's population density is around 35 million persons per square kilometer. However, it is expected to reach 92 by 2060, when East and West Africa will, at 161, be four times more densely populated than Southern Africa.

Three countries are projected to experience the largest increase in population: Ethiopia, Nigeria, and Tanzania. Ethiopia will add almost 2 million people a year in the coming decades. Nigeria could grow from about 158 million people in 2010 to between 396 million and 462 million people by 2060. Tanzania could potentially grow from 45 million people in 2010 to about 200 million people by 2060. These projects have ranges of uncertainty. With Nigeria, for example, the high-variant projection puts the total population at 617 million in 2060, while the low-variant one puts it at 465 million.

In contrast, some countries in Southern Africa are projected to experience slow increases or even decreases in population, as fertility is already low and projected to fall further. For example, low-variant assumptions project that South Africa's population will decline from 50 million to 45 million during 2010–60, but the medium- and high-variant assumptions project that it will increase to 57 million and 71 million. Botswana and Zimbabwe already have low fertility rates, and trends in these two countries are expected to resemble those in South Africa.

Stages of the Demographic Transition

Regions within Sub-Saharan Africa vary. North and Southern Africa are well into their demographic transition. Their fertility was already low, and the working-age share of the population was more than 60 percent in 2010. These regions may already be reaping the first demographic dividend: in South Africa, the demographic transition is estimated to add around 0.5 percent of additional growth of GDP per capita each year (Oosthuizen 2013). In contrast, the transition in Middle, West, and East Africa has yet to take off (figure 1.11). UN medium-variant projections suggest that the working-age share will increase to 55–60 percent in these three regions by 2035.

Figure 1.11 Actual and Projected Proportion of the Population 15–64 Years of Age in Africa, by Region, 1950–2060

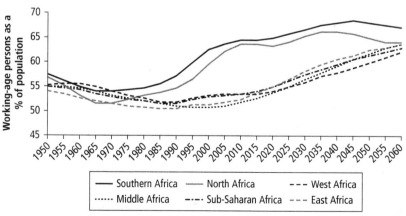

Source: UN Population Division 2012.
Note: Data after 2010 are projections based on medium-variant fertility.

Figure 1.12 Size of the Population 15–64 Years of Age in Africa, by Region, 1950, 2010, and 2060

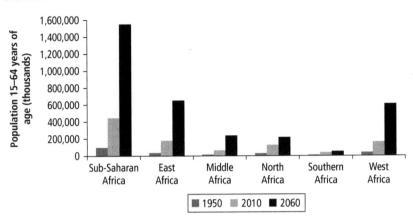

Source: UN Population Division 2012.
Note: Data after 2010 are projections based on medium-variant fertility.

The size of the working-age population in Sub-Saharan Africa is projected to rise from 450 million in 2010 to 1.56 billion in 2060 (figure 1.12). In 2060, most of that working-age population will live in East and West Africa, which will have close to 1 billion working-age adults, compared with 342 million in 2010.

Under-Five Mortality

Differences in under-five mortality within Sub-Saharan Africa are wide. Under-five mortality in Southern Africa has been low for years, while rates in Middle and in West Africa are about twice as high. Although mortality is declining across Sub-Saharan Africa, thanks in part to the mass-scale distribution of anti-retroviral treatments for HIV/AIDS, the gap in under-five mortality between regions is still very wide and, though projected to narrow, is unlikely to disappear (figure 1.13).

Under-five mortality also varies greatly between countries (map 1.2). For example, in Angola, Chad, the Democratic Republic of Congo, Mali, and Somalia, it is higher than 150 deaths per 1,000 live births; in some countries in North and Southern Africa, it is 17–50.

Within countries, urban areas usually have lower under-five mortality rates than rural areas (figure 1.14). In Niger, for example, twice as many children under the age of five die in rural areas as in urban areas. These differences are also evident within wealth quintiles and household education levels in most countries.

Figure 1.13 Actual and Projected Under-Five Mortality Rate in Africa, by Region, 1995–2050

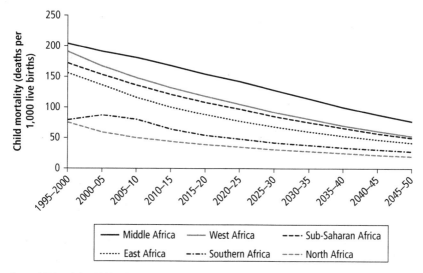

Source: UN Population Division 2012.
Note: Data after 2010 are projections based on medium-variant fertility. The period covers July 1 of the first year to June 30 of the second year.

Fertility and Rural-Urban Residence

Fertility varies substantially within Sub-Saharan Africa. UN Population Division data suggest that in the 1950s the TFR, across the continent, was around 6–7. Differences among Africa's regions were small during that decade and into the early 1960s, after which fertility began to decline rapidly in the southern and northern parts of the continent and to rise in eastern, western, and middle parts. In Middle Africa, rates increased until the mid-1990s and then started to decline. In West Africa, they peaked in the early 1980s at just under 7. In East Africa, they peaked in the late 1960s to early 1970s at about 7. In Africa as a whole, the TFR is now around 5, but it is much lower in Southern Africa, at about 2.5; it is about 5.5 in West and Middle Africa and about 4.5 in East Africa (map 1.3).

As with under-five mortality, rural and urban areas (notably capital cities) show wide variations in fertility (figure 1.15). Heterogeneity is most apparent in Ethiopia, where fertility in the capital, Addis Ababa, is below replacement at 1.5, compared with 2.9 in other urban areas and 5.5 in rural areas.

Moreover, as shown in figure 1.16, the rural-urban gap in fertility is much wider in Sub-Saharan Africa (though varying by country) than in most of the non-African countries (with the exception of Brazil).

Map 1.2 Under-Five Mortality Rate in Africa, by Country, 2010

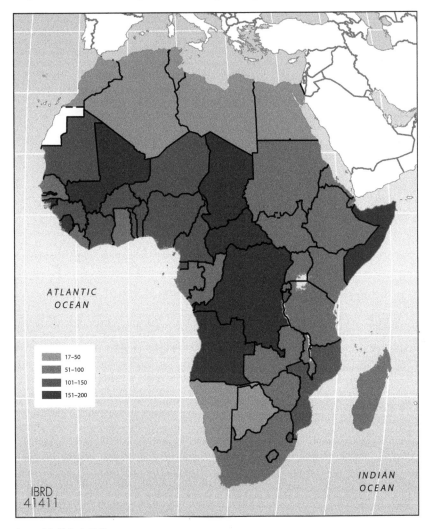

ATLANTIC
OCEAN

	17–50
	51–100
	101–150
	151–200

INDIAN
OCEAN

IBRD
41411

Source: World Bank 2013.

Migration and Urbanization

Africa is urbanizing heavily (figure 1.17). In the vast majority of Sub-Saharan African countries, 30–35 percent of the population is in urban areas. Before the demographic transition, high mortality in cities tended to result in excess deaths over births, and the urban population grew only because of migration

Figure 1.14 Under-Five Mortality Rate in Select African Countries, by Urban-Rural Residence, Various Years, 2007–09

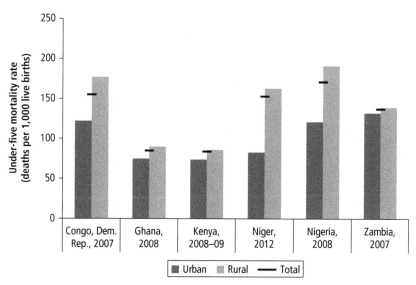

Source: Based on the most recent demographic and health survey for the country.

from rural areas. Today, urban areas have both lower mortality and lower fertility than rural areas.

A striking feature of the modern era in developing countries outside Africa has been the reduction in the absolute number of workers in agriculture, despite growing populations and growing demand for food. Technological progress and mechanization of farming have essentially removed the Malthusian check. Africa is expected to follow this pattern, as its agricultural productivity continues to improve. Thus urbanization is a response partly to demographic forces and partly to economic incentives that come from economic growth (Jones 2003). As more people move to urban areas and urban areas continue to exhibit lower mortality and fertility than rural areas, fertility is expected to fall more rapidly in countries that are more urbanized than in those that are more rural.

The majority of growth in Africa's urban centers is due to the natural increase from a higher birth than death rate—perhaps up to 60–75 percent—with the rest due to rural-urban migration (UN Population Division 2008; UN Population Fund 1996). This migration often has a circular pattern, with many migrants retaining links with their household of origin through visits and remittances and, in all parts of Africa, a great deal of return (urban-rural) migration.

Map 1.3 Total Fertility Rate in Africa, by Country, 2010

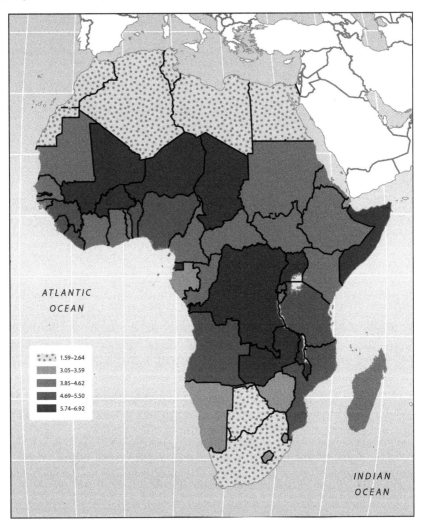

ATLANTIC
OCEAN

	1.59–2.64
	3.05–3.59
	3.85–4.62
	4.69–5.50
	5.74–6.92

INDIAN
OCEAN

Source: UN Population Division 2012.

In addition to seasonal migration for work, the uncertainty of employment prospects in urban areas means that rural-urban migrants may move back and forth as economic conditions change. This pattern of migration is important because it may play a role in slowing the fertility decline associated with urban areas or accelerate the fertility decline associated with rural areas.

Figure 1.15 Total Fertility Rate in Ethiopia, Ghana, and Kenya, by Rural-Urban Residence, Various Years

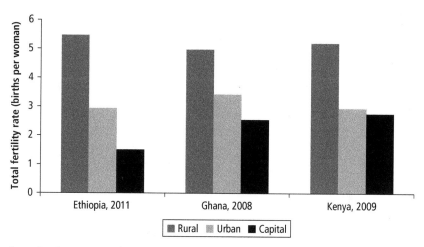

Source: Based on most recent demographic and health survey for the country.

Implications for the Demographic Dividend

Sub-Saharan Africa has two potential problems in realizing a demographic dividend. The first is that its demographic transition is projected to be very slow—compare the lethargic ascent of the line for Sub-Saharan Africa in figure 1.18 to the sharp rise in the line for Latin America and the Caribbean and for East Asia between 1970 and 2010.

The jump for East Asia closely parallels the region's economic takeoff, and indeed about one-third of the economic growth during its "economic miracle" can be attributed to the demographic dividend (Bloom, Canning, and Malaney 2000; Bloom and Williamson 1998). In contrast, the slow decline in fertility projected for Sub-Saharan Africa suggests that the rise of the working-age share, which started in 1990, will not peak until 2080—90 years later. Moreover, the ratio of working-age population per dependent will be below 2 at its peak. In short, the projected impact of population growth in Sub-Saharan Africa is likely to be slow and small.

Two key questions are evident from this analysis. First, can the fertility decline in Sub-Saharan Africa be accelerated and, if so, how? This subject is tackled in chapter 2. Second, given that economic growth does not automatically follow changes in population structure (Urdal 2006), how can the potential of the demographic dividend be realized? This subject is tackled in chapters 3 and 4.

Figure 1.16 Total Fertility Rate in Sub-Saharan Africa and Seven Countries from Other Regions, by Urban-Rural Location, Various Years

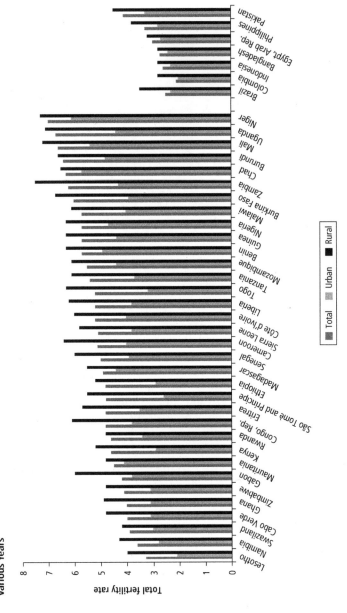

Source: Based on data from the most recent demographic and health survey for the country, Madhavan and Guengant 2013.

Figure 1.17 Urban as a Share of Total Population, by World Region, 1960–2012

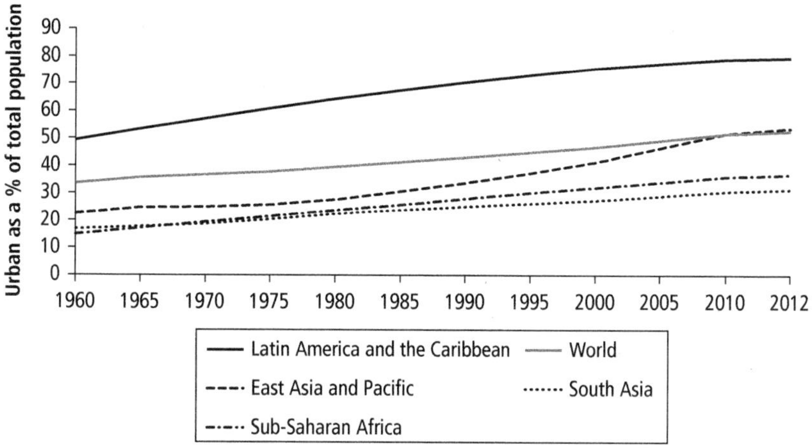

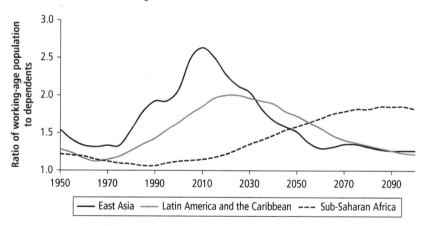

Source: Simkins 2013.

Figure 1.18 Actual and Projected Ratio of Working-Age Population 16–64 Years of Age to Dependents in Select World Regions, 1950–2100

Source: UN Population Division 2013.
Note: Data after 2010 are projections based on medium-variant fertility.

Notes

1. The forecast is based on the United Nation's medium-variant fertility projections, which assume that average family size will fall fairly slowly (UN Population Division 2012).
2. The launch of mass-scale anti-retroviral treatment appears to be reversing the impact of HIV on adult mortality.

References

Acemoglu, D., and S. Johnson. 2007. "Disease and Development: The Effect of Life Expectancy on Economic Growth." *Journal of Political Economy* 115 (6): 925–85.

Bakilana, A. 2013. "State of Demographics." Background paper for this book, World Bank, Washington, DC, October.

Bleakley, H. 2003. "Disease and Development: Evidence from the American South." *Journal of the European Economic Association* 1 (1-2): 376–86.

———. 2010. "Malaria Eradication in the Americas: A Retrospective Analysis of Childhood Exposure." *American Economic Journal: Applied Economics* 2 (2): 1–45.

Bloom, D. E., D. Canning, and G. Fink. 2009. "Disease and Development Revisited." NBER Work Paper 15137, National Bureau of Economic Research, Cambridge, MA.

Bloom, D. E., D. Canning, and P. Malaney. 2000. "Demographic Change and Economic Growth in Asia." *Population and Development Review* 26 (supplement): 257–90.

Bloom, D. E., D. Canning, R. K. Mansfield, and M. Moore. 2007. "Demographic Change, Social Security Systems, and Savings." *Journal of Monetary Economics* 54 (1): 92–114.

Bloom, D., D. Canning, and J. Sevilla. 2003. *The Demographic Dividend: A New Perspective on the Economic Consequences of Population Change.* Santa Monica, CA: RAND Corporation.

———. 2004. "The Effect of Health on Economic Growth: A Production Function Approach." *World Development* 32 (1): 1–13.

Bloom, D. E., and J. G. Williamson. 1998. "Demographic Transitions and Economic Miracles in Emerging Asia." *World Bank Economic Review* 12 (3): 419–55.

Hayami, Y. 1997. "Induced Innovation and Agricultural Development in East Asia." Population Working Paper 88-4, East-West Center, Program on Population, Honolulu, August 31. http://www.popline.org/node/532439.

Jones, G. 2003. "Urbanization." In *Encyclopedia of Population*, edited by P. Demeny and G. McNicoll. New York: Macmillan Reference.

Kelley, A. C., and R. M. Schmidt. 1995. "Aggregate Population and Economic Growth Correlations: The Role of the Components of Demographic Change." *Demography* 32 (4): 543–55.

Madhavan, S., and J. P. Guengant. 2013. "Proximate Determinants of Fertility." Background paper for this book, World Bank, Washington, DC, March.

Malthus, T. R. 1888. "An Essay on the Principle of Population: Or, a View of Its Past and Present Effects on Human Happiness." Reeves and Turner.

Mason, A. 2001. *Population Change and Economic Development in East Asia: Challenges Met, Opportunities Seized.* Stanford, CA: Stanford University Press.

———. 2003. "Population Change and Economic Development: What Have We Learned from the East Asia Experience?" *Applied Population Policy* 1 (1): 3–14.

———. 2005. "Demographic Transition and Demographic Dividends in Developed and Developing Countries." Paper for United Nations expert group meeting on social and economic implications of changing population age structures.

Müller, R., and F. Woellert. 2013. "Late Bloomer: Why Brazil Did Not Make Appropriate Use of Its Demographic Bonus." Case study for this book, World Bank, Washington, DC, March.

O'Neilla, B. C., M. Daltonb, R. Fuchsc, L. Jianga, S. Pachauric, and K. Zigovad. 2010. "Global Demographic Trends and Future Carbon Emissions." *Proceedings of the National Academy of Sciences* 107 (41): 17521–26.

Oosthuizen, M. 2013. "South African National Transfer Accounts 2005: Version 1." National Transfer Accounts Project. http://www.ntaccounts.org.

Pradhan, E. 2013. "Social Determinants of Fertility." Background paper for this book, World Bank, Washington, DC, April.

Rodriguez-Wong, L., and J. A. M. de Carvalho. 2004. "Age Structural Transition in Brazil: Demographic Bonuses and Emerging Challenges." Paper presented to the seminar on "Age-Structural Transitions: Demographic Bonuses, but Emerging Challenges for Population and Sustainable Development," Paris, February 23–26.

Simkins, C. 2013. "Urbanization and Fertility." Background paper for this book, World Bank, Washington, DC, April.

UN (United Nations) Population Division. 2008. *An Overview of Urbanization, Internal Migration, Population Distribution, and Development in the World.* New York: United Nations Population Division. http://www.un.org/esa/population/meetings/EGM _PopDist/P01_UNPopDiv.pdf.

———. 2012. *World Population Prospects: The 2011 Revision.* New York: United Nations, Population Division, Department of Economic and Social Affairs.

———. 2013. *World Population Prospects: The 2012 Revision, Methodology of the United Nations Population Estimates and Projections.* New York: United Nations, Population Division, Department of Economic and Social Affairs.

UN Population Fund. 1996. *Sources of City Growth.* New York: UN Population Fund. http://www.unfpa.org/swp/1996/index.htm.

Urdal, H. 2006. "A Clash of Generations? Youth Bulges and Political Violence." *International Studies Quarterly* 50 (3): 607–29.

World Bank. 2001. *East Asian Miracle: Economic Growth and Public Policy.* Washington, DC: World Bank.

———. 2011. World Development Indicators 2011. Washington, DC: World Bank.

———. 2013. Health, Nutrition, and Population Statistics. Washington, DC: World Bank.

Chapter 2

Speeding the Demographic Transition

Introduction

The necessary precursor of a demographic dividend is a demographic transition in which a country or region moves from high to low levels of mortality and fertility. As detailed in chapter 1, the mortality transition in Sub-Saharan Africa is well under way, with child mortality rates falling rapidly in most countries. Yet the fertility transition is slow in some places and stalled in others. This chapter examines the prospects for accelerating the fertility decline and the policy tools available, but first it tackles two questions.

The first question is, Should the state intervene to quicken the fertility transition for economic reasons? Some countries have been criticized for using coercive policies to achieve national population targets. For example, the International Conference on Population and Development in Cairo in 1994 condemned such policies and adopted a woman-centered, rights-based approach to family planning (Bongaarts and Sinding 2009). This chapter takes the view that the economic benefits of smaller family size accrue mainly to the family and that fertility decisions should be made by the family. While there are economic costs to having larger families, there are also benefits, including the direct enjoyment that parents get from their children; these are not included in standard measures of gross domestic product (GDP) per capita, but they will and should influence families' decisions.

Within this framework there is still scope for public policy. One policy area addresses factors that help families to achieve their desired family size, in particular, through access to family planning methods that allow women to avoid unwanted fertility. A second touches on factors that affect the demand for fertility. A portion of fertility is to replace or insure against child mortality, but it is clearly better to reduce child mortality and the need for replacement births than to have high child mortality and high desired fertility. Further, interventions that empower women (education, labor market opportunities, and information on the health benefits of delaying first births and spacing births) increase the capabilities and decision-making power of women and can improve their welfare. Enlarging the choices available is good for women, but individual women have to decide what choices they wish to make.

The second question is, Are the economic benefits of a rapid fertility transition really greater than those of a slow transition? And, even if they are, is it prudent to intervene to speed the fertility transition? The rapid fertility transition in East Asia was accompanied by a rapid and sharp increase in the working-age share of the population as youth dependency rates dropped. However, this gain was short-lived, lasting around 40 years. The population is now aging, and the working-age share of the population will drop in the near future as old-age dependency rises. Projected rates of fertility decline in Sub-Saharan Africa suggest that the rise in working-age share will be slow in coming, will have a modest peak, and will last a long time. If the working-age share were the only factor in the demographic dividend, then a rapid decline in fertility and a large rise in income per capita for a short period would not necessarily be better than having a slower decline in fertility and a smaller rise in income per capita for a longer period.

However, the rise in the working-age share is not the only effect of the fertility transition. The reduction in fertility is not just a decline in total fertility; it is usually associated with improvements in the timing and spacing of births. Teenage pregnancy and short intervals between births are associated with poor health outcomes for both mothers and children (Conde-Agudelo et al. 2012; Finlay, Özaltin, and Canning 2011), which can have a negative impact on a country's economy. In contrast, a decline in fertility can allow women to enter the labor force, which increases the working-age share of the population, among other benefits (Bloom et al. 2009; Goldin 1994; Soares and Falcão 2008). These health and female labor supply effects are likely to be permanent and to bring long-term economic benefits.

Moreover, economic benefits are not the only factors that affect welfare calculations. Another important consideration regarding policies that speed the transition is that fertility choices are personal rather than instruments for macroeconomic policy. The decisions regarding family planning and size should remain with the individual family unit since the benefits and costs of the demographic dividend accrue at the household level (Bloom et al. 2012). The health, educational, and economic benefits of lower family size accrue directly to the families that choose to have fewer children. Families should make an informed choice about the right number of children to have. There is also high infertility and sterility in the region due to health problems, and infertility, particularly childlessness, can have enormous social consequences for women (Hollos and Larsen 2008; Larsen 2000). The family-centered approach advocated here means that the state should respond both to the women who want to reduce their fertility and to those who want to overcome infertility.

Despite recent declines, fertility rates in Sub-Saharan Africa remain the highest in the world. While declines in fertility have followed declines in child mortality in the rest of the world, the pace of the decline has varied across countries, and it is not automatic that a rapid fertility transition will occur in Sub-Saharan Africa. Social, economic, and cultural forces play an important part in desired fertility for families in Africa. Household fertility rates within the same population tend to move together, independent of individual family incentives. This behavior suggests that fertility is highly influenced by social interactions and group norms (Bongaarts and Watkins 1996). In addition, even within the household, decision makers may have different preferences, and the observable outcome may be the result of negotiations that depend on the strength of bargaining power (Ashraf, Field, and Lee 2010; Manser and Brown 1980). Therefore, the factors that affect the empowerment of women, such as women's education, may change the incentives that families encounter as well as the bargaining outcomes that affect fertility.

Once desired fertility falls, women need to have knowledge of and access to mechanisms that help them to control their fertility. These mechanisms are known as the proximate determinants of fertility and include the age of marriage or sexual debut, contraception, abortion, sterility, and postpartum infecundity due to long periods of breastfeeding after giving birth (Bongaarts 1978). When considering how to lower fertility rates, two important policy areas arise. The first is the need to overcome social customs that force girls into early marriage and childbirth. A delay in the age of marriage and childbirth will give girls the option to stay in school and work prior to marriage. The second is the need to make family planning services widely available to women who desire to limit or space births. When men and women have different fertility preferences, family planning costs may substantially weaken a woman's bargaining position if she does not have her own income (Glick and Linnemayr 2013).

The rest of this chapter highlights areas where policies can make a difference to fertility outcomes. It first reviews the evidence linking fertility with child health (including the impacts of declines in mortality and the effects of child spacing and the age of mothers), investments in female education, social norms, gender equity, female labor force participation, and urbanization. This is followed by a review of evidence regarding the proximate determinants of fertility, including age of marriage and use of contraception. A final section describes the factors related to effective family planning programs, including costs and public subsidies.

Child Health and Fertility

At the aggregate level, a reduction in mortality is a prerequisite for and a major driver of fertility decline (Dyson 2011). In Europe the reduction in child and infant mortality was the most important factor in fertility decline, with higher wages being responsible for only about one-third of the decline (Coale 1986; Eckstein, Mira, and Wolpin 1999; Galloway and Lee 1998; Preston 1978). Despite substantial declines, child mortality levels are much higher in Sub-Saharan Africa than in the rest of the world.

Child Mortality

The desire to have surviving children drives the fertility decisions of families. Households have two main mechanisms through which changes in child mortality affect fertility—replacement and insurance. When a child dies, one expects to see replacement fertility as the household adjusts to the shock. However, a child's death may not always be "replaced," as fertility declines with age. This means that, in addition to replacement fertility, families may also engage in insurance fertility. In some regions families have more children than they actually want—known as hoarding—expecting that some of these children will die and not be replaceable. Hoarding is more common in societies where children are important for continuing and expanding the genetic lineage, for providing old-age support, and for transferring family assets.

Estimates of the replacement effect are usually 0.2–0.3 (Haines 1998; Maglad 1994; Olsen 1980; Palloni and Rafalimanana 1999; Schultz 1997). That is, on average, a child death leads to replacement fertility in less than one-third of cases. The insurance effect is potentially larger, estimated at 0.5–1.0 (Hossain, Phillips, and LeGrand 2007; LeGrand and Phillips 1996; LeGrand et al. 2003), but it is hard to measure (Ben-Porath 1976; Sah 1991; Schultz 1969, 1976) because it depends on the perceived risk of child mortality rather than on actual child mortality. The drop in fertility due to the insurance effect usually lags behind the drop in child mortality. It takes a while for households to realize that child mortality has fallen and to stop bearing additional children for insurance purposes.

Apart from historical longitudinal evidence from the European Fertility Project (Coale and Watkins 1986), cross-sectional data from the World Development Indicators show a negative relationship between under-five mortality and fertility. Countries with low under-five mortality today also have low fertility rates (figure 2.1). Countries in Sub-Saharan Africa have both higher fertility *and* higher under-five mortality than elsewhere in the world. The importance of lower child mortality in fertility decline suggests that African countries with high child mortality rates should focus first on improving child health and then on reducing fertility. The responsiveness of fertility to a decline in mortality also means that health interventions that save children's lives cause an increase in population; however, this period of population growth is temporary and counterbalanced by falling fertility in the long run.

Figure 2.1 Correlation between Under-Five Mortality Rate and Total Fertility Rate in Sub-Saharan Africa and Rest of the World, 2012

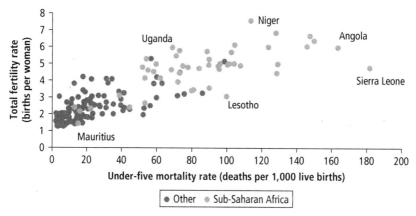

Source: World Bank 2012.

Birth Intervals and Age of Mother at Birth

Short intervals between births have negative effects on maternal, infant, and child health. Folate depletion in mothers can adversely affect children born after short birth intervals. Women bearing children in short intervals are also at risk of cervical insufficiency, which increases the chance of preterm birth or miscarriage. Children born after shorter birth intervals have a higher risk of death and ill health due to mother-to-child transmission of infection, suboptimal lactation (because of overlap between periods of breastfeeding and pregnancy), and sibling competition (Conde-Agudelo, Rosas-Bermúdez, and Kafury-Goeta 2006; Conde-Agudelo et al. 2012).

Birth spacing is critical in reducing infant mortality. Even after adjusting for mother's age, parents' education, urban or rural location, and other household indexes of relative wealth, children born after shorter birth intervals are at a significantly higher risk of dying: children born after an interval of 7–11 months are 4.3 times more likely to die than children born after an interval of 36–47 months (figure 2.2). The risk of death decreases as birth intervals increase and is lowest when a child is born at an interval of 48–59 months.

Young motherhood has a strong negative effect on the health outcomes of mothers and children that is independent of birth spacing, order, and household socioeconomic factors (figure 2.3). Young mothers are more likely to die as a result of childbirth, and children born to young mothers are more likely to die or suffer from ill health. A teenage girl's pelvis is not fully formed

Figure 2.2 Adjusted Relative Risk of Infant Mortality in Sub-Saharan Africa, by Birth Interval, 1987–2011

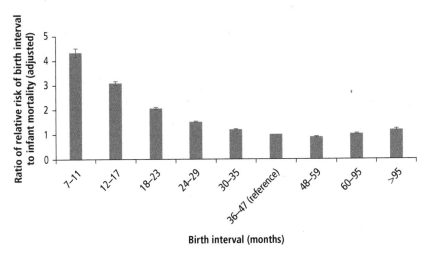

Source: Finlay and Canning 2013.
Note: Depicts the relative risk of infant mortality in Sub-Saharan Africa from the time since the previous birth, adjusting for other household characteristics.

Figure 2.3 Ratio of Adjusted Relative Risk of Infant Mortality to Age of Mother at Birth in Sub-Saharan Africa, 1987–2011

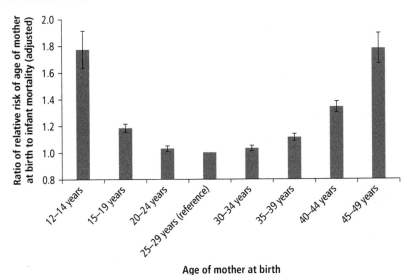

Source: Finlay and Canning 2013.

to support pregnancies. Moreover, young mothers may not know how to provide child care and might not have adequate financial support. The effect of a mother's age on child health is nonlinear, as older mothers can also yield poor child health outcomes through the biological mechanism.

Contraceptives enable households to ensure adequate birth spacing. A family planning intervention in Matlab, Bangladesh, not only resulted in a fertility decline of 17 percent, but also saw added benefits of increased birth spacing, lower child mortality, greater use of preventative health measures, and improved women's status. A secondary benefit of the Matlab intervention was a decline in child mortality because of better birth spacing. This hypothesis is consistent with the findings of Joshi and Schultz (2007), who discovered that increased access to family planning does not delay age at first birth, but rather increases birth spacing. A paper by Finlay, Özaltin, and Canning (2011) asserts that promoting delayed age of childbearing requires viable economic and educational alternatives for women rather than increased access to family planning.

The young age of a mother at birth—common in Sub-Saharan Africa—also lengthens her reproductive life, which is counterproductive in accelerating the fertility transition. Sub-Saharan Africa needs to make serious headway in increasing the age of mothers at first birth. One means is through national policies setting the legal marital age, and another is through policies increasing education levels for girls and women. In the United States, for example, the average age of first birth increased from 21 to 25 years in 1970–2000. Though not preceded by explicit policy changes, this change is attributable to increased education—and labor market opportunities—for women.

Female Education and Fertility

Increased female education decreases total fertility. Both economic theory and the ideational theory of fertility change identify mechanisms through which female education leads to fertility decline. The economic theory of fertility posits an incentive effect—more educated women have higher opportunity costs of bearing children in terms of labor income forgone, and, as is evident in Sub-Saharan Africa, men often want larger families than their wives (Bankole and Singh 1998). The household bargaining model suggests that women with more education can support themselves better and have more bargaining power than women with less education, which creates a better opportunity to achieve lower desired fertility.

According to the ideation theory, women with more education may have better access to global communication networks and, through school and community, have different ideas of desired family size. They also may have increased access to, and awareness of, family planning methods, although recent surveys reveal a wide spread of knowledge in most socioeconomic groups in Africa (Khan et al. 2007). Additionally, women with more education also have better knowledge of prenatal care and child health and hence might have lower fertility through the indirect mechanism of lower expected child mortality.

The negative relationship between female education and fertility stands out clearly in Ethiopia, Ghana, and Kenya (figure 2.4). The differences in the total fertility rate (TFR) between women with no schooling and women with a high school education are striking. In Ghana in 2008, for example, women with a high school education (12 years of schooling) had a TFR of 2–3, whereas women with no education had a TFR of around 6. In Ethiopia in 2011, women with a high school education had a TFR of 1.34, while women with no education had a TFR of 5.61.

The strong association between education and fertility is suggestive of a causal relationship, but it may be the result of confounding—women who prefer to have small families may also prefer to acquire a good education. In addition,

Figure 2.4 Total Fertility Rate in Ethiopia, Ghana, and Kenya, by Female Years of Schooling, 1990–2010

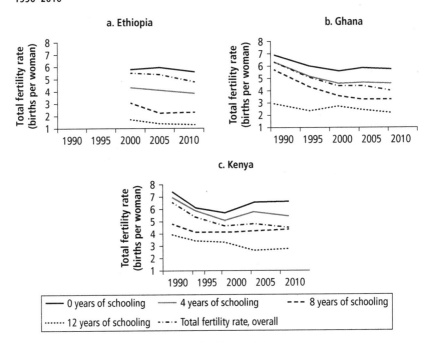

Source: Based on the most recent demographic and health survey for the country.

early childbearing can be a reason for dropping out of school. However, strong empirical evidence from Sub-Saharan Africa supports the causal role of female education in fertility decline (box 2.1). An education reform in Kenya that increased the length of primary education by one year increased female educational attainment and delayed the age of marriage and first birth (Chicoine 2012). A randomized control trial by Duflo et al. (2006), also in Kenya, finds that reducing the cost of school uniforms not only lowered dropout rates but also cut teenage marriage and childbearing. Osili and Long (2008) examine education reform in Nigeria and find that increasing female education by one year reduced early fertility by 0.26 birth.

The large impact of education on fertility is related to the potential earnings of women and the opportunity cost of raising children. However, there are also other possible mechanisms, including ideation and raising the bargaining power of women. Lavy and Zablotsky (2011) present evidence that female education lowers fertility without changing female labor force participation rates. Using the abrupt end of military rule, which greatly restricted the mobility of Arabs in Israel until the mid-1960s, as their instrument, the authors find that the change caused a very large increase in female schooling attainment. Consequently, the increase in schooling led to a decline in completed fertility. They further showed that female labor force participation in that population had remained stable and concluded that education reduced fertility by increasing the bargaining power of those women in the household through access to contraceptives and preference for healthier and educated children.

In addition to female education, male education also has a role in determining fertility. Breierova and Duflo (2004) find that female education matters more than male education in increasing age at marriage and delaying fertility. Male education may in fact raise fertility by increasing the economic resources of the household and may strengthen men's bargaining position within marriage, but these effects seem to be smaller than the effect of female education. While fertility falls when both men's and women's education rises together, figure 2.5 shows the large gap between male and female secondary enrollment in Sub-Saharan Africa, which means that achieving equality in educational attainment in Sub-Saharan Africa could have a substantial effect on fertility rates. Moreover, as shown in figure 2.6, countries where women have more schooling have lower fertility rates, which adds an association-based argument for educating girls, over and above its effect on human capital, female labor force participation, and economic growth.

In 1980 and 2010, African nations with high levels of female education had lower total fertility than countries with lower levels of female education. The difference between the lines in figure 2.6 are consistent between the two years, which suggests that other factors, such as increased access to family planning methods, decreased child mortality, and better access to labor market

BOX 2.1

The Effect of Education Reform on Teenage Fertility in Ethiopia

Ethiopia has wide variations in fertility by education level. These variations also are evident in teenage fertility, as 61 percent of women with no schooling have a child before turning 20, compared with only 16 percent of women with eight years of schooling.

Do these variations reflect a causal effect? The 1994 education reform in Ethiopia removed school fees, instituted school lunches in rural areas, increased the education budget, and allowed classes to be taught in the local vernacular rather than in Amharic.

Figure B2.1.1 shows the average years of schooling of women in Ethiopia by birth cohort based on the 2011 demographic and health survey (DHS). The cohort born in 1987 was exposed to the reform at age seven when entering school, while the cohort born in 1986 came of school age under the old system. As shown, the reform led to a substantial jump in female education, increasing female schooling of the cohorts born in or after 1987 by 0.8 year.

Pradhan and Canning (2013a) use a regression discontinuity approach to estimate the effect of this exogenous shock to educational attainment on teenage marriage, fertility, and sex. They estimate that each additional year of schooling leads to about a

Figure B2.1.1 Average Years of Schooling in Ethiopia, by Birth Cohort and Reform Coverage, 1960–90

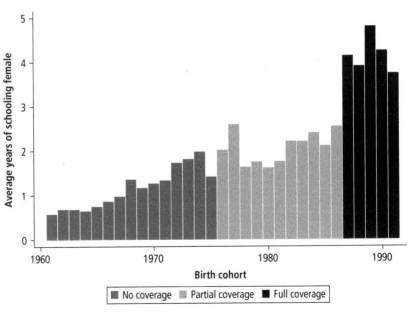

Source: Pradhan and Canning 2013a.

(continued next page)

Box 2.1 (continued)

7 percentage point reduction in the probability of teenage birth (figure B2.1.2) and a 6 percentage point decrease in the probability of teenage marriage (table B2.1.1). These effects are large (though the effect on teenage sex appears statistically insignificant). They suggest that women with eight years of schooling should have a fertility rate 53 percentage points lower than that of women with no schooling.

Reductions in early childbearing indicate that overall fertility rates in this cohort will be lower and that the direct benefits of avoiding early childbearing, such as improved maternal and child health, will be greater.

Figure B2.1.2 Probability of Giving Birth before 20 Years of Age in Ethiopia, by Birth Cohort and Reform Coverage, 1960–90

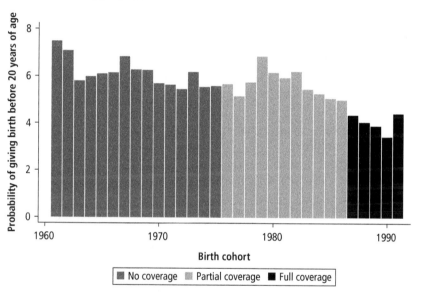

Source: Pradhan and Canning 2013a.

Table B2.1.1 Effect of Education on Adolescent Reproductive Behavior in Ethiopia

Variable	Teenage birth	Teenage marriage	Teenage sex
Years of schooling	−0.067***	−0.060***	−0.014
	(0.006)	(0.009)	(0.049)
Time trend	0.016	0.015	−0.028
	(0.014)	(0.014)	(0.027)
Number of observations	2,740	2,740	2,740

Source: Pradhan and Canning 2013a.
Note: Compares women born in the two years after 1987 who were fully exposed to the new policies with those born in the two years before. Standard errors are in parentheses. All regressions control for religion, ethnicity, number of siblings that the woman had, and her birth order.
*** *p* <.01. Standard errors in parentheses. All regressions controlled for religion, ethnicity, number of siblings that the woman had, and her birth order.

Figure 2.5 Gap in Male-Female Secondary Enrollment in Sub-Saharan Africa, Latest Year Available

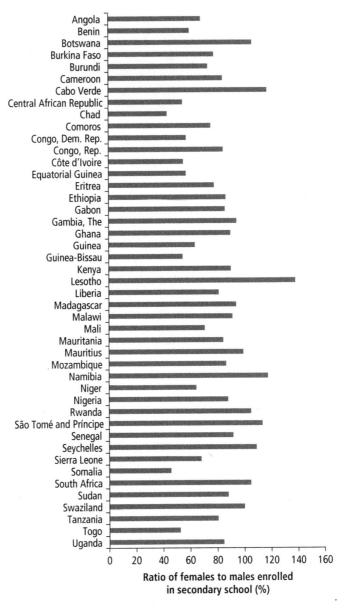

Source: World Bank 2011.
Note: Data are not available for Zambia and Zimbabwe.

Figure 2.6 Total Fertility Rate and Average Years of Female Schooling in Sub-Saharan Africa, 1980 and 2010

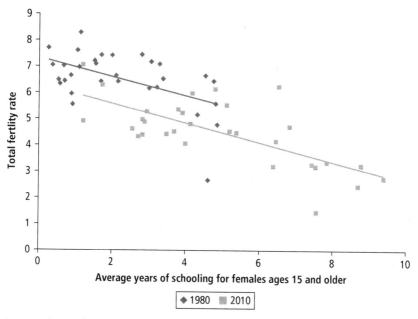

Source: Fertility rates from World Bank 2011; average years of female schooling from Barro and Lee 2013.

opportunities, may also have played a role in lowering fertility. Education, while important, is not the whole story. Education is a "distal" determinant of fertility, which can only act by delaying age at marriage and childbearing and by achieving desired birth spacing. Family planning is important to reducing fertility.

Social Norms and Fertility

Social norms are important determinants of fertility. This premise first appeared in the analysis of the European Fertility Project in which several papers show that once fertility begins to decline in a particular area, other areas sharing a common language or culture experience similar declines (Coale and Watkins 1986; Knodel and Van de Walle 1979; Watkins 1987). Knowledge of the risks and benefits of different contraceptive methods, and the costs and benefits of having fewer children, seems to diffuse through social networks.

Social norms spread through two mechanisms—social learning and social influence (Montgomery and Casterline 1993, 1996). Social learning occurs when personal interactions with peers change fertility norms. Households face many uncertainties in determining optimal family size. For example, they face uncertainty about the costs and benefits of contraception or the costs of and returns to education for their children. Discussions with other members of the same social group help to resolve this uncertainty, and many social groups reach their own informal consensus on the ideal number of children, contraceptive practice, and so forth. Social influence, in contrast, deals with normative influences on preferences and behavior, highlighting the effect of the social environment on personal preferences.

Through either or both of these two mechanisms, social networks usually lead to higher aggregate effects than individual effects. For example, increasing a woman's education may lower both her fertility and her neighbor's fertility—this spillover effect gives rise to a social multiplier leading to policy effects that affect fertility more in the aggregate than at the individual level. In a multi-country analysis, Canning et al. (2013) find that increasing a woman's schooling by one year reduced her completed fertility by 0.1 child, while raising average schooling in the country by one year reduced average completed fertility by about 0.3 child. Similarly, as child survival affects fertility not only through replacement but also through insurance effects, the societal level of child mortality has a significant effect on expected mortality and thus fertility. In accord with this theory, Canning et al. find that every third child who dies is replaced at the household level, whereas a decline in child mortality at the national level decreases fertility one for one.

Important for reproductive decisions, social norms may differ among a society's groups. Munshi and Myaux (2006), for example, show that contraceptive and reproductive decisions were similar for households from the same religion in Matlab, Bangladesh, but varied among households from different religions (but with similar access to family planning services within the same village). This suggests that the diffusion of reproductive choices through network effects depends on how women and families are linked.

Efforts to introduce "cross-talks" in social networks may be important in increasing the effect of family planning campaigns. In a longitudinal study in Bangladesh, Kincaid (2000) finds that women who participated in group discussions about reproductive behavior showed an increase in rates of modern contraceptive use five times higher than women who were visited individually by health workers. The highly heterogeneous makeup of African societies with multiple religious, ethnic, and language groups may slow the diffusion of new social norms for reproductive decisions.

Marketplace or large community events are some of the channels through which households from different social networks interact. In Kenya, Kohler, Behrman, and Watkins (2001) find that women who share social networks with other women who use contraceptives are more likely to use contraceptives themselves. Further, they find that, in areas with high levels of family planning services and take-up, social networks affect contraceptive decisions through social learning. Behrman, Kohler, and Watkins (2002) find that social networks among men might be influential in changing ideations about contraceptive behavior and ideal family size. They note that both men and women (in their study) remarked that decisions about family size are men's domain and that men are more likely to be influenced by their network partners than women.

Religion provides important social norms in Africa that affect fertility, particularly when the religion expressly favors large families and discourages family planning (Caldwell and Caldwell 1987; McQuillan 2004). Traditional religions in Africa are not dogmatic about family planning (Adongo, Phillips, and Binka 1998), but there are differences in fertility between religious groups. Heaton (2011) finds that Muslims have substantially higher fertility than Christians in the region and that Protestants and Catholics have similar fertility. However, around the world there is increasing evidence that Muslim societies follow the same path in fertility as other countries where religion plays an important role, at most delaying fertility decline rather than preventing it (Groth and Sousa-Poza 2012).

Can government policies change preferences and affect demand for family planning? In Bangladesh, the Islamic Republic of Iran, and the Republic of Korea, the timing of government policies corresponds with their fertility decline.

Figure 2.7 shows the time path of fertility and the timing of government population policies in three African countries (Robinson and Ross 2007). In Kenya, steep fertility decline followed the launch of a strong national family planning program in the early 1970s. Total fertility fell about 40 percent in 1980–2000. Population policies in Ghana that began around the same time also saw steep declines in fertility. In Uganda, however, the first national population policy, which began in 1995, was less successful (Uganda Ministry of Finance, Planning, and Economic Development 2008).[1] However, even in places where the timing of policies is closely aligned with changes in fertility, it is difficult to infer causality.

Gender Equity and Fertility

The economic model discussed so far considers household's unitary decision makers. In a unitary household model, a couple is assumed to have a single set of preferences. In a bargaining model, the husband and wife have different preferences. They bargain over outcomes, including the number of children, and are successful depending on their relative bargaining power. The relative age, education, and private economic resources of the couple will affect their bargaining power and may affect fertility decisions. Gender inequality can be an important determinant of fertility.

Figure 2.7 Impact of Family Planning Campaigns on Total Fertility in Ghana, Kenya, and Uganda, 1960–2014

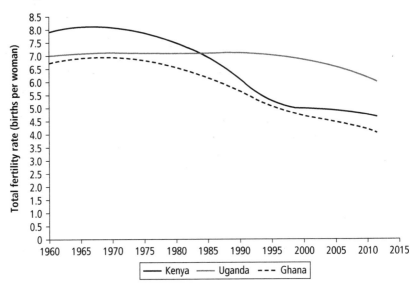

Source: World Bank 2011.

Men and women have different fertility preferences in Sub-Saharan Africa. Husbands consistently prefer larger families than their wives (Shapiro and Gebreselassie 2008; Westoff 1992). Further data from Demographic and Health Surveys (DHSs) suggest that the proportion of husbands or partners who approve of contraceptive use is much lower than the proportion of women who do; this spread is larger in Sub-Saharan Africa than in other regions. Ethnographic studies have shown that women often hide contraceptive use from their partner (Castle et al. 1999; Fapohunda and Todaro 1988; McCarraher, Martin, and Bailey 2006). A field experiment in Zambia by Ashraf, Field, and Lee (2010), for example, finds that women are more likely to use contraceptives and less likely to bear children if they are offered contraceptives that they can conceal from their partner than if they are offered contraceptives in their husband's presence. Because men in many African households have more bargaining power than women (Woldemicael and Beaujot 2011), addressing gender inequity could accelerate fertility decline.

Female Labor Market Opportunities and Fertility

The economic theory of fertility stresses the potential earnings of women. When deciding about child care and ideal family size, a household evaluates the opportunity cost of child care for the husband and the wife. If the potential earnings of women are much lower than the potential earnings of men, a household might decide that women will perform child care rather than join the low-earnings labor market. As the relative wages for women rise, women and households face time trade-offs between child care and labor market participation. Hence high female labor market participation results in lower fertility. However, the direction of causality (between female labor market participation and fertility) is hard to isolate—only the association is clear (Hout 1978; Kupinsky 1977).

The type of work that women do may be even more important for fertility than whether they work. Most women in Sub-Saharan Africa work inside their home or on the family farm, not for pay, and often alongside raising children. Women working in more formal sectors, such as manufacturing or services, outside the home, and for pay may be unable to care for children at the same time and so may face tighter time constraints than other working women. When a developing country has a comparative advantage in labor-intensive manufacturing and trade raises the demand for female labor in manufacturing, fertility may decline (Goh 1999). In rural China, for example, Fang et al. (2010) find that female employment in nonfarm work reduced completed fertility by 0.64 child and the probability of bearing more than one child by 54.8 percent, compared with female employment in farm work.

Sub-Saharan Africa is exceptional in that both female labor force participation *and* fertility are high (figure 2.8). Disaggregating the same data by country,

Figure 2.8 Total Fertility Rate and Female Labor Force Participation in Sub-Saharan Africa and Other Regions, 2011

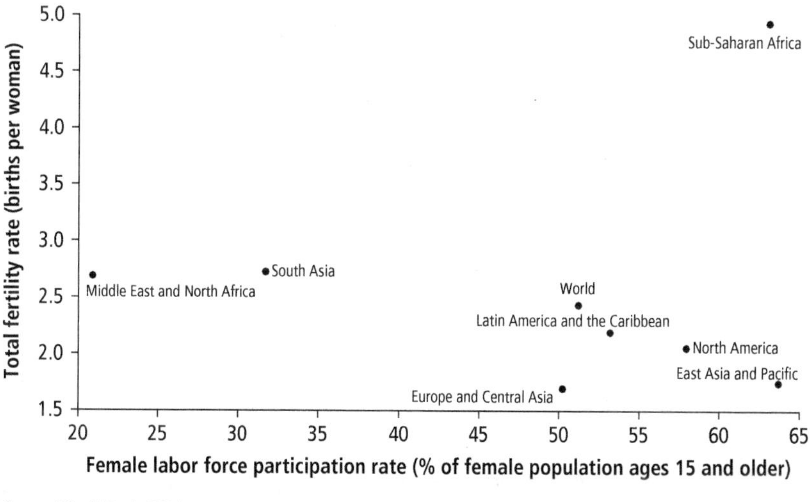

Source: World Bank 2011.

Figure 2.9 Total Fertility Rate and Female Labor Force Participation in Select Sub-Saharan African Countries, 2011

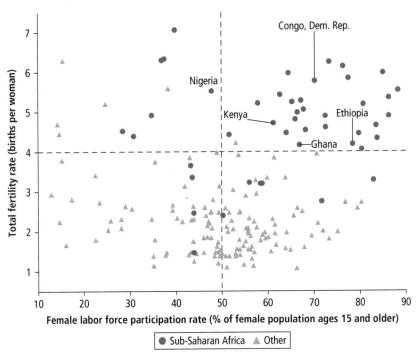

Source: World Bank 2011.

figure 2.9 places the majority of African countries in the top-right quadrant of high female labor force participation and high fertility. There are two reasons for this: women participate in the informal labor market where there is a minimal time trade-off between market participation and child care, and working mothers have the support of an extended social network for child care (Fapohunda and Todaro 1988). Other evidence from Africa suggests that increased female labor force participation only leads to lower fertility for highly educated women in urban areas (Ashraf, Field, and Lee 2010; Castle et al. 1999; McCarraher, Martin, and Bailey 2006).

Urbanization and Fertility

As described in chapter 1, total fertility rates are consistently much higher in urban than in rural settings in Sub-Saharan Africa, and the rural-urban differences in TFR are far greater in Africa than in other world regions. Even among women with no education, those residing in the capital city have much lower fertility (2.02) than those residing in rural areas (5.89). Although the effect of urbanization is most pronounced among women with low levels of education, the effect of education is even greater, as the TFR is much lower for women with a high school education than for women with any other level of education, regardless of place of residence. Nevertheless, as more people move to urban areas, fertility is expected to fall more rapidly.

The reasons for the rural-urban gap in fertility are many and varied. Where only the male head of household moves to the city for work or where migration to the city is temporary (seasonal work), coital frequency (fecundability) can decline. Age of first marriage may be higher in cities because both women and men choose to pursue schooling or employment, thereby delaying family formation. Access to modern methods of contraception and abortion services is likely greater in urban than in rural areas.

All of these factors can affect quantum or temporal shifts in fertility such that women have fewer children overall and begin childbearing later. Social norms regarding fertility preferences and contraceptive use also vary greatly between urban and rural areas, with assimilation over time among new rural migrants to cities. However, it is unclear whether the rural-urban difference in fertility is mainly because of differences in social norms or because of differences in socioeconomic conditions. According to the literature on rural-urban migrants, the two mechanisms tend to reinforce each other, having different effects in different settings.

In agricultural communities, having many children could mean higher productivity on the household farm. Children are both a production and a consumption good, and the ideal family size—larger in these agricultural economies—is determined by weighing the productivity of each additional child against the resources the child consumes. Rural households may optimally decide to have more children. At the same time, rural areas often have less access to and knowledge of family planning methods, and so rural households that want to control their fertility may be unable to access contraceptives and achieve their desired family size.

Having more children might be more costly in urban than in rural settings, as urban areas have higher costs for child care and for housing. Better labor market opportunities in urban areas also mean a higher opportunity cost of time. Urban economies tend to be industrial or service based, and work tends to be outside the home, making it difficult for women to combine work with child care. In addition, the lack of a local extended family in urban areas may make child care more difficult.

In urban areas, economic constraints and ideations seem to be important in lowering the fertility rates of women without any education. Women with low education in urban areas may learn from and copy their better educated neighbors, or the social control mechanisms that encourage high fertility may be weakened. In addition, urban areas may have better access to family planning services and methods, which allows women to reduce their fertility but also can affect their preferences through advertising and other sources of information.

During the early phases of urbanization, rural to urban migration is difficult, and migrants who move to urban areas are selectively different from persons who stay in rural areas. Chattopadhyay, White, and Debpuur (2006) find that the fertility behavior of rural-urban migrants in Ghana resembles that of urban natives more closely than that of persons who stay in rural areas, both before and after migration. This suggests that urbanization selects women who would have low fertility in any case.

However, Brockerhoff and Eu (1993) in their analysis of DHS data from Burundi, Ghana, Kenya, Mali, Nigeria, Senegal, Togo, and Uganda, find that migration among women in these countries is higher for women who are unmarried, are in their 20s, or have formal education. Brockerhoff (1998), using data from 14 DHSs in Sub-Saharan Africa, finds that the pattern of conception and contraceptive use of rural-urban migrant women who have been in urban areas for around two years resembles that of urban natives.

Proximate Determinants of Fertility

Bongaart's model of the proximate determinants of fertility lays out various mechanisms through which fertility can change (Bongaarts 1978). The proportion of women married or sexually active, contraceptive use (and effectiveness), postpartum insusceptibility, and induced abortion explain almost all of the variations in fertility observed over time. The other determinants—fecundability, intrauterine mortality, and sterility—are biological and health-related factors rather than choices.

Figure 2.10 shows a conceptual model for making the biological limit of fertility—the fecundity rate—fall to the actual observed fertility rate. The model asserts that all distal determinants of fertility act through these proximate determinants, providing a useful framework for decomposing fertility rates and better understanding its immediate drivers.

This framework allows us to quantify the role of each of the proximate determinants in lowering fertility. Assuming a biological maximum of fertility, figure 2.11 identifies the proximate determinants that lowered actual fertility from the biological maximum for Sub-Saharan African countries with demographic and health surveys after 2000 compared with select low- and middle-income countries in other regions. It provides a snapshot of how fertility is controlled in these countries.

Figure 2.10 Conceptual Framework of Proximate Determinants of Fertility

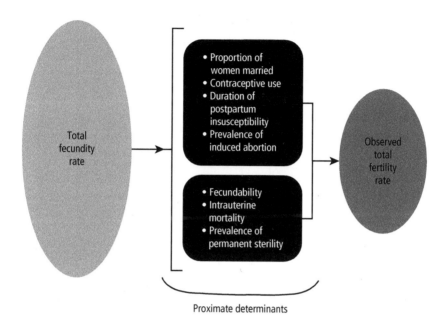

Proximate determinants

Source: Madhavan and Guengant 2013, adapted from Bongaarts 1978.

Delayed age at marriage and postpartum insusceptibility—due to high fertility rates and postpartum practices—play a large role in modulating fertility in Sub-Saharan Africa. In the comparator countries, delayed age of marriage also plays a large role, but contraceptive use plays a proportionally greater role than in Sub-Saharan Africa.

The proportion of unmarried women, due to late marriage, plays a critical role in lowering fertility. The African countries that have achieved low fertility have done so mainly through nonmarriage. With the exception of Burundi, Madagascar, Niger, and the Philippines, countries with lower fertility have higher proportions of unmarried women and higher levels of contraceptive use. However, contraception and abortion play a smaller role in most African countries than in countries in other regions, such as Bangladesh, the Arab Republic of Egypt, Pakistan, and the Philippines.

Although induced abortion plays a smaller role in lower fertility than nonmarriage and contraceptive use, it plays a sizable role in some countries in Sub-Saharan Africa (Eritrea, Ghana, Kenya, Liberia, Senegal, and Togo) and in the comparator sample (Bangladesh, Egypt, Pakistan, and the Philippines). In Eritrea and Togo, abortion plays a proportionately larger role in determining fertility than contraceptive use.

Figure 2.11 Total Fertility Rate in Sub-Saharan Africa and Select Low- and Middle-Income Countries in Other Regions, by Proximate Determinant, 1996–2011

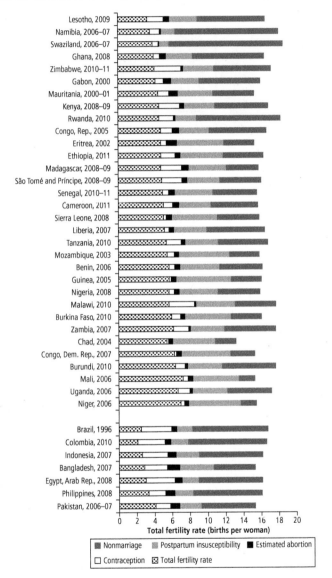

Source: Madhavan and Guengant 2013, using data from various demographic and health surveys (DHSs).
Note: The actual level of total fecundity is seen to vary from country to country (that is, the bars do not stack up to 15.3) because the residuals are not shown. This is not considered significant because the usefulness of this analysis stems from the ability to view the proportional contributions of the proximate determinants themselves at varying levels of total fertility rate. Data on fertility, marriage, postpartum insusceptibility, and contraceptive use come directly from DHSs. Abortion rates are imputed based on data from other sources, because, although terminations can be reported in DHSs, there may be underreporting due to stigma.

To illustrate the decomposition analysis, the proximate determinants of fertility change in rural and urban areas of five countries in Sub-Saharan Africa are decomposed. The countries are the Democratic Republic of Congo, Ethiopia, Ghana, Kenya, and Nigeria (figure 2.12). The five cities considered—Accra, Addis Ababa, Kinshasa, Lagos, and Nairobi—had populations in 2010 ranging from 2.5 million (Accra) to 10.8 million (Lagos), representing between 14 and 36 percent of the country's urban population (UN Population Division 2012). For all countries, the TFR is considerably lower in urban areas and in key cities than in rural areas, with the TFR in Addis Ababa at a remarkable 1.51. Moreover, the role of delayed age of first marriage—signified by the "nonmarriage" bar—features most prominently across all countries and residential areas, indicating that this is the primary fertility-inhibiting behavior. Key cities have the highest proportion of nonmarriage, followed by urban areas in general and then by rural areas. Conversely, induced

Figure 2.12 Total Fertility Rate in Five Sub-Saharan African Countries, by Proximate Determinant and Rural-Urban Residence, Various Years

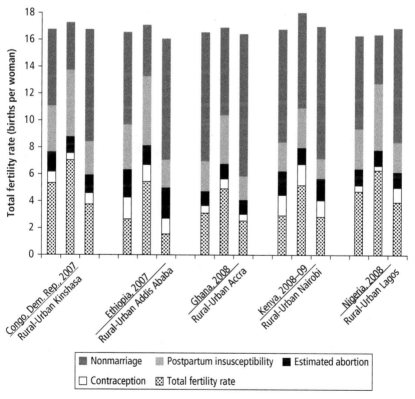

Source: Madhavan and Guengant 2013, using data from various demographic and health surveys.

abortion and contraceptive use appear to have a proportionally small effect on fertility. Postpartum abstinence or lactational amenorrhea (or postpartum insusceptibility) exhibits the second most powerful effect. As expected, the proportion of postpartum insusceptibility is highest where nonmarriage is lowest and fertility is highest—that is, in rural areas. The key cities have the lowest share of postpartum insusceptibility (to match the high share of nonmarriage).

The changes in TFR in four of these countries were then decomposed across residential areas to attribute changes in fertility to proximate determinants over time (figure 2.13). A key driver of fertility decline across all residential locations is contraceptive use in Ethiopia. In Kenya, it is both delayed age at marriage and contraceptive use, whereas in Ghana, it is delayed age at marriage. In Nigeria, however, the overall decline has been insignificant, and postpartum insusceptibility and contraceptive use seem to be the major determinants. Once again, in urban areas and major cities, delayed age at marriage is the most important proximate determinant of fertility.

Figure 2.13 Change in Total Fertility Rates in Four Sub-Saharan African Countries, by Proximate Determinant and Rural-Urban Residence, 2008–11

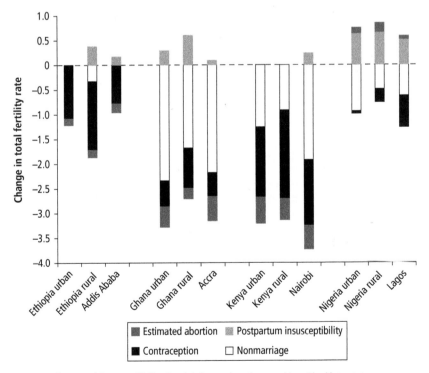

Source: Madhavan and Guengant 2013, using data from various demographic and health surveys.

Declines in TFR in countries in Sub-Saharan Africa and other regions are largely associated with increases in contraceptive use and age of first marriage— and, as seen, investments in female education can reduce fertility through both of these channels. Educated women are likely to marry later and to use contraceptives to space births and limit the number of children. Contraceptive use is still a minor factor in total fecundity in Sub-Saharan Africa, especially for countries with high fertility. In fact, contraceptive prevalence rates in most countries in Sub-Saharan Africa are quite low compared with rates in seven countries in other regions (figure 2.14).

Figure 2.15 presents a side-by-side comparison of TFR regressed onto the contraceptive prevalence rate for rural and urban Sub-Saharan Africa. While the association is slightly stronger for the rural analysis, with less variance from the mean, the more striking finding is that the entire scale for TFR is on the order of 2.0 points higher in rural than in urban areas. Moreover, the range for the contraceptive prevalence rate in rural areas (0–60 percent) is lower than the range for urban areas (10–70 percent). Similarly, the TFR is as high as 7.0 for rural areas, with many countries above 6.0, while the TFR in urban areas is below 4.5 for most countries, with just a few outliers above that.

Effective Family Planning: Barriers, Costs, and Public Subsidies

Family planning policies can increase contraceptive use by changing social norms—both individual preferences and social acceptability—regarding the use of contraceptives and by reducing the barriers to access (Magnani et al. 1999). Family planning encompasses not only the supply of contraceptives but also educational and outreach campaigns to encourage smaller family size (Bongaarts 1994). In a panel study, Magnani et al. (1999) find that in a family planning program in Morocco increased contraceptive use was associated with changes in social norms regarding family planning.

An intensive family planning experiment was conducted in Matlab, Bangladesh, that included the door-to-door provision of contraceptives by health workers. Health workers distributed contraceptives and provided households with information on the means and benefits of family planning. The intervention took place in some areas of Matlab, while other areas acted as controls. Results from this community-level intervention suggest that the provision of family planning services reduced fertility by about 1 child per woman in program areas versus control areas (Joshi and Schultz 2007; Schultz 2009).

In a Navrongo family planning program in northern Ghana, which had a similar design of treatment and control areas, an intervention that combined

Figure 2.14 Use of Modern Methods of Contraception in Sub-Saharan Africa and Seven Countries in Other Regions, by Rural-Urban Residence, Various Years

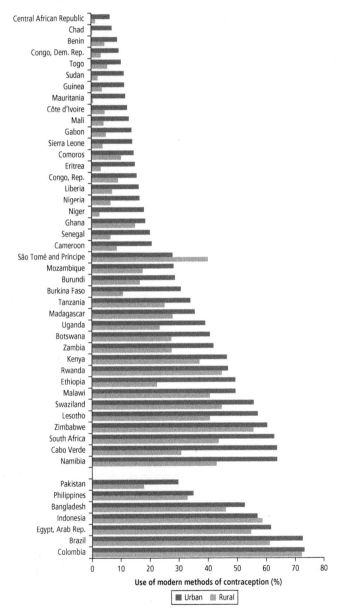

Source: Madhavan and Guengant 2013, using data from the most recent demographic and health survey in the country.

Figure 2.15 Association between Total Fertility Rate and Contraceptive Prevalence Rate in Sub-Saharan Africa, by Rural-Urban Location, Various Years

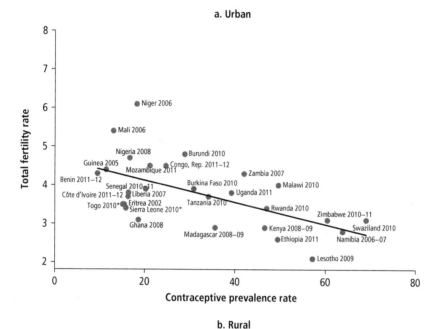

a. Urban

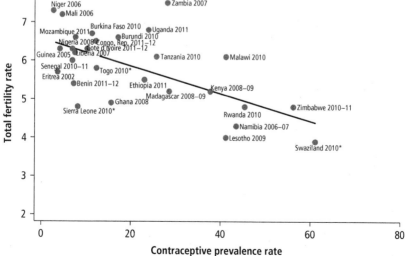

b. Rural

Source: Simkins 2013.

household visits by trained nurses with mobilization of traditional resources (including men) increased birth spacing in the first few years of the program relative to control communities (Phillips et al. 2012), with a similar reduction of about 1 child per woman.

Evidence from Rwanda suggests that an intensive family planning campaign can rapidly increase contraceptive use. A program launched in 2007 with a public education component and a budget six times as much as the previous program saw the contraceptive prevalence rate rise from 17 to 52 percent between 2005 and 2010, while fertility fell from 6.1 to 4.6 births per woman. DHSs also reveal substantial, if somewhat less dramatic, increases in contraceptive use in Ethiopia and Malawi, two countries with aggressive national family planning programs.

Evidence from the randomized experiments in Matlab and Navrongo suggests that intensive family planning programs can increase contraceptive use, reduce fertility, and hence speed the demographic transition.

Barriers to Uptake and Policy Responses

Sub-Saharan Africa has the highest percentage of women with unmet need for contraception: approximately 25 percent of women in the region—some 49 million women—either use traditional methods or use no method at all (Gribble 2012). The reasons for nonuse are varied—from being unmarried or having infrequent sexual intercourse to being concerned about health-related risks (figure 2.16).

Inadequate Supply

Inadequate supply of family planning services encompasses availability of contraceptives and counseling. Women in Sub-Saharan Africa are not as knowledgeable about family planning services or methods of contraception as women in other regions, based on the most recent DHS data from a sample of countries from Sub-Saharan Africa[2] and a sample of countries from Asia, Latin America, and the Middle East and North Africa.[3]

Data from the most recent DHS of 25 African countries show that, among women ages 15–49 who are not using contraceptives, 70 percent in urban areas and 56 percent in rural areas know of at least one source of family planning method. Relative to the comparator sample, of women not using contraception, 84 percent in urban areas and 73 percent in rural areas know of a method of family planning. Knowledge of a method is used here as a crude measure of availability of family planning services due to the lack of rigorous information on indicators of availability such as stock-outs and distance to and costs of accessing services (Creanga et al. 2011).

A natural experiment from Ghana provides causal evidence of the effect of contraceptive availability on fertility outcomes. Jones (2013) investigates the impact of changes in the supply of U.S.-funded contraceptives caused by the global gag rule that affected aid to local nongovernmental organizations providing a large share of contraceptives for Ghanaian households. Using this exogenous shock, Jones shows that pregnancies increased during the periods in which contraceptives were less available, although wealthier or more educated women offset this impact through abortions. Contraceptive stock-outs could therefore have a direct impact on fertility, underlining the importance of funding for sustainable family planning.

Poor Quality of Services

Another supply-side barrier is the quality of services—especially in health care, client-provider interactions, and products—as well as little (or no) choice of method. Studies show that the provision of information to clients and the

Figure 2.16 Reasons for Not Using Family Planning Services to Limit or Space Births in Sub-Saharan Africa, 2004–11

a. Reason for not using family planning to limit births

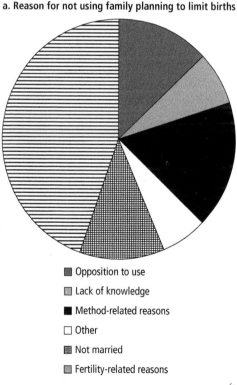

■ Opposition to use
▨ Lack of knowledge
■ Method-related reasons
□ Other
▦ Not married
▧ Fertility-related reasons

(continued next page)

Figure 2.16 (continued)

b. Reason for not using family planning to space births

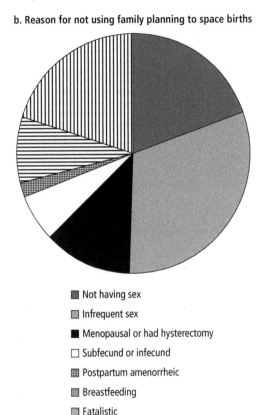

- ▨ Not having sex
- ▨ Infrequent sex
- ■ Menopausal or had hysterectomy
- ☐ Subfecund or infecund
- ▥ Postpartum amenorrheic
- ▤ Breastfeeding
- ▨ Fatalistic

Source: Demographic and health surveys for 25 countries in Sub-Saharan Africa (2004–11). See http://www.statcompiler.com.

technical competence of providers have a statistically significant effect on contraceptive use (Dieleman et al. 2011).

Provision of information on side effects and on various methods of contraception is low in Sub-Saharan Africa, but differs little from the rest of the sample countries with higher contraceptive prevalence rates. About 37 percent of African women were informed of side effects when obtaining contraceptives, compared with 31 percent of other women. Similarly, 44 percent of married women in Sub-Saharan Africa indicated that they were informed of other methods while deciding which method to use. Using the metrics available in DHSs, it appears that the quality of care is similar in the African sample and in the samples with higher contraceptive use.

Lack of Awareness

A possible explanation for unwanted fertility is that women are simply unaware of modern methods of contraception. The contraceptive knowledge gap varies across and within African countries. Most women in Africa are aware of modern contraception—90 percent of currently married women 15–49 years of age can name at least one method and 79 percent can name at least three. However, contraceptive knowledge is decidedly poorer in West African countries such as Chad, Niger, and Nigeria, where only 25, 45, and 48 percent of married women, respectively, can name at least three methods.

Similarly, differences in knowledge across wealth and education levels (and urban or rural residence) are striking in many of these countries. West African countries display the most extreme differences. For example, only 4.5 percent of the women in Chad's poorest households know of at least three methods compared with 55 percent in the richest. In Nigeria, 23 percent of women without schooling know of at least three methods versus 80 percent with some high school education. Knowledge of contraception is generally higher in Sub-Saharan Africa than in other regions that also have relatively high contraceptive use.

Elementary knowledge of contraceptive methods does not seem to be a high barrier to access and use. Lack of basic knowledge may account for some of the low use in some geographic regions, but not all. Based on the DHS sample for Sub-Saharan Africa, it appears that most women who reported that they were not using contraception despite not wanting to become pregnant (at least not now) did not lack elementary knowledge. Only 6 percent of the women who were married or co-habitating, not using contraception, but not wanting to become pregnant reported that they were not using contraception because they did not know of a method.

Knowledge of contraceptive side effects seems to play a larger role in women not using contraception in Africa than in the sample countries in other regions. Among women not using contraception despite not wanting to get pregnant, 14 percent reported fear of side effects and 6 percent reported health reasons as reasons for not using contraceptives. These shares are similar to the comparator sample, where 13 percent cited side effects and 10 percent cited health reasons for not using contraception; 50 percent of these women in Sub-Saharan Africa mentioned fertility-related reasons such as infrequent sex or infertility. Seen against some of the other reasons, the knowledge barriers—while not trivial—do not seem very high.

Knowledge here, however, is defined in very narrow terms and does not encompass the knowledge of the full costs and benefits of family planning, not only for maternal and child health but also for household wealth. Demand-generating family planning programs combined with the provision of contraceptive services, as in Matlab (Joshi and Schultz 2007) or more recently in

Zambia (Neukom et al. 2011), could increase contraceptive use and improve fertility and child health outcomes.

Lack of Affordability

Affordability includes not only the direct costs of contraceptives, but also the opportunity costs of securing them, such as travel and waiting time. Affordability is certainly a plausible barrier for poor households, with the average contraceptive prevalence rate in the poorest and richest households in Africa being 14 and 32 percent, respectively. The gap in use, albeit consistent with affordability, is also linked to differences in desired fertility and accessibility of contraceptives across wealth levels.

Married or co-habitating women who said that they did not want to become pregnant did not report price as a major reason for not using contraception.[4] In the African DHS samples, 3 percent of these women cited price as a factor, but that proportion was as high as 7 percent in many West African countries, including Benin, Burkina Faso, and Cameroon.

However, the price sensitivity of poorer households may be higher when one compares preventive technologies such as contraceptives to other consumable goods. Studies show that households fail to act on their intentions and desires when purchasing goods whose payoff is in the future (Kremer and Holla 2009). Literature from behavioral economics suggests that people fail to act in their interest for a wide range of reasons, and several "nudge" interventions have succeeded in encouraging households to follow through on their intent. Family planning services would be underconsumed if these behavioral biases were present. Studies of six family planning programs from Ghana, India, Sri Lanka, Thailand, and the United States suggest that modest incentives such as a tin of powdered milk could encourage the use of family planning services (Heil, Gaalema, and Herrmann 2012).

Gender Inequity

The opportunity costs of bearing children are borne largely by women, who generally prefer to have smaller families than their husband or partner prefers. However, in most African settings, husbands or partners have more bargaining power in the household, resulting in underconsumption of family planning services and larger family sizes than women desire. Hence focusing on gender could improve the impact of family planning initiatives.

Costs and Cost-Effectiveness of Family Planning Programs

The Matlab and Navrongo studies suggest that intensive family planning programs can affect fertility as well as maternal and child health. However, the costs of programs that combine extensive health worker–client relationships with contraceptive products can be high. Estimating both costs and cost-effectiveness of such programs is fraught with complications, as seen in the literature.

Capturing all of the costs and benefits of family planning programs can prove difficult. Similarly, the costs of providing family planning include the costs of contraceptives, trained providers, and a reliable supply chain. Full cost-effectiveness studies also compare program costs across countries, considering quality of services provided, using a common methodology, defining common service packages, and estimating administrative costs of the program (Murray et al. 2000).

Most cost-effectiveness studies on family planning, however, fail to capture the myriad costs and benefits of the intervention and instead report estimates in "couple-year of protection" (CYP), which captures the annual costs of providing contraception to a couple. Costs of contraceptives alone can be very different across settings: for example, an FHI360 analysis of five studies that examines the costs of delivering family planning services in Kenya finds large differences in estimates, with one year of CYP for an intrauterine device ranging from US$2.16 to US$13.99 in 1997. The estimates for other methods also tend to have similarly large spreads.

A recent Guttmacher Institute study reports direct costs for Africa that range from US$1.01 CYP for an intrauterine device, US$4.15 for condoms, US$8.72 for pills, and US$8.61 for injectables (Singh et al. 2010). These costs include the costs of commodities, supplies, and labor, including visits, examinations, and procedures. In addition to the direct costs, the report estimates indirect costs of family planning programs. For Africa, the total per user cost of providing a modern method is estimated at US$11.26 CYP.

And so the costs and impact of a "bare-bones" family planning program that supplies only contraceptives could be very different from those of a comprehensive program that provides a range of methods, offers competent providers who counsel on the various choices of method and potential side effects, and offers information about the adopted choice. The Guttmacher report provides estimates for such comprehensive programs, noting that the CYP increases from US$11.26 to US$26.90 for Africa. The increase is aligned with the costs in the Zambia study, where midwives were trained, hired, and placed at public health facilities to improve take-up of long-acting reversible methods. The added cost of such a comprehensive and high-quality program was estimated at US$13 per CYP.

Targeted media campaigns designed to convey family planning–related messages may also be quite cost-effective. CYP estimates of such campaigns range from US$1.36 in Turkey (Kincaid et al. 1993), US$3.26 in Egypt (Robinson and Lewis 2003), and US$3.57 in Zimbabwe (Piotrow et al. 1992).

As these campaigns are important for a comprehensive family planning program, their costs should be added to the direct costs of providing family planning.

Rationales for Public Support of Family Planning

Even though the estimated costs of providing family planning services are not trivial in developing economies, the rationale for public subsidies is compelling, especially for a human rights–based approach that enables women to make their own reproductive choices.

Market failure is a standard economic rationale for subsidizing a good whose net social benefits exceed the individual benefits. Households in agrarian economies benefit from having large families, but these costs fall not only on the household. Family planning subsidies also can lead to smaller families with well-spaced births where the positive externalities of better educated and healthier children can significantly add to the quality of human capital.

Another market failure is that women and households lack information needed to make their reproductive choices. Households might not be aware of the long-term costs and benefits of having fewer or more widely spaced births, especially for children's survival and future prospects. Subsidizing family planning would temper the undervaluation of contraceptives that occurs when households decide on family size and birth spacing. Subsidizing family planning could make contraceptives more cost-beneficial for households than they are now. Beyond gender disparities, socioeconomic disparities could be mitigated by public subsidies, as when an equity-based approach focuses more on poorer and more rural households.

Notes

1. Average incomes are higher in Kenya than in Uganda. Since income could affect access to family planning services, part of the lower fertility rates in Kenya could be attributed to higher average incomes in Kenya as compared to Uganda.
2. The sample of countries in Sub-Saharan Africa includes Benin, Burkina Faso, Burundi, Cameroon, Chad, the Democratic Republic of Congo, Ethiopia, Ghana, Guinea, Kenya, Liberia, Madagascar, Malawi, Mali, Mozambique, Namibia, Niger, Nigeria, Rwanda, Senegal, Sierra Leone, Tanzania, Uganda, Zambia, and Zimbabwe.
3. The sample of countries in other regions includes Bangladesh, Bolivia, Brazil, Colombia, the Dominican Republic, Egypt, Indonesia, Jordan, Morocco, Nicaragua, Pakistan, Peru, the Philippines, and Vietnam.
4. In the DHS, women, not men, were asked about the reasons for not using contraceptives. It is possible that men would be more likely to cite cost (including opportunity cost of women's time) as a reason for not using them.

References

Adongo, P. B., J. F. Phillips, and F. N. Binka. 1998. "The Influence of Traditional Religion on Fertility Regulation among the Kassena-Nankana of Northern Ghana." *Studies in Family Planning* 29 (1): 23–40.

Ashraf, N., E. Field, and J. Lee. 2010. "Household Bargaining and Excess Fertility: An Experimental Study in Zambia." Harvard University, Cambridge, MA. http://fmwww .bc.edu/ec-j/SemF2011/Field.pdf.

Bankole, A., and S. Singh. 1998. "Couples' Fertility and Contraceptive Decision-Making in Developing Countries: Hearing the Man's Voice." *International Family Planning Perspectives* 24 (1): 15–24.

Barro, R. J., and J. W. Lee. 2013. "A New Data Set of Educational Attainment in the World, 1950–2010." *Journal of Development Economics* 104 (C): 184-98.

Behrman, J. R., H. P. Kohler, and S. C. Watkins. 2002. "Social Networks and Changes in Contraceptive Use over Time: Evidence from a Longitudinal Study in Rural Kenya." *Demography* 39 (4): 713–38.

Ben-Porath, Y. 1976. "Fertility Response to Child Mortality: Micro Data from Israel." *Journal of Political Economy* 84 (2): S163–78.

Bloom, D. E., D. Canning, G. Fink, and J. Finlay. 2009. "Fertility, Female Labor Force Participation, and the Demographic Dividend." *Journal of Economic Growth* 14 (2): 79–101.

———. 2012. "Microeconomic Foundations of the Demographic Dividend." PGDA Working Paper 93, Harvard University, Program on the Global Demography of Aging, Cambridge, MA.

Bongaarts, J. 1978. "A Framework for Analyzing the Proximate Determinants of Fertility." *Population and Development Review* 4 (1): 105–32.

———. 1994. "The Impact of Population Policies: Comment." *Population and Development Review* 20 (3): 616–20.

Bongaarts, J., and S. Sinding. 2009. "A Response to Critics of Family Planning Programs." *International Perspectives on Sexual and Reproductive Health* 35 (1, March): 29–44.

Bongaarts, J., and S. C. Watkins. 1996. "Social Interactions and Contemporary Fertility Transitions." *Population and Development Review* 22 (4): 639–82.

Breierova, L., and E. Duflo. 2004. "The Impact of Education on Fertility and Child Mortality: Do Fathers Really Matter Less Than Mothers?" NBER Working Paper w10513, National Bureau of Economic Research, Cambridge, MA. http://www.nber .org/papers/w10513.

Brockerhoff, M. 1998. "Migration and the Fertility Transition in African Cities." In *Migration, Urbanization, and Development: New Directions and Issues, Proceedings of the Symposium on Internal Migration and Urbanization in Developing Countries, January 22–24, 1996.* New York: Springer.

Brockerhoff, M., and H. Eu. 1993. "Demographic and Socioeconomic Determinants of Female Rural to Urban Migration in Sub-Saharan Africa." *International Migration Review* 27 (3): 557–77.

Caldwell, J. C., and P. Caldwell. 1987. "The Cultural Context of High Fertility in Sub-Saharan Africa." *Population and Development Review* 13 (3): 409–37.

Canning, D., I. Günther, S. Linnemayr, D. Bloom. 2013. "Fertility Choice, Mortality Expectations, and Interdependent Preferences: An Empirical Analysis." *European Economic Review* 63 (C): 273–89.

Castle, S., M. K. Konaté, P. R. Ulin, and S. Martin. 1999. "A Qualitative Study of Clandestine Contraceptive Use in Urban Mali." *Studies in Family Planning* 30 (3): 231–48.

Chattopadhyay, A., M. J. White, and C. Debpuur. 2006. "Migrant Fertility in Ghana: Selection versus Adaptation and Disruption as Causal Mechanisms." *Population Studies* 60 (2): 189–203.

Chicoine, L. E. 2012. "Education and Fertility: Evidence from a Policy Change in Kenya," IZA Discussion Paper 6778, Institute for the Study of Labor, Bonn. http://econpapers .repec.org/paper/izaizadps/dp6778.htm.

Coale, A. J. 1986. *The Decline of Fertility in Europe since the Eighteenth Century as a Chapter in Demographic History*. Princeton, NJ: Princeton University Press.

Coale, A. J., and S. C. Watkins. 1986. *The Decline of Fertility in Europe: The Revised Proceedings of a Conference on the Princeton European Fertility Project*. Princeton, NJ: Princeton University Press.

Conde-Agudelo, A., A. Rosas-Bermudez, F. Castaño, and M. H. Norton. 2012. "Effects of Birth Spacing on Maternal, Perinatal, Infant, and Child Health: A Systematic Review of Causal Mechanisms." *Studies in Family Planning* 43 (2): 93–114.

Conde-Agudelo, A., A. Rosas-Bermúdez, and A. C. Kafury-Goeta. 2006. "Birth Spacing and Risk of Adverse Perinatal Outcomes." *JAMA (Journal of the American Medical Association)* 295 (15): 1809–23.

Creanga, A. A., D. Gillespie, S. Karklins, and A. O. Tsui. 2011. "Low Use of Contraception among Poor Women in Africa: An Equity Issue." *Bulletin of the World Health Organization* 89 (4): 258–66.

Dieleman, M., S. Kane, P. Zwanikken, and B. Gerretsen. 2011. "Realist Review and Synthesis of Retention Studies for Health Workers in Rural and Remote Areas." Technical Report 1, World Health Organization, Geneva.

Duflo, E., P. Dupas, M. Kremer, and S. Sinei. 2006. "Education and HIV/AIDS Prevention: Evidence from a Randomized Evaluation in Western Kenya." Working Paper 4024, World Bank, Washington, DC. http://ideas.repec.org/p/wbk/wbrwps/4024.html.

Dyson, T. 2011. "The Role of the Demographic Transition in the Process of Urbanization." *Population and Development Review* 37 (S1): 34–54.

Eckstein, Z., P. Mira, and K. I. Wolpin. 1999. "A Quantitative Analysis of Swedish Fertility Dynamics: 1751–1990." *Review of Economic Dynamics* 12 (1): 137–65.

Fang, H., K. N. Eggleston, J. A. Rizzo, R. J. Zeckhauser. 2010. "Female Employment and Fertility in Rural China." NBER Working Paper w15886, National Bureau of Economic Research, Cambridge, MA. http://www.nber.org.ezp-prod1.hul.harvard.edu/papers /w15886.

Fapohunda, E. R., and M. P. Todaro. 1988. "Family Structure, Implicit Contracts, and the Demand for Children in Southern Nigeria." *Population and Development Review* 14 (4): 571–94.

Finlay, J. E., and D. Canning. 2013. "The Association of Fertility Spacing, Timing, and Parity with Child Health." Background paper for this book, World Bank, Washington, DC.

Finlay, J. E., E. Özaltin, and D. Canning. 2011. "The Association of Maternal Age with Infant Mortality, Child Anthropometric Failure, Diarrhoea, and Anaemia for First Births: Evidence from 55 Low- and Middle-Income Countries." *BMJ Open* 1 (2): n.p. doi:10.1136/bmjopen-2011-000226.

Galloway, P. R., and R. D. Lee. 1998. "Urban Versus Rural: Fertility Decline in the Cities and Rural Districts of Prussia, 1875 to 1910." *European Journal of Population* 14 (3): 209–64.

Glick, P., and S. Linnemayr. 2013. "Family Planning in Sub-Saharan Africa: The Role of Supply and the Rationale for Public Action." Background paper for this book, World Bank, Washington, DC.

Goh, A. 1999. "Trade, Employment, and Fertility Transition." *Journal of International Trade and Economic Development* 8 (2): 143–84.

Goldin, C. 1994. "The U-Shaped Female Labor Force Function in Economic Development and Economic History." NBER Working Paper 4707, National Bureau of Economic Research, Cambridge, MA.

Gribble, J. 2012. "Fact Sheet: Unmet Need for Family Planning." Population Reference Bureau, Washington, DC, July.

Groth, H., and A. Sousa-Poza. 2012. *Population Dynamics in Muslim Countries: Assembling the Jigsaw*. New York: Springer.

Haines, M. R. 1998. "The Relationship between Infant and Child Mortality and Fertility: Some Historical and Contemporary Evidence for the United States." In *From Death to Birth: Mortality Decline and Reproductive Change*, edited by M. Montomery and B. Cohen, 227–53. Washington, DC: National Academy Press.

Heaton, T. B. 2011. "Does Religion Influence Fertility in Developing Countries?" *Population Research and Policy Review* 30 (3): 449–65.

Heil, S. H., D. E. Gaalema, and E. S. Herrmann. 2012. "Incentives to Promote Family Planning." *Preventive Medicine* 55 (S1): S106–12.

Hollos, M. and U. Larsen. 2008. "Motherhood in Sub-Saharan Africa: The Social Consequences of Infertility in an Urban Population in Northern Tanzania." *Culture, Health, and Sexuality* 10 (2): 159–73.

Hossain, M. B., J. F. Phillips, and T. K. LeGrand. 2007. "The Impact of Childhood Mortality on Fertility in Six Rural Thanas of Bangladesh." *Demography* 44 (4): 771–84.

Hout, M. 1978. "The Determinants of Marital Fertility in the United States, 1968–1970: Inferences from a Dynamic Model." *Demography* 15 (2): 139–59.

Jones, K. M. 2013. "Contraceptive Supply and Fertility Outcomes: Evidence from Ghana." International Food Policy Research Institute, Washington, DC.

Joshi, S., and P. Schultz. 2007. "Family Planning as an Investment in Development: Evaluation of a Program's Consequences in Matlab, Bangladesh," Discussion Paper 951, Economic Growth Center, Yale University, New Haven, CT.

Khan, S., V. Mishra, F. Arnold, and N. Abderrahim. 2007. *Contraceptive Trends in Developing Countries*. Calberton: Macro International.

Kincaid, D. L. 2000. "Social Networks, Ideation, and Contraceptive Behavior in Bangladesh: A Longitudinal Analysis." *Social Science and Medicine* 50 (2): 215–31.

Kincaid, D. L., S. H. Yun, P. T. Piotrow, and Y. Yaser. 1993. "Turkey's Mass Media Family Planning Campaign." *Family Planning Management* 2: 68–92.

Knodel, J., and E. Van de Walle. 1979. "Lessons from the Past: Policy Implications of Historical Fertility Studies." *Population and Development Review* 5 (2): 217–45.

Kohler, H. P., J. R. Behrman, and S. C. Watkins. 2001. "The Density of Social Networks and Fertility Decisions: Evidence from South Nyanza District, Kenya." *Demography* 38 (1): 43–58.

Kremer, M., and A. Holla. 2009. "Pricing and Access: Lessons from Randomized Evaluations in Education and Health." In *What Works in Developing: Thinking Big, Thinking Small,* edited by J. Cohen and W. Easterly. Washington, DC: Brookings Institution Press. http://www.brookings.edu/events/2008/05/~/media/Events/2008/5/29%20global%20development/2008_kremer.PDF.

Kupinsky, S. 1977. "The Fertility of Working Women in the United States: Historical Trends and Theoretical Perspectives." In *The Fertility of Working Women: Synthesis of International Research,* edited by S. Kupinsky, 188–249. New York: Praeger.

Larsen, U. 2000. "Primary and Secondary Infertility in Sub-Saharan Africa." *International Journal of Epidemiology* 29 (2): 285–91.

Lavy, V., and A. Zablotsky. 2011. "Mother's Schooling and Fertility under Low Female Labor Force Participation: Evidence from a Natural Experiment." NBER Working Paper 16856, National Bureau of Economic Research, Cambridge, MA. http://www.nber.org/papers/w16856.

LeGrand, T. K., T. Koppenhaver, N. Mondain, and S. Randall. 2003. "Reassessing the Insurance Effect: A Qualitative Analysis of Fertility Behavior in Senegal and Zimbabwe." *Population and Development Review* 29 (3): 375–403.

LeGrand, T. K., and J. F. Phillips. 1996. "The Effect of Fertility Reductions on Infant and Child Mortality: Evidence from Matlab in Rural Bangladesh." *Population Studies* 50 (1): 51–68.

Madhavan, S., and J. P. Guengant. 2013. "Proximate Determinants of Fertility." Background paper for this book, World Bank, Washington, DC.

Maglad, N. E. 1994. "Fertility in Rural Sudan: The Effect of Landholding and Child Mortality." *Economic Development and Cultural Change* 42 (4): 761–72.

Magnani, R. J., D. R. Hotchkiss, C. S. Florence, and L. A. Shafer. 1999. "The Impact of the Family Planning Supply Environment on Contraceptive Intentions and Use in Morocco." *Studies in Family Planning* 30 (2): 120–32.

Manser, M., and M. Brown. 1980. "Marriage and Household Decision-Making: A Bargaining Analysis." *International Economic Review* 21 (1): 31–44.

McCarraher, D. R., S. L. Martin, and P. E. Bailey. 2006. "The Influence of Method-Related Partner Violence on Covert Pill Use and Pill Discontinuation among Women Living in La Paz, El Alto, and Santa Cruz, Bolivia." *Journal of Biosocial Science* 38 (2): 169–86.

McQuillan, K. 2004. "When Does Religion Influence Fertility?" *Population and Development Review* 30 (1): 25–56.

Montgomery, M. R., and J. B. Casterline. 1993. "The Diffusion of Fertility Control in Taiwan: Evidence from Pooled Cross-Section Time-Series Models." *Population Studies* 47 (3): 457–79.

————. 1996. "Social Learning, Social Influence, and New Models of Fertility." *Population and Development Review* 22 (supplement): 151–75.

Müller, R., and F. Woellert. 2013a. "At a Second Glance: Obstacles to Ghana's Demographic Success Story." Case study for this book, World Bank, Washington, DC, March.

————. 2013b. "The Demographic Bonus within Reach: Ethiopia's Heterogeneous Success Story of Fertility Decline." Case study for this book, World Bank, Washington, DC, March.

————. 2013c. "Disillusion after Years of Progress Stall in Kenya's Fertility Decline: Uncertain Future despite Resource Wealth." Case study for this book, World Bank, Washington, DC, March.

————. 2013d. "Same Trajectories, Diverging Results: How Bangladesh Overtook Pakistan in the Demographic Transition." Case study for this book, World Bank, Washington, DC, March.

————. 2013e. "Why Nigeria Is Caught in a High Fertility Trap." Case study for this book, World Bank, Washington, DC, March.

Munshi, K., and J. Myaux. 2006. "Social Norms and the Fertility Transition." *Journal of Development Economics* 80 (1): 1–38.

Murray, C. J., D. B. Evans, A. Acharya, and R. M.P.M. Baltussen. 2000. "Development of WHO Guidelines on Generalized Cost-Effectiveness Analysis." *Health Economics* 9: 235–51.

Neukom, J., J. Chilambwe, J. Mkandawire, R. K. Mbewe, and D. Hubacher. 2011. "Dedicated Providers of Long-Acting Reversible Contraception: New Approach in Zambia." *Contraception* 83 (5): 447–52.

Olsen, R. J. 1980. "Estimating the Effect of Child Mortality on the Number of Births." *Demography* 17 (4): 429–43.

Osili, U. O., and B. T. Long. 2008. "Does Female Schooling Reduce Fertility? Evidence from Nigeria." *Journal of Development Economics* 87 (1): 57–75.

Palloni, A., and H. Rafalimanana. 1999. "The Effects of Infant Mortality on Fertility Revisited: New Evidence from Latin America." *Demography* 36 (1): 41–58.

Phillips, J. F., E. F. Jackson, A. A. Bawah, B. MacLeod, P. Adongo, C. Baynes, and J. Williams. 2012. "The Long-Term Fertility Impact of the Navrongo Project in Northern Ghana." *Studies in Family Planning* 43 (3): 175–90.

Piotrow, P. T., D. L. Kincaid, M. J. Hindin, C. L. Lettenmaier, I. Kuseka, T. Silberman, A. Zinanga, F. Chikara, D. J. Adamchak, M. T. Mbizvo. 1992. "Changing Men's Attitudes and Behavior: The Zimbabwe Male Motivation Project." *Studies in Family Planning* 23 (6): 365–75.

Pradhan, E., and D. Canning. 2013a. "The Effect of Educational Reform in Ethiopia on Girls' Schooling and Fertility." Background paper for this book, World Bank, Washington, DC.

————. 2013b. "Socioeconomic Determinants of Fertility." Background paper for this book, World Bank, Washington, DC, March.

Preston, S. H. 1978. *The Effects of Infant and Child Mortality on Fertility*. New York: Academic Press.

Robinson, W. C., and G. L. Lewis. 2003. "Cost-Effectiveness Analysis of Behaviour Change Interventions: A Proposed New Approach and an Application to Egypt." *Journal of Biosocial Science* 35 (4): 499–512.

Robinson, W. C., and J. A. Ross. 2007. *The Global Family Planning Revolution: Three Decades of Population Policies and Programs.* Washington, DC: World Bank.

Sah, R. K. 1991. "The Effects of Child Mortality Changes on Fertility Choice and Parental Welfare." *Journal of Political Economy* 99 (3): 582–606.

Schultz, T. P. 1969. "An Economic Model of Family Planning and Fertility." *Journal of Political Economy* 77 (2): 153–80.

———. 1976. "Interrelationships between Mortality and Fertility." In *Population and Development: The Search for Selective Interventions,* edited by R. G. Ridker, 239–89. Baltimore, MD: Johns Hopkins University Press.

———. 1997. "Demand for Children in Low-Income Countries." In *Handbook of Population and Family Economics,* edited by M. R. Rosenzweig and O. Stark, 349–30. Amsterdam: Elsevier.

———. 2009. "How Does Family Planning Promote Development? Evidence from a Social Experiment in Matlab, Bangladesh, 1977–1996." Yale University, Economic Growth Center, New Haven, CT.

Shapiro, D., and T. Gebreselassie. 2008. "Fertility Transition in Sub-Saharan Africa: Falling and Stalling." *African Population Studies* 23 (1): 3–23.

Simkins, C. 2013. "Urbanization and Fertility." Background paper for this book, World Bank, Washington, DC, April.

Singh, S., J. E. Darroch, L. S. Ashford, and M. Vlassoff. 2010. "Adding It Up: The Costs and Benefits of Investing in Family Planning and Maternal and Newborn Health." Guttmacher Institute, New York.

Soares, R. R., and B. L. S. Falcão. 2008. "The Demographic Transition and the Sexual Division of Labor." *Journal of Political Economy* 116 (2): 1058–104.

Uganda Ministry of Finance, Planning, and Economic Development. 2008. "National Population Policy for Social Transformation and Sustainable Development." Government of Uganda, Kampala.

UN (United Nations) Population Division. 2012. *World Population Prospects: The 2011 Revision.* New York: United Nations, Population Division, Department of Economic and Social Affairs.

Watkins, S. C. 1987. "The Fertility Transition: Europe and the Third World Compared." *Sociological Forum* 2 (4): 645–73.

Westoff, C. F. 1992. "Age at Marriage, Age at First Birth, and Fertility in Africa." Technical Paper 169, World Bank, Washington, DC.

Woldemicael, G., and R. Beaujot. 2011. "Currently Married Women with an Unmet Need for Contraception in Eritrea: Profile and Determinants." *Canadian Studies in Population* 38 (1-2): 61–81.

World Bank. 2011. World Development Indicators. Washington, DC: World Bank.

———. 2012. World Development Indicators. Washington, DC: World Bank.

Chapter 3

Education Effects of the Demographic Dividend

The concept of the demographic dividend was originally constructed to explain the links between the demographic transition, changes in age structure, and economic growth. While the main focus of the literature has been on economic outcomes, the demographic transition also has had profound impacts on human development, regardless of the economic return. This chapter presents a framework for understanding how lower fertility can lead to a schooling dividend. It briefly describes the trends in schooling and the relations between fertility and investments in education, describes the pathways through which fertility may create a dividend, presents a decomposition analysis of macro-level factors, and suggests opportunities for creating a virtuous cycle and harnessing Africa's promising dividend.

Trends in Schooling and Fertility in Sub-Saharan Africa

The analysis begins by looking at trends in schooling. Sub-Saharan Africa still falls short of its Millennium Development Goal targets in schooling, but the region has recorded gains in recent decades. Between 1990 and 2010, net primary enrollments rose from 52 to 75 percent and secondary enrollments doubled from 22 to 41 percent (Lloyd and Hewett 2003; World Bank 2013).[1] Gains were also achieved in gender parity, with the female-to-male ratio rising from .74 to .82 in secondary enrollments and from .47 to .62 in tertiary enrollment. Gender parity in primary enrollment has now been achieved in nearly 20 of 48 African countries, up from 9 in 1990. Reductions in socioeconomic disparities are less documented, but enrollments among poor and rural families have benefited from policies offering tuition-free enrollment, even if these gains mask differences in school quality.

Correlational analyses at a regional level show strong associations between fertility, school enrollment, and completion rates (figure 3.1, panels a–c).

In the last two decades, higher fertility rates were associated with lower rates of primary enrollment (R^2 = 0.26), primary school completion (R^2 = 0.59), and secondary enrollment (R^2 = 0.72).

Age dependency rates are correlated not only with fertility but also with education spending per child. For instance, figure 3.2 shows the correlations between changes in age dependency and changes in public education spending per pupil between 1990 and 2010. During that period, age dependency declined steeply in South Africa (−0.22), Botswana (−0.30), and Swaziland (−0.31) and rose modestly in Niger (+0.09). As seen, countries registering the largest declines in age dependency also showed the largest increases in public spending per child (R^2 = 0.31), with a 0.01 unit decline in age dependency being associated, on average, with a US$14.50 gain in public spending per child.

These patterns suggest that lower fertility is associated with a schooling dividend, but more evidence is needed to establish causality.

Figure 3.1 Macro Correlations between Fertility and Schooling in Sub-Saharan African Countries, 1990–2010

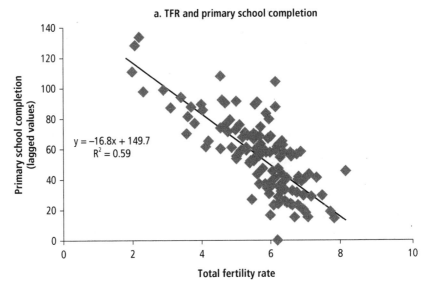

a. TFR and primary school completion

$y = -16.8x + 149.7$
$R^2 = 0.59$

(continued next page)

Figure 3.1 (continued)

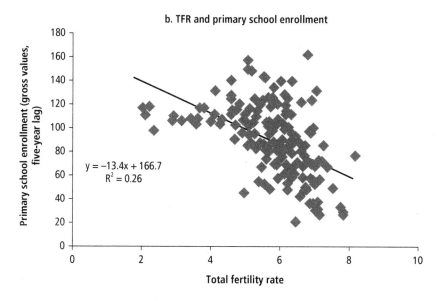

b. TFR and primary school enrollment

$y = -13.4x + 166.7$
$R^2 = 0.26$

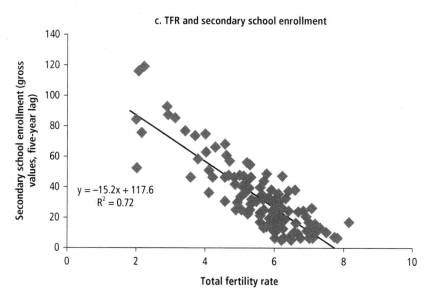

c. TFR and secondary school enrollment

$y = -15.2x + 117.6$
$R^2 = 0.72$

Source: Eloundou-Enyegue 2013.
Note: TFR = total fertility rate.

Figure 3.2 Nominal Change in Public Spending per Child and Age Dependency in Sub-Saharan African Countries, 1990–2010

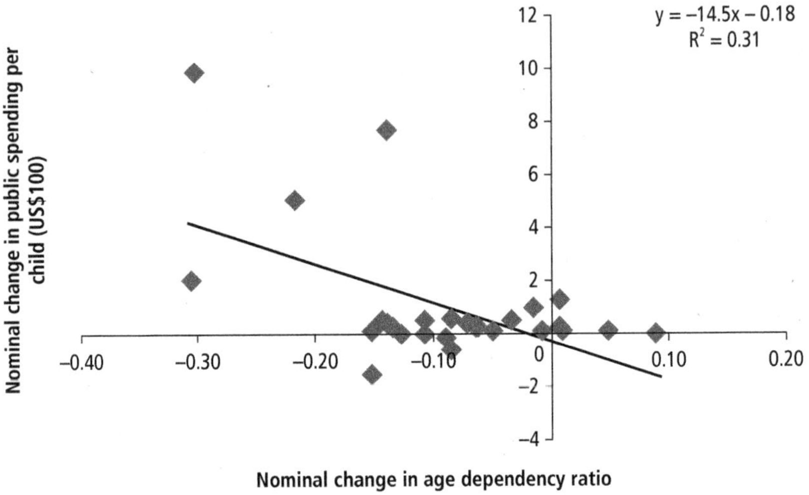

Source: Eloundou-Enyegue 2013.
Note: Age dependency ratio is the ratio of young to adult population.

Fertility and Investments in Education

Lower fertility can boost investments in education in several ways. Perhaps the best known is the quantity-quality trade-off, through which fertility decisions and investments in human capital are determined jointly (Hanushek 1992). The demographic-economic relationship between fertility and education implies that lower fertility is both a cause and a consequence of increased investments in education. In particular, both fertility and schooling are determined by a common set of factors that affect families' incentives and preferences.

This effect may be particularly pronounced for girls' schooling because girls in households with high fertility are frequently kept out of school to care for their younger siblings. The effects of lower fertility are strongly observed in a study in Matlab, Bangladesh, where a family planning intervention helped to decrease fertility rates and to improve child health and educational outcomes (Schultz 2009). A study in Sub-Saharan Africa finds that the birth of an unintended child reduced the enrollment of young children and increased the dropout rate of older children, suggesting that additional births may tighten the constraints on family resources (Eloundou-Enyegue and Williams 2006; Koissy-Kpein, Kuepie, and Tenikue 2012).

Aggregate spending on children in many countries is a fairly constant share of national resources and is independent of the size of the youth cohort (Mason et al. 2009), which implies that lower fertility would increase the amount of resources available to each child. If youth cohorts are smaller, governments can increase the amount of educational funding per child (Eloundou-Enyegue and Giroux 2013), leading to higher schooling enrollment as well as better-quality education.

The quantification of this education dividend faces numerous methodological hurdles of internal validity, generalization, and aggregation. Because fertility and schooling are jointly determined, their correlation could be spurious, and only a few studies from Africa meet the stringent statistical standards needed to determine the direction of causality. Further concerns arise from a possible ecological fallacy stemming from a discrepancy between levels of analysis and inference when studying fertility effects: rigorous research on the subject requires a micro-level focus (Cassen 1994), whereas much of the policy interest rests squarely on the national bottom line: "How do changes in a country's fertility shape *national* schooling outcomes?" Finally, the paucity of rigorous studies precludes strong generalization, thus presenting reviewers with the dilemma of choosing between internal validity (considering only the few strong studies) or generalization (drawing from a wider pool of studies).

The rest of this chapter attempts to mitigate the limitations of current studies by highlighting the relative contribution of various factors to public spending per child. It does so by combining and expanding on the evidence from both micro- and macro-level perspectives. The micro-level evidence is derived from studies of the effects of sibsize and teenage fertility on schooling in Sub-Saharan Africa. Some of these studies have begun to address causation issues, but results have not been aggregated to assess macro-level implications. This shortcoming is addressed by discussing possible methods of aggregation. The macro-level evidence is derived from decomposition analyses of the contributions of changing age structure and the size of child cohorts on public education spending per child. These analyses offer direct evidence that fertility decline is correlated with a schooling dividend. Although the decomposition analysis highlights the relative contribution of various factors, it does not establish causality between them.

Pathways of Achieving a School Dividend

Fertility transitions can affect national schooling outcomes through reductions in the number of siblings (sibsize), pregnancy-related dropouts, age dependency, and (though not applicable to Sub-Saharan Africa) cohort size (figure 3.3).

There is a fundamental distinction between macro- and micro-level influences of fertility on education. The key macro-level influence is age

Figure 3.3 Fertility Transitions and Pathways to the Schooling Dividend

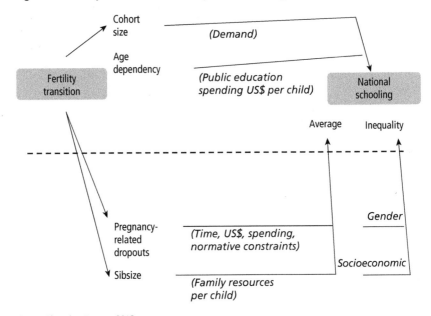

Source: Eloundou-Enyegue 2013.

structure, specifically age dependency and cohort size. By temporarily reducing age dependency rates, swift declines in birth rates create an environment favorable to educational expansion. Strategic investments during that period spur gains in schooling before the population ages (Bloom, Canning, and Sevilla 2003). Reductions in absolute cohort size are another macro-level mechanism (Flinn 1993), but they are not applicable to Sub-Saharan Africa because the population momentum from past high fertility continues to produce large cohorts there.[2]

At the micro level, fertility transitions imply a reduction in average family size and in the share of children born within very large families. Fewer children are thus subjected to the severe resource constraints facing large families, and this compositional change mechanically improves national schooling outcomes (Knodel and Wongsith 1991; Knodel, Havanon, and Sittitrai 1990). Also operating at the micro level are delays in first births, which reduce the incidence of pregnancy-related dropouts. In countries where such dropouts are common, delaying first births would raise women's educational attainment.

Eloundou-Enyegue (2013) offers a detailed examination of the many influences between fertility and education and summarizes the rich literature exploring their differences and complementarities. The gains driven by macro processes accrue to all families regardless of the direct implications of the change, while the gains from micro processes accrue mostly to the families and individuals participating in the transition. The two processes represent a complementarity between private and public responses.

A country's total education dividend is the sum of these pathway-specific influences. As such, it is likely to be larger, more multifaceted, but also more complex than the effect from any single pathway. Since some of the pathways predominantly affect average schooling while others predominantly affect schooling inequality, there is a tension between the full effects of a fertility transition on average schooling and on school inequality.

Sibsize

Smaller sibsize is a classic theoretical pathway for explaining the effects of fertility transitions on schooling. The premise is that high fertility dilutes parental resources and lowers the amount of resources available per child. Moreover, girls are often taken out of school to care for their younger siblings, and so high fertility has an adverse impact on their schooling. Smaller families have more resources per child, and this has a positive effect on schooling outcomes (Blake 1981, 1989). Although the argument seems intuitive, it has been questioned on multiple grounds, including the economies of scale captured by a family, Africa-specific heterogeneity in the structure and definition of families, overgeneralizations, and the risk of ecological fallacies.

The evidence on sibsize effects in Sub-Saharan Africa is best summarized chronologically to reflect the steady improvements in the methodologies used in this research. Early studies in Africa had mixed results, finding both nonsignificant or even positive associations between large sibsize and schooling (Chernichovsky 1985; DeLancey 1990; Gomes 1984). Subsequent efforts refined the measures of sibsize. Some of these refinements considered the implications of discrimination by birth order or by gender as well as the implications of polygamy and fertility outside of marriage for the distinct progenies of marital partners. Other studies used event-history data to gauge the time dependency of sibsize (Eloundou-Enyegue and Williams 2006; Lloyd and Gage-Brandon 1994). Together, these studies reveal large inequalities in sibsize experiences within families. Their results confirm and refine earlier findings by revealing internal variation: sibsize has larger effects on female and older children, children in households headed by a male, and children in households with limited access to networks of kinship assistance (Case, Paxson, and Ableidinger 2004; Lloyd and Gage-Brandon 1994). Studies using time-varying measures of sibsize also find slightly larger effects than cross-sectional studies.[3]

The next wave of studies addressed the endogeneity of fertility and schooling using improved research designs, two-stage estimation, or instrumental variables, such as twin births, the sex composition of early births, or unwanted births (Black, Devereux, and Salvanes 2005; Conley and Glauber 2006; Kuepie and Tenikue 2012). These studies still found negative effects of sibsize on educational attainment in developing settings, even if these effects were smaller than those found using simpler estimation methods (Black, Devereux, and Salvanes 2005; Conley and Glauber 2006; Desai 1995). Unfortunately, few of these cutting-edge studies focus on Sub-Saharan Africa. Especially relevant here is a study by Koissy-Kpein, Kuepie, and Tenikue (2012) that uses demographic and health survey (DHS) data from 30 African countries to examine how recent unintended births affected school entry and dropout. This exogenous fertility is found to increase the odds of dropout by 20 percent. As the authors point out, these annual effects must be compounded to reflect their cumulative influence on schooling.

Micro-level estimates of sibsize effects, however rigorous, are a poor proxy for macro-level estimates because they do not aggregate these effects across all children and do not take into account national resource constraints in public education. Knodel and various colleagues (Knodel and Wongsith 1991; Knodel, Havanon, and Sittitrai 1990) pioneered efforts to show how aggregate effects depend on the distribution of fertility declines across subpopulations. However, aggregate effects also depend on concurrent changes in the effects of sibsize and family structure. Large effects need not imply large dividends if the fertility transition is driven by high socioeconomic groups or is accompanied by adverse changes in family structure or if the sibsize effects decline nationwide during the course of the transition (Eloundou-Enyegue and Giroux 2013).

Teenage Pregnancy

Teenage pregnancy is a second pathway of influence. In theory, unwanted teen pregnancies lead girls to drop out of school prematurely. Therefore, reductions in teen pregnancies boost female education attainment rates. Similar to the dilution argument, the details of this position are open to scrutiny. Concerns relate to the reliability of reports on dropouts and issues related to school regulations, school climate, and timing.

Efforts to assess causality have used event-history methods that consider schooling performance before pregnancy but also the possibility that young mothers might return to school after the birth of a child. These methods might also consider long-standing concerns that correlations associating teenage fertility and women's educational attainment merely reflect the socioeconomic disadvantage of poorer teens (Grant and Hallman 2008; Madhavan and Thomas 2005). The percentage of pregnancy-related dropouts can be used to gauge potential impact, but this indicator is weak, and it also must consider the timing of pregnancies and the extent to which girls drop out of school at higher rates than boys for other reasons. Schooling life tables help to integrate data on the incidence, timing, and causes of dropouts, yielding aggregate effects at the population level. With accurate data on the timing and reasons for dropping out, such tables also can be used in simulations of the theoretical impact of reducing pregnancy-related dropouts (Lloyd and Mensch 2008).[4]

Pregnancy-related dropouts are common in many African countries. In a 2007 study of 23 countries, pregnancy accounted, on average, for 17.7 percent of all female dropouts at the secondary level (Eloundou-Enyegue and Stokes 2004). It was the leading cause of female dropouts in the Central African Republic (37 percent), Mozambique (25.8 percent), and South Africa (36.1 percent) and the second leading cause in six additional countries: Cameroon (22 percent), Chad (20 percent), Gabon (29.8 percent), Kenya (30.8 percent), Uganda (28 percent), and Zambia (25.9 percent). Simulations based on schooling life tables estimated the likely impact of hypothetical reductions in pregnancy-related dropouts on the gender gap in educational attainment. For a few countries (Cameroon, Gabon, and Kenya), reducing pregnancy-related dropouts could help to close the gender gap. Such reductions were not necessary in South Africa, where the gap had already been bridged, and they were ineffective in countries (such as Benin, Chad, and Niger) with more basic constraints to girls' education. Country-specific results showed stronger impacts for countries at the intermediate stages of educational and fertility transitions, including where teen fertility was normatively high or educational attainment for girls was low and pregnancy was not an independent constraint to their education. It became important only when educational pursuits and the normative age of marriage and motherhood overlapped in the life course of teens.

However, the evidence from this study is dated. In a follow-up study, Lloyd and Mensch (2008) suggest that pregnancy-related dropouts are less common. This possibility and the broader doubts about causation suggest that reducing teenage pregnancy will likely produce a modest schooling dividend today.

Event-history analyses warrant caution in interpreting the correlation between educational attainment and teenage pregnancy. Causation is in doubt when the prior educational performance of pregnant teens is inordinately poor or when teens return to school after childbirth (Grant and Hallman 2008). In sum, teen pregnancy is most disruptive where families are less supportive of girls' education and where school systems expel pregnant students or restrict continued schooling for teen mothers. It is least important during the early and late stages of fertility transition because there is variability in pregnancy and in outcomes. Only in the middle stages is there room for an effect.

Age Structure

Although sibsize and teenage pregnancy offer plausible routes between fertility and education, age structure is the most specific pathway invoked in the

Figure 3.4 Framework for Achieving a Schooling Dividend via Changes in Age Structure

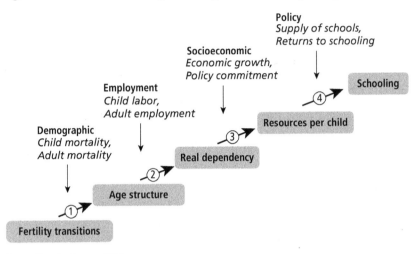

Source: Eloundou-Enyegue 2013.

dividend argument. This pathway (shown in figure 3.4) can be described as a sequence in which declines in fertility affect (1) "demographic" age dependency, then (2) "real" dependency,[5] then (3) public education resources available per pupil, and eventually (4) schooling outcomes.

This simple framework yields three useful insights. First, it highlights individual steps and their unique constraints, which may include child mortality levels, adult mortality levels, and the pace of fertility decline; the prevalence of child labor and adult unemployment; national economic performance and budget allocation priorities; and effective schooling policy (that is, the extent to which existing resources are used effectively and efficiently).

The framework can be used to pinpoint the step(s) where the process of generating a dividend breaks down. This can be done by calculating crude conversion coefficients for each step. For instance, if a country experiences a 15 percent decline in the total fertility rate between 1975 and 1990, and this change is followed 15 years later by a 10 percent decline in demographic age dependency, the conversion coefficient for the first step is estimated to be 0.67 (10/15). As a general rule, large positive coefficients imply efficient conversion; small positive ones indicate less efficient conversion; and negative coefficients indicate ineffective or counterproductive conversion. It is thus possible to identify country-specific bottlenecks. This detailed analysis helps to clarify why some countries fail to achieve a schooling dividend despite declining fertility.

Decomposition Analysis: Demographic Changes and Educational Resources per Child

Changes in educational resources per child can be decomposed into the following three factors: growth in income per capita, increase in the proportion of national resources devoted to education, and improvements in the child dependency ratio. Such a decomposition is useful for assessing how historical changes in public education resources per child reflect changes in youth dependency, economic growth, or a reallocation of resources toward education. Analysis of the data from 1990 to 2010 on spending on public education in 29 countries in Sub-Saharan Africa varies widely from country to country (Eloundou-Enyegue 2013).

The general implication is that, in addition to boosting average schooling inputs, fertility transitions might widen educational inequality across countries. Similar divergence is occurring in countries where fertility transitions have begun among the urban middle classes. If these trends extend into the future, a self-reinforcing cycle of schooling and fertility change becomes plausible. Given the effects of schooling on fertility (Bledsoe et al. 1998; Bongaarts 2003; Kravdal 2002), Africa's initial schooling dividend might spur additional declines in fertility. The cycle might be "virtuous" insofar as it stokes continuous gains in average education. However, it might include a more "vicious" element if uneven gains in schooling reinforce the current concentration of fertility among the lower socioeconomic groups. The challenge lies in tempering the cycle of divergence while bolstering the cycle of average schooling growth.

Why did some countries fail to achieve large gains in public spending per child? The framework in figure 3.4 helps to pinpoint the country-specific bottlenecks. For Sub-Saharan Africa as a whole, fertility declined about 10 percent between 1975 and 1990. This translated, 15 years later, into a 10 percent fall in age dependency, a 9 percent decline in real dependency, a 60 percent gain in schooling resources per child, and a 41 percent growth in gross enrollments (Eloundou-Enyegue and Giroux 2013). On average, all of these mechanisms worked effectively for the region as a whole during that period.[6]

The same was not true for individual countries, most of which took at least one counterproductive step to achieving a schooling dividend through changes in age structure, as laid out in figure 3.3. The most common bottleneck was real dependency (12 cases), followed by fertility transitions (5 cases), resources per child (5 cases), and age structure (3 cases). Only Somalia had more than one problematic step. However, resources per child (step 4) were not the most common problem; most countries could convert additional resources into better schooling outcomes, albeit with varying degrees of efficiency. Of course, step 4 might be more problematic at later stages of transition. Nonetheless, the implications for government policy are first to initiate the decline in fertility, later to shift resources to policies aimed at translating the lower age dependency into more resources per capita, and then to shift resources to policies aimed at improving final schooling outcomes.

In theory, contemporary fertility transitions in Sub-Saharan Africa can improve the region's schooling through all four pathways. Consistent with this expectation, strong correlations are found between national fertility rates and basic schooling outcomes. Some of these correlations persist when analyses extend to the corresponding variables of change. For instance, fertility declines in the last two decades are correlated with gains in public education resources per pupil. However, cross-country correlations are not a compelling source of evidence. Studies continually strive to address the causality, aggregation, and generalization issues plaguing this area of research.

Policies to Reap Africa's Promising Schooling Dividend

Africa's schooling dividend is not only likely but *already* visible in a few vanguard countries. The most plausible pathways for achieving a dividend are changes in age structure and sibsize. The cumulative effects of changing age structure and sibsize will improve average schooling for countries that achieve swift and broad-based transitions. Quantifying these impacts is much harder, given the limited efforts to aggregate the micro effects of changing sibsize or to assess the causal nature of changes associated with declining age dependency.

Despite the inability to establish causation, the prerequisites and conditions for a schooling dividend are increasingly understood. The following conditions include features of the transitions themselves as well as those of the contextual environment:

- *Transition features.* In achieving a dividend via sibsize, transitions must be broad based rather than driven by higher socioeconomic groups. They must also be accompanied by favorable trends in family structure. These include circumstances that either enhance the available family resources (parental presence and employment) or channel a greater share of household resources to children (greater control of household budget decisions by women). A dividend via age dependency likewise requires a swift and steady transition that opens a clear period of low age dependency; transitions must also feature continued progress in adult, especially maternal, survival.

- *Contextual features.* Dividends via sibsize require steady returns to investments in school quality. Dividends via age structure require favorable economic conditions and continued policy commitment to education. The detailed analysis of this pathway suggests that, among countries achieving a notable fertility decline since 1990, the most common stumbling block was the ability to translate low age dependency into increased spending per pupil, perhaps because of adverse economic conditions.

Beyond securing a national dividend, the issue of inequality arises. Cross-country inequality in public spending per capita has increased 12 percent since 1990. These inequalities are fueled by the strong asymmetry in contemporary African transitions. In most African countries that conducted DHSs after 2000, fertility levels among the lowest-socioeconomic group were at least double those in the highest-socioeconomic group. In the absence of corrective policies, the dividend will likely widen schooling inequality across and within countries.

Nevertheless, it is possible to envision a self-reinforcing cycle for Africa in which early schooling dividends spur further reductions in fertility, which prolong the dividend. This scenario is most plausible in settings where the drive for school quality intensifies and the returns to schooling are substantial. Indeed, despite a steep rise in unemployment among graduates and new questions about the returns to education (Boyle 1996), many urban families have increased their investment in private education, tutoring, and other discretionary spending on children's human capital (Boyle 1996; Buchmann 2001). Adolescents and young adults also show a preference for smaller families and a propensity to curtail fertility and opt for quality rather than quantity (Casterline 2009).

Both trends portend a virtuous cycle in the expansion of schooling. However, this cycle will also depend on the economy and policy. Countries experiencing the largest gains in public spending per child (US$460 on average) did so with a balanced mix of reduced age dependency (39 percent), economic growth (36 percent), and public commitment to education (25 percent). These macro-level factors will remain key, as will processes within the family, including family structure, gender discrimination in educational investments, and women's control of domestic resources.

Shadowing this virtuous cycle, however, is the specter of an equally plausible "vicious cycle" of inequality. As noted, the propensity to invest in school quality and to curtail fertility is greater among urban middle classes. Whether other groups follow suit is key to the intergenerational reproduction of inequality. On that score, recent fertility statistics raise concern. Most of the 23 countries show at least a 2:1 ratio in the fertility of low versus high socioeconomic groups. While some of this gap reflects differences in unmet need for family planning, some also reflects strategic decisions of the poor to choose larger, rather than smaller but better endowed, progenies as a way to reduce economic uncertainty.

Some of these conditions are hard to legislate or to affect directly by policy, but many are amenable at least indirectly to policy influence. Policies for fertility decline include investments in programs to meet the demand for fertility limitation, especially among younger, rural, and poor women. Delays in the onset of fertility shape the demographic momentum and increase the likelihood of women having a stronger say in household budget allocation, including investments in the education of children. Policies for maternal survival include addressing the primary factors that have been found to raise maternal mortality, including delayed and widely spaced births, as well as prenatal health care. Policies for raising returns to investments in schooling may include a strong push to raise education standards and secure a high premium to education in the labor market, while also addressing the resource inequalities hampering the ability of poor families to compete in educational investments. Policies to maintain or raise national education budgets may be helpful as well. Beyond direct investments in education, indirect investments in maternal health and programs to increase access to family planning among teens and rural and poor women will help to spur a virtuous (rather than a vicious) cycle of schooling expansion. Policies must, of course, be country specific, but countries can build on the simple framework highlighted in figure 3.4 to pinpoint their main bottlenecks and plan the chronology of their interventions.

Notes

1. Secondary enrollment rates divide the number of children enrolled by the age-appropriate child population. They may be inflated by children older than the usual age range who are repeating grades.
2. For Sub-Saharan Africa, although the total fertility rate declined 21 percent and the share of the population between the ages of 0 and 14 declined 4 percent between 1990 and 2010, the absolute size of this age group increased 63 percent. During that period, the size of youth cohorts declined in only a handful of small countries (Cape Verde, Mauritius, and the Seychelles).
3. Eloundou-Enyegue and Williams (2006) find that children whose sibsize was estimated to be 7 at the time of survey did, in fact, experience an average sibsize of 6.17, with annual values ranging from 2 to 10. The study also shows that failure to consider this time dependency leads to slightly underestimated sibsize effects.
4. Simulations for the effects of reducing pregnancy-related dropouts on gender gaps in educational attainment can be based on a formulation of gender gaps.
5. A distinction is made between "demographic" age dependency (the proportion of children 0–14 years old relative to working-age individuals 15–64 years old) and "real" age dependency (the ratio of dependent children to working adults). Dependent children are only a subset of all children in countries where child labor and child-headed households are common. Working adults are likewise a subset of the total working-age population.
6. Declines in the total fertility rate were associated with reduced age dependency (+1.02), reduced age dependency was accompanied by reduced real dependency (+0.89), and reduced real dependency was accompanied by improved resource per child (+6.58), which itself was accompanied by gains in enrollments (+0.68).

References

Black, S., P.J. Devereux, and K.G. Salvanes. 2005. "The More the Merrier? The Effect of Family Composition on Children's Education." *Quarterly Journal of Economics* 120 (2): 669–700.

Blake, J. 1981. "Family Size and the Quality of Children." *Demography* 18 (4): 421–42.

———. 1989. *Family Size and Achievement*. Berkeley: University of California Press.

Bledsoe, C. H., J. B. Casterline, J. A. Johnson-Kuhn, and J. G. Haaga, ed. 1998. *Critical Perspectives on Schooling and Fertility in the Developing World*. Washington, DC: National Academies Press.

Bloom, D. E., D. Canning, and J. Sevilla. 2003. *The Demographic Dividend: A New Perspective on the Economic Consequences of Population Change*. Population Matters Monograph MR-1274. Santa Monica, CA: RAND Corporation.

Bongaarts, J. 2003. "Completing the Fertility Transition in the Developing World: The Role of Educational Differences and Fertility Preferences." *Population Studies* 57 (3): 321–35.

Boyle, P. M. 1996. "Parents, Private Schools, and the Politics of an Emerging Civil Society in Cameroon." *Journal of Modern African Studies* 34 (4): 609–22.

Buchmann, C. 2001. "Getting Ahead in Kenya: The Role of Shadow Education and Social Capital in Adolescents' School Success." In Annual Meeting of the Population Association of America. Washington, DC, 2001: 31.

Case, A., C. Paxson, and J. Ableidinger. 2004. "Orphans in Africa: Parental Death, Poverty, and School Enrollment." *Demography* 41 (3): 483–508.

Cassen, R. 1994. *Population and Development: Old Debates, New Conclusions*. New Brunswick, NJ: Transaction Publishers.

Casterline, J. B. 2009. "Fertility Desires and the Prospects for Fertility Decline in Africa." Paper presented at the annual meeting of the Population Association of America, Detroit, April 30–May 2.

Chernichovsky, D. 1985. "Socioeconomic and Demographic Aspects of School Enrolment and Attendance in Rural Botswana." *Economic Development and Cultural Change* 33 (2): 319–32.

Conley, D., and R. Glauber. 2006. "Parental Educational Investment and Children's Academic Risk: Estimates of the Impact of Sibship Size and Birth Order from Exogenous Variation in Fertility." *Journal of Human Resources* 41 (4): 722–37.

DeLancey, V. 1990. "Socio-Economic Consequences of High Fertility for the Family." In *Population Growth and Reproduction in Sub-Saharan Africa*, edited by G. Acsadi, G. Johnson Acsadi, and R. Bulatao. Washington, DC: World Bank.

Desai, S. 1995. "When Are Children from Large Families Disadvantaged? Evidence from Cross-National Analyses." *Population Studies* 49 (2): 195–210.

Eloundou-Enyegue, P. M. 2013. "A Demographic Dividend for Africa's Schooling? Theory and Early Evidence." Background paper for this book, World Bank, Washington, DC, October.

Eloundou-Enyegue, P. M., and S. C. Giroux. 2013. "Schooling Dividends from Fertility Transitions. Early Evidence for Sub-Saharan Africa, 1990–2005." *Journal of Children and Poverty* 19 (1): 21–44.

Eloundou-Enyegue, P. M., and C. S. Stokes. 2004. "Teen Fertility and Gender Inequality in Education: A Contextual Hypothesis." *Demographic Research* 11 (art. 11): 305–34.

Eloundou-Enyegue, P. M., and L. B. Williams. 2006. "Family Size and Schooling in Sub-Saharan African Settings: A Reexamination." *Demography* 43 (1): 25–52.

Flinn, C. J. 1993. "Cohort Size and Schooling Choice." *Journal of Population Economics* 6 (1): 31–55.

Gomes, M. 1984. "Family Size and Educational Attainment in Kenya." *Population and Development Review* 10 (4): 647–60.

Grant, M. J., and K. K. Hallman. 2008. "Pregnancy-Related School Dropout and Prior School Performance in KwaZulu-Natal, South Africa." *Studies in Family Planning* 39 (4): 369–82.

Hanushek, E. A. 1992. "The Trade-Off between Child Quantity and Quality." *Journal of Political Economy* 100 (1): 84–117.

Knodel, J., and M. Wongsith. 1991. "Family Size and Children's Education in Thailand: Evidence from a National Sample." *Demography* 28 (1): 119–31.

Knodel, J., N. Havanon, and W. Sittitrai. 1990. "Family Size and the Education of Children in the Context of Rapid Fertility Decline." *Population and Development Review* 16 (1): 31–62.

Koissy-Kpein, S. A., M. Kuepie, and M. Tenikue. 2012. "Fertility Shock and Schooling." CEPS/INSTEAD Working Paper 2012-12, Centre for Population, Poverty, and Public Policy Studies, Luxembourg. http://ideas.repec.org/p/irs/cepswp/2012-12.html.

Kuepie, M., and M. Tenikue. 2012. "The Effect of the Number of Siblings on Education in Sub-Saharan Africa: Evidence from a Natural Experiment." CEPS/INSTEADWorking Paper 2012-28, Centre for Population, Poverty, and Public Policy Studies, Luxembourg.

Kravdal, Ø. 2002. "Education and Fertility in Sub-Saharan Africa: Individual and Community Effects." *Demography* 39 (2): 233–50.

Lloyd, C. B., and A. Gage-Brandon. 1994. "High Fertility and Children's Schooling in Ghana: Sex Differences in Parental Contributions and Educational Outcomes." *Population Studies* 48 (2): 293–306.

Lloyd, C. B., and P. C. Hewett. 2003. *Primary Schooling in Sub-Saharan Africa: Recent Trends and Current Challenges.* New York: Population Council.

Lloyd, C. B., and B. S. Mensch. 2008. "Marriage and Childbirth as Factors in Dropping Out from School: An Analysis of DHS Data from Sub-Saharan Africa." *Population Studies* 62 (1): 1–13.

Madhavan, S., and K. Thomas. 2005. "Childbearing and Schooling: New Evidence from South Africa." *Comparative Education Review* 49 (4): 452–67.

Mason, A., R. Lee, A.-C. Tung, M.-S. Lai, and T. Miller. 2009. "Population Aging and Intergenerational Transfers: Introducing Age into National Accounts." In *Developments in the Economics of Aging*, edited by D. A. Wise. Chicago: University of Chicago Press.

Schultz, T. P. 2009. "How Does Family Planning Promote Development? Evidence from a Social Experiment in Matlab, Bangladesh, 1977–1996." Yale University, Economic Growth Center, New Haven, CT.

World Bank. 2013. *World Development Indicators 2013*. Washington, DC: World Bank.

Chapter 4

Economic Effects of the Demographic Dividend

The concept of the demographic dividend was originally constructed to explain the links between the demographic transition and economic growth, and the main focus of the literature has been on economic outcomes. Demographic change has a direct impact on the economy through the effect of age structure on the supply of labor and the effect of aggregate savings on household and public investment. This chapter briefly outlines trends in Africa's recent economic performance and then examines the links between fertility and both age structure and aggregate savings. It describes a model that uses data for Nigeria to simulate economic growth and development outcomes under a baseline scenario in which fertility falls slowly. This model is useful for identifying the channels through which fertility declines affect economic growth. The chapter concludes by suggesting policies to reap the economic dividend of the fertility transition.

Trends in Africa's Recent Economic Performance

The growth and overall economic performance of Sub-Saharan Africa in the 1970s and 1980s were disappointing for various reasons and have been described as a "growth tragedy" (Easterly and Levine 1997). There are many explanations for Africa's poor economic performance in the past: its colonial past, conflicted history, and geography (Sachs and Warner 1997), ethnic and linguistic diversity (Easterly and Levine 1997; Montalvo and Reynal-Querol 2005), resource curse (Sachs and Warner 1995), and lack of social capital (Temple 1998) all loom large.

However, there are also reasons for optimism, as reflected in recent publications such as "Lion on the Move" (McKinsey Global Institute 2010), "The Sun Shines Bright" (Economist 2011), and "African Growth Miracle" (Young 2012). After a period of slow growth, Africa's economic performance has taken

Figure 4.1 Growth of GDP and GDP per Capita in Sub-Saharan Africa, 1965–2010

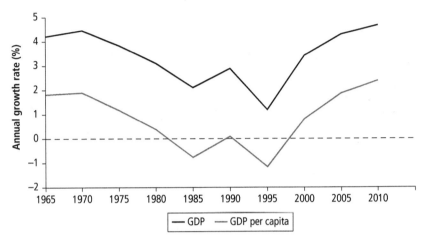

Source: Cho and Tien 2013.
Note: Sample of 29 balanced countries. GDP = gross domestic product. The period covers July 1 of the first year to June 30 of the second year.

off in the last decade (figure 4. 1), and recent reports cautiously predict that growth will continue (see IMF 2012). Is this a short-run blip or a fundamental change? If the latter, it could be the start of a long-run improvement in economic performance and growth that can provide jobs for the large working-age cohorts that are coming.

What factors have contributed to Africa's recent economic growth? As shown in figure 4.2, three features provide clues to the economic turnaround experienced since the mid-1990s: the share of working-age population increased, the amount of capital per worker rose sharply, particularly in 2005–10, and total factor productivity (TFP) grew steeply (Arbache and Page 2010). Although education and age structure were favorable to growth (Cho and Tien 2013), their effects are slow moving and do not sufficiently explain the recent takeoff. To understand the reasons for the takeoff better, one needs to look at the investment rate, capital flows, and technological progress.

Economic growth is strongly associated with public investment, provided that countries manage their debt sustainably. For this reason, public investment in infrastructure is often used to boost the economy and promote growth (Buffie et al. 2012). However, given their high levels of debt and limited fiscal space, African countries have not had the option of using public investment to stimulate the economy, and private investment has played a larger role than public investment in overall investment. This may be changing, however, as countries

Figure 4.2 Decomposition of GDP per Capita in Sub-Saharan Africa, 1960–2010

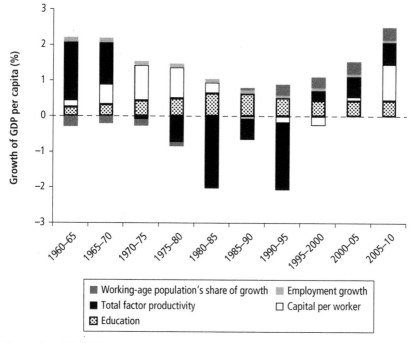

Source: Cho and Tien 2013.
Note: $\alpha = 0.33$; $\beta = 0.67$; $\gamma = 0.1$. Average of 32 Sub-Saharan African countries, presented by five-year periods with annualized figures. GDP = gross domestic product. The period covers July 1 of the first year to June 30 of the second year.

have had less debt, a stronger fiscal environment, generally healthier economies, and stronger resource revenues since the late 2000s.

Beginning in the mid-1990s, investment in Sub-Saharan Africa increased, while savings remained almost unchanged (figure 4.3, panel a).[1] By 2010, investment constituted 23 percent of gross domestic product (GDP), largely as a result of international financial flows, including foreign direct investment (FDI), overseas development assistance (ODA), remittances, and net exports.

It is widely believed that resources play a critical role in attracting capital to the region. The main channels include FDI for resource extraction and exports due to the rise of international commodity prices and improved terms of trade since the mid-1990s. Resource-rich countries—oil and non-oil—have benefited from increased FDI, but so have resource-poor countries (figure 4.4), suggesting that the presence of natural resources is not the only explanation for increased capital inflows. The nature of FDI is important because it affects the likelihood of investments that will produce jobs and because generating

Figure 4.3 Saving and Investment Gap and Source of Capital Inflows in Sub-Saharan Africa, 1980–2010

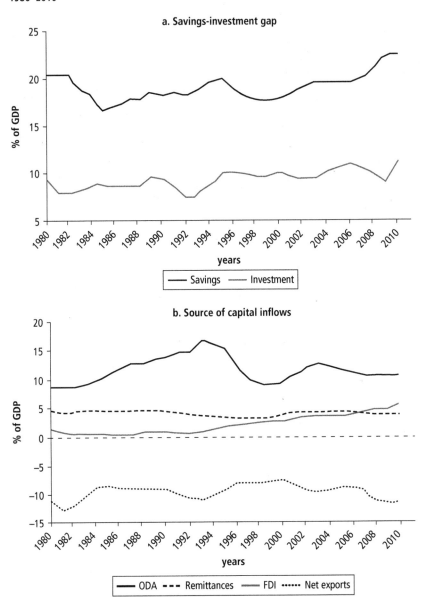

Source: Cho and Tien 2013.
Note: GDP = gross domestic product; ODA = overseas development assistance; FDI = foreign direct investment.

Figure 4.4 FDI as a Share of GDP in Sub-Saharan African Countries, by Resource Status, 1980–2010

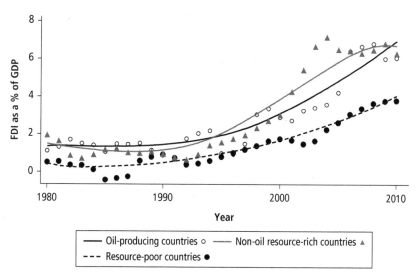

Source: Cho and Tien 2013.
Note: Based on 30 countries in Sub-Saharan Africa, excluding two outliers: Chad (oil exporting) and Lesotho (non-oil exporting); lowess smooth lines were used. FDI = foreign direct investment; GDP = gross domestic product.

high-paying jobs for the youth bulge moving into working age is essential to capturing the economic payoffs of the demographic transition.

Finally, the region has experienced substantial gains in TFP as a result of the shift from low- to high-productivity sectors of employment as well as improved political stability (Lewis 1954). Productivity is generally believed to be lower in agriculture than in other sectors, although TFP growth can take place even without structural transformation.[2] While the correlation is admittedly imperfect, structural transformation seems to be associated with TFP growth. This transformation was slow in Africa up until the mid-1990s, with the contribution of agriculture, industry, and services to GDP quite steady. Since the mid-1990s, however, the share of agriculture has declined sharply and that of industry has risen at the same time that the population has become increasingly urbanized.

Although the demographic transition has played a small role in Africa's economic takeoff to date, does it have the potential to reap jobs and savings payoffs in African countries and thus to support sustainable economic growth? This subject is discussed in the next two sections.

Jobs Payoffs

Demographic change affects the economy through age structure and labor force participation. Economic growth is driven by increasing the amount of inputs used for production or by increasing the productivity of these inputs, and labor is one of the most important inputs in the production process, accounting for about two-thirds of all output produced (Hall and Jones 1999).

However, most models of economic growth assume a fixed number of workers per capita. And indeed, the proportion of the working population is bounded above by 1 (when every single person in the population is working), so increasing the number of workers per capita cannot power growth in the *very* long run. Still, there are substantial variations in the number of workers per capita over time, and these variations can have significant impacts on GDP growth rates. For example, in East Asia the number of workers per capita has risen sharply over the last 40 years. This increase in labor supply, combined with increases in physical and human capital inputs (as opposed to increases in total factor productivity), accounts for most of the economic growth and development associated with the Asian economic miracle (Young 1995).

Increases in the size of the workforce per capita stem primarily from two sources. One is a change in the age structure of the population, which determines the ratio of working-age people to total population. The second is a change in labor force participation. While participation rates for men of working age tend to be uniformly high over time, participation rates for women can fluctuate dramatically, which can lead to rapid changes in the number of workers and consequently output per capita.

Aggregate demographic forces can also affect the productivity of workers. An increase in the aggregate size of the labor force can reduce the amount of available land and capital stock per worker, thereby lowering productivity. In the long run, a shortage of capital can be corrected by investment; however, this is not the case with land. In addition, if the size of a youth cohort affects its educational attainment—for example, a larger youth cohort receives fewer resources and schooling—this poorer accumulation of human capital may adversely affect its productivity when the cohort enters the labor force.

Effect of Age Structure

Age structure affects an economy in the following way: if age-specific behavior stays the same, aggregate behavior will depend on the number of people at each age. Age-specific patterns of consumption, work, and labor income are fairly stable over time and across countries or economies—figure 4.5 compares Kenya and Taiwan, China—which makes the direct effect of changes in age structure fairly predictable. In Africa, for example, consumption exceeds labor income until people are in their 20s and after they are in their early 60s, and consumption of education is higher for youth, while consumption for health care is higher for the elderly (figure 4.6).

Figure 4.5 Labor Income and Consumption per Capita in Kenya and Taiwan, China, by Age, 1994

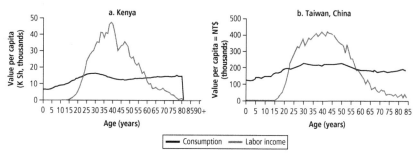

Source: National Transfer Accounts (http://www.ntaccounts.org/web/nta/show).

Figure 4.6 Age-Specific Consumption in South Africa, 2005

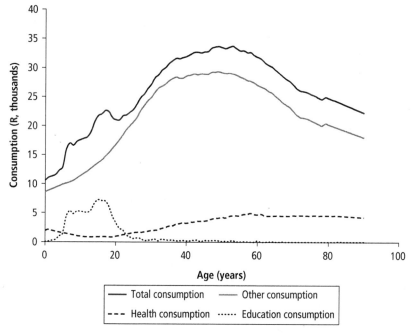

Source: Oosthuizen 2013.

Figure 4.7 Ratio of Working-Age Population 16–64 Years of Age to Dependents and Total Fertility Rate in Africa, 2010

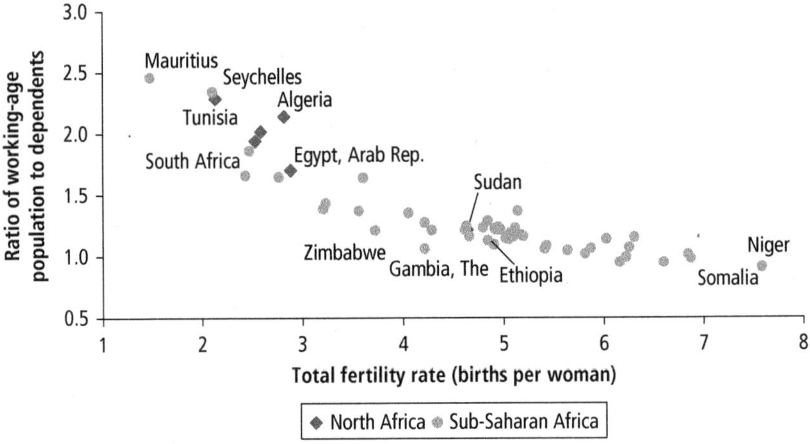

Source: Pradhan and Canning 2013.

Demographic change has the most direct effect on the economy through the effect of age structure on labor supply (figure 4.7). Here, the working-age range is conventionally defined to be the population between ages 16 and 64, although it is often narrower in practice. In countries with high fertility rates, the level of youth dependency is high—the ratio of working-age population to dependents is around 1. As fertility falls, the youth dependency rate declines, and the ratio of working-age population to dependents rises. There are around 2.5 workers per dependent when fertility falls to the replacement level of 2.0 children per woman. At the same time, if output per worker stays constant, then a rise in the working-age share of the population from 1.0 worker per dependent to 2.5 workers per dependent would lead to a 43 percent rise in income per capita.

Effect of Cohort Size and Youth Employment

As the ratio of working-age population to dependents rises, the absolute number of young workers entering the labor force also rises, creating large youth cohorts. Being born into a large cohort, known as generational crowding, may reduce wages and lead to large-scale unemployment among youth (Korenman and Neumark 2000). However, in Sub-Saharan Africa, it is more likely that large numbers of young workers will be forced to work in low-productivity sectors such as agriculture and informal household enterprises. Large inflows of youth into the informal labor market also make it difficult for developing countries to generate the investment needed to foster industrialization. Many youth enter the labor market early, typically as apprentices in self-employed jobs or as helpers in family businesses. Social safety nets are rare, which, combined with low wages, means that income is very low. The key issue in realizing the demographic dividend is to ensure that people are employed in productive, well-paid work. Although little research exists for developing countries, evidence from advanced countries suggests that poor initial outcomes can persist well into adulthood (Gindling and Newhouse 2014; Welch 1979), raising the possibility that if members of large cohorts are disadvantaged when they are young, they will have lower incomes as they enter the workforce.

This section uses employment and population data from a variety of sources owned by the World Bank to analyze the relationship between cohort size and four outcomes for Sub-Saharan Africa in the period 1990–2010.[3] The outcomes are primary activity, school attendance, sector of work, and employment status. Primary activity is divided into three categories: employed, unemployed, or inactive. Inactive youth between 15 and 24 are further divided into inactive students and inactive nonstudents. Because reliable information on hours of work is not available, the analysis uses the standard definition of the International Labour Organization, which defines employment as having worked at least one hour during the previous seven days. Because youth who work while attending school are classified as employed, school attendance is examined separately.

Sector of work is split into agriculture, services, and industry. Agriculture is generally the sector with the lowest productivity and tends to be associated with worse labor market outcomes than industry or services. The final indicator is employment status, which includes unpaid workers, self-employed workers, wage-employed workers, and employers.

As shown in figure 4.8, size of the youth cohort varies substantially among large African countries. While youth cohorts in Ethiopia and Nigeria are growing, population growth has begun to slow in Kenya and South Africa. However, because birth rates are high, youth cohorts in many African countries will continue expanding in the near future (figure 4.9).

Labor market outcomes are also very heterogeneous. For instance, the share of working youth ages 15–24 varies from 5 percent in South Africa to 80 percent in Cameroon. Most youth work in agriculture or as unpaid or self-employed workers, but richer African countries like Mauritius and South Africa have a much higher share of wage-employed workers than poorer countries. The employment status and sector of work are meaningful correlates of job quality, as persons working in agriculture or as unpaid or self-employed workers tend to work in lower-productivity, poorly paid jobs (O'Higgins 2001; World Bank 2009).

How does the variation in population growth explain the variation in labor market outcomes? Countries where the population is growing more slowly or has declined have seen moderate declines in youth employment. In particular,

Figure 4.8 Size of the Youth Cohort 15–24 Years of Age in Select Sub-Saharan African Countries, 1960–2010

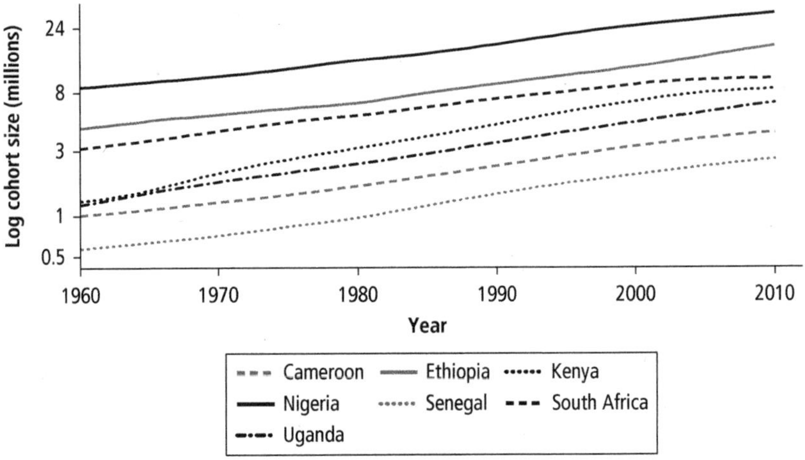

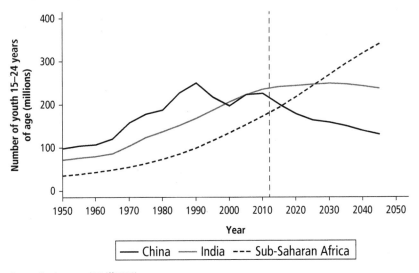

Source: Newhouse and Wolff 2013b.

Figure 4.9 Projected Growth of Youth Population 15–24 Years of Age in Sub-Saharan Africa, China, and India, 1950–2050

Source: Newhouse and Wolff 2013b.

a 10 percent decline in cohort size is associated with a 2.5 percentage point reduction in the share of working youth. Given the small number of countries in the sample, however, the effect is not precisely estimated. Substantial increases in employment—of less than 5 percentage points—are within the margin of error. However, the moderate reduction in work for smaller cohorts does not appear to translate into higher rates of school attendance.

For persons who are working, a 10 percent decline in cohort size is associated with virtually no change in the share of workers in wage jobs or the share of workers in agricultural jobs. Smaller cohorts seem to be associated with a small shift from industry to service jobs, but it is difficult to know whether or by how much the shift benefits workers.

Finally, the link between cohort size and employment outcomes does not become stronger as the cohort ages: the relationship between cohort size and primary activity is, in fact, weaker for individuals 25 to 34 years old, who have already finished school, than it is for youth. Smaller cohorts are associated with a smaller share of unpaid workers in middle age, but the result is not statistically significant.

The two youngest age groups (15–19 and 20–24) react differently to declines in cohort size, with larger effects on school attendance, in part because a larger share of youth attends high school than college (table 4.1). For individuals

Table 4.1 Effect of a 10 Percent Decline in Cohort Size on Employment among Youth 15–19 and 20–24 Years Old in Sub-Saharan Africa, 2008–11
percentage point change

Indicator	Youth 15–19 years of age	Youth 20–24 years of age
Labor market activity		
Student or inactive	5.6	−1.1
Working	−5.7	0.2
Unemployed	0.1	0.9*
Distribution of work		
Wage employed	−1.3	0.3
Unpaid work	3.9	−0.3
Self-employed	−2.6	0.0
Sector of work		
Agriculture	+0.7	+0.1
Industry	−1.6	−4.0**
Services	+0.9	+3.9**
School attendance	−6.0*	−2.4**

Source: Newhouse and Wolff 2013b.
*p <.10, **p <.05.

15–19 years old, a 10 percent reduction in cohort size is associated with a 6.0 percentage point fall in the share of youth in school; for those 20–24 years old, it is associated with only a 2.4 percentage point fall, but it is more precisely estimated. Overall, if anything, youth in smaller cohorts appear to be less likely to attend school.

There is little evidence that African youth in smaller cohorts are more likely to work or, if they work, are more likely to work in either salaried or nonagricultural jobs, which tend to be more productive. Furthermore, as workers age, any effects of cohort size decline and largely disappear for persons 35–44 years old. This suggests that, for smaller cohorts, any negative effects of a reduction in school attendance are small.

Of course, cohort size is determined by factors that can also influence labor market outcomes. For example, labor market conditions are a key driver of migration, which affects the size of the cohort at a particular time. Additionally, cohort size is affected by child mortality rates, which are also related to employment outcomes. The results were cross-checked by examining the relationship between cohort size at birth, which is not endogenous in these ways, and labor market outcomes. There is little difference in the results when using cohort size at birth rather than at the time of entering working age.

Identifying the various channels through which cohort size affects labor market outcomes is an important issue that is difficult to quantify. Households decide to have children based on a variety of factors, including current social and economic conditions and the pace of economic development. It is therefore possible that the relationship between cohort size and employment outcomes is partly colored by the effects of different rates of development. For example, Botswana and Mauritius developed quickly, which could have reduced fertility at a time when their growing economies were creating productive jobs. However, the size of a youth cohort depends on fertility 20 years before it enters the labor market. Ultimately, the complex process of development may mean that the factors affecting fertility in the past may be affecting job creation today.

These estimated effects could also reflect the impact of human capital investment that stems from changes in fertility. Fewer children may allow households to invest more per child, and the size of the birth cohort may affect the public provision of education and health services per child, if total public spending on these sectors does not adjust completely to cohort size (which it rarely does). Children in larger cohorts may therefore receive lower investments in health and education, making them less competitive in the labor market, and this disadvantage persists into adulthood. While, in theory, smaller youth cohorts allow higher investment per child, in some cases exogenous shocks—for example, famines—may reduce fertility and increase child mortality. These types of shocks can reduce the size of a youth cohort and have long-term negative effects on that cohort's physical and cognitive development, thereby reducing its labor productivity. The effects on cohort size include both the direct effect of generational crowding in the labor market and the effect of investments in children.

Effect of Female Labor Force Participation

Economic theory argues that changes in fertility can affect a woman's contribution to the labor market in many ways. One effect refers to the specialization effect of childrearing, which is derived from the fact that the primary responsibility for child care, particularly at early ages, tends to fall on women (Becker 1985). An increase in fertility will force women to spend a larger portion of their energy and time on child care; the responsibility to care for a child restricts the time that a mother can devote to labor. Consequently, reduced fertility can increase the female labor supply by allowing women to devote more of their time and efforts to labor market activities rather than to childrearing activities. Having more children may also increase the marginal value of a woman's time as an input in child care, which adds to the cost of childrearing and can limit women's opportunities outside the home—this is known as the home-intensive effect (Lundberg and Rose 2000).

In addition, childbearing may have dynamic, path-dependent effects on working. Wages partly reflect work experience, so withdrawal from the labor force reduces the experience that a worker can accrue. This, in turn, can reduce a worker's wages, possibly below the reservation wage and below the fixed cost of entering the labor market and searching for a job (Lundberg, Sinha, and Yoong 2010). Therefore, absence from the labor market reinforces continued absence, given lower wages and higher costs of job search.

In all of these cases, female labor supply and subsequent earnings decrease in response to an increase in fertility, as women either look for part-time or less demanding types of work or drop out of the labor force entirely to meet familial obligations (Jacobsen, Pearce, and Rosenbloom 1999). At the same time, additional income may be needed to cover the costs of raising an extra child, which implies that female labor supply may even increase in response to fertility (Iacovou 2001). Consequently, the actual effect of an additional child on female labor supply depends on the relative magnitude of these competing substitution and income effects.

The Endogeneity Problem

From an empirical perspective, it is difficult to measure the impact of fertility on women's labor supply and earnings because both fertility decisions and labor supply behavior are jointly endogenous consequences of the household resource allocation problem (Barro and Becker 1989; Schultz 1978, 1990). Thus any observed associations between fertility and either labor supply or earnings may be biased and not be interpreted causally. In particular, a woman's fertility and labor supply decisions may be affected by other variables, including education, health, household composition, husband's income, or other socioeconomic determinants; failure to account for these variables will result in biased estimates of the effect of fertility on labor supply.

Additionally, it may be difficult to disentangle the causal effect of fertility on women's work because fertility and labor supply may be simultaneously determined and may reinforce each other through reverse causal pathways (Browning 1992; Rosenzweig and Schultz 1985). Other unobserved factors, such as heterogeneity in couples' preferences for children, must also be proxied for in the empirical estimation. For these and other reasons, the main challenge lies in constructing an exogenous measure of fertility as a means to analyze the impact of fertility on female labor supply.

Some studies have found that labor market participation rates of married women have increased and fertility rates have declined in most developed countries over the last few decades. These studies use a range of approaches, specifically instrumental variable methods in the case of cross-sectional data, to correct for the inherent endogeneity and to identify the causal effect of fertility changes on employment, women's work, and other behavioral outcomes. For example, microeconomic studies by Angrist and Evans (1998) and by Rosenzweig and Wolpin (1980) use twin births and the sex composition of previous births, respectively, as sources of exogenous variation in fertility. Similarly, Iacovou (2001) uses pooled cross-sectional data to find that unanticipated fertility effects from twin births significantly affect women's labor supply in the years immediately following an unplanned birth, although these effects attenuate over time. That said, the authors find that twin births are associated with a substantial short-run loss in earnings.

In a similar fashion, changes in legislation have also been used as instruments for fertility. In particular, Angrist and Evans (1996) find that a decline in fertility induced by changes in abortion laws in the United States led to a decrease in fertility, which, in turn, led to an increase in the labor force participation of African American women. Country-level evidence from Bloom et al. (2009) also finds that removing legal restrictions on abortion significantly reduced fertility and increased female labor force participation; on average, a birth reduced a woman's labor supply by almost two years over the course of her reproductive lifetime. Recently, several studies have also exploited differences in access to modern contraception and to family planning as proxies for fertility; for example, Bailey (2006) uses state-level variations in legislation on access to the contraceptive pill as an instrument for fertility, finding a positive effect of lower fertility on female labor supply in the United States.

Apart from using instrumental variable methods, some studies have attempted to resolve the endogeneity problem by directly estimating the determinants of fertility and labor supply within a simultaneous equations framework. For example, Rosenzweig and Schultz (1985) and Schultz (1978) develop a structural framework to disentangle a couple's supply of births from their demand for births in order to assess the effect of varying fertility on household allocation and labor supply decisions. Although the studies yield different parameter estimates for the effect of fertility, both studies demonstrate that the effect of fertility decisions on labor supply can be identified even when fertility is endogenous to a woman's decision to work.

Developing-Country Studies

Few studies have examined the impact of fertility on female labor supply in developing-country contexts, particularly in Sub-Saharan Africa. Perhaps the best evidence of the fertility–labor supply relationship in middle-income countries is presented by Cruces and Galiani (2007), who duplicate the twin births instrumental variables design in Argentina and Mexico and find comparable effects to the U.S. study by Angrist and Evans (1998). Similarly, Chun and Oh (2002) use cross-sectional data from the Republic of Korea and instrument fertility decisions using the sex of the first child, finding that having an additional child reduces women's labor force participation by almost 28 percent. Investigations in Indonesia (Kim and Aassve 2006) and Morocco (Assaad and Zouari 2003) use women's education and age of marriage as instruments for fertility and find similar results.

In contrast, Lundberg, Sinha, and Yoong (2010) find little impact of fertility on female labor force participation in Matlab, Bangladesh, although they acknowledge that this weak association may be because a third factor, such as sector of employment, may be driving both fertility and labor force participation decisions.

While most studies in developed countries have found an inverse relationship between fertility and female labor supply, the same relationship may not be true in Sub-Saharan Africa, where household composition and the division of labor among household members is very different than in developed settings (Westeneng and D'Exelle 2011). In particular, households in many African societies tend to extend well beyond the nuclear family unit. When young adults find a partner, they often continue to reside in their parents' home and only separate once they have sufficient earning capacity. Likewise, older family members may join the households of their children as they become increasingly dependent on their children's support.

These differences in household composition are particularly important to intra-household labor market decisions, as differences in the number of adults residing in the household may explain differences in labor supply.

For example, having more male adults in the household may lower the need of women to participate in the labor market. However, having more female adults may allow some women (as well as older children) in the household to assume the role of "mother substitutes" to younger children, providing an opportunity for the remaining women to reenter the labor market (Wong and Levine 1992). Depending on the number of adults in the household, the effect of fertility on female labor supply may reduce or even become positive with each additional child.

Besides household size and composition, it may also be important to consider the status of women in the household when identifying their contribution to labor supply. In most developed-country contexts, marital status and the time and cost associated with pregnancy, childbearing, and childrearing together have a significant effect on female labor supply (Becker 1985; Westeneng and D'Exelle 2011; Wong and Levine 1992). More specifically, couples are more likely to leave their parental household following marriage, and women's careers are often interrupted for a significant time after pregnancy and childbirth. In Sub-Saharan Africa, couples often continue to reside with their parents and are more likely to share child care responsibilities following childbirth. Moreover, women who recently started their own household are expected to participate less in income-generating activities, at least initially. When higher status is ascribed to their motherhood, however, women gain more bargaining power and access to social networks and may eventually be able to spend more time in the labor market.

Women in Sub-Saharan Africa tend to be strongly attached to the labor market, working less during pregnancies but returning to the labor market right after giving birth. When they give birth, the impact of that birth on their other children and their own labor force participation depends on the type of work they do and the type of child care support they have. Because many women in Sub-Saharan Africa are either self-employed or work in the informal sector, mothers can often bring their young children to work with them. Therefore, an additional birth may not have a large impact on a woman's labor force participation in Africa.

In Sub-Saharan Africa, although the average labor force participation rate is higher for women living with a child under two years of age than for women not living with a small child (figure 4.10, panel a), women living with a young child are more likely to work in agriculture or other informal sectors (figure 4.10, panel b) and less likely to be employed in wage labor (figure 4.10, panel c). Moreover, female labor force participation is lower for more educated women, and women who are educated are more likely to work in less productive jobs following the birth of a child. In this manner, these women may continue to contribute to household income by taking jobs that are available (jobs in agriculture or other informal sectors) and flexible (jobs that allow

Figure 4.10 Female Labor Force Participation and Fertility in Sub-Saharan Africa, 2008–11

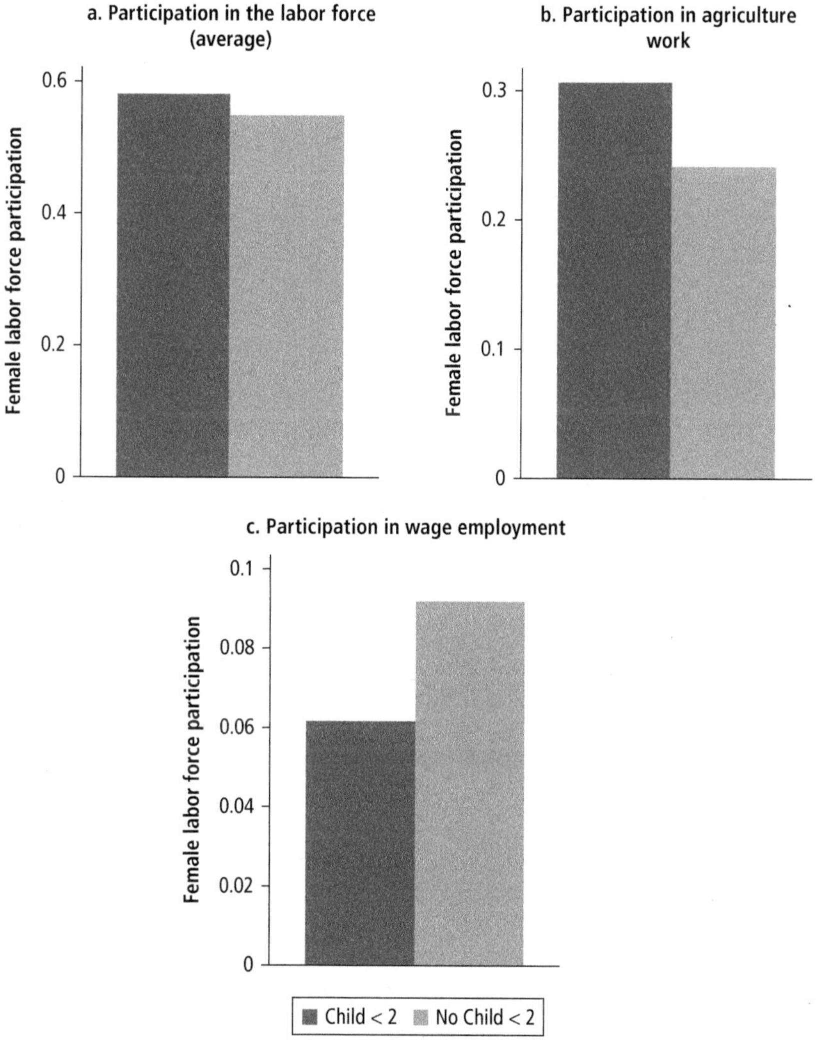

a. Participation in the labor force (average)

b. Participation in agriculture work

c. Participation in wage employment

■ Child < 2   ■ No Child < 2

Source: Newhouse and Wolff 2013a.

them to be self-employed). But it is more likely that having more children will shift a mother's work-life balance toward child care and away from economic activities in the long term, which, in turn, will reduce her ability to be in the labor force.

Women in low-income African countries contribute greatly to the labor force. However, as the type of work shifts from informal sector labor, such as

Figure 4.11 Female Labor Force Participation in Sub-Saharan African Countries and the Rest of the World, by GDP and Country, 2011

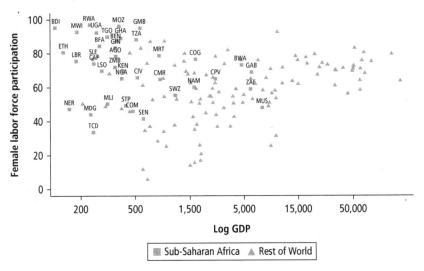

Source: Newhouse and Wolff 2013a.
Note: GDP = gross domestic product.

agriculture, to formal sector labor, such as manufacturing, women's labor supply begins to decline even as per capita income increases. However, as the formal service sectors begin to dominate the labor market, female labor force participation increases as income per capita increases, forming a U-shaped relationship, shown in figure 4.11 (Goldin 1994).

Attempts to Resolve the Endogeneity Problem: Studies in South Africa and Tanzania

In two recent longitudinal studies, David Newhouse and Claudia Wolff attempt to verify the robustness of the effect of fertility on women's labor supply using panel data collected from South Africa and Tanzania. In these studies, the authors compare the labor market outcomes of women ages 15–55 who have had a child in the past two years to women who have not had a child in the past two years, controlling for several observable characteristics.

In their analysis of South Africa, Newhouse and Wolff use data from the 2008 and 2011 National Income Dynamic Study, a large-scale, high-quality panel study that surveyed more than 3,000 South African women. Information on employment history, birth history, socioeconomic background, and other individual-specific controls (including marital status, age, and education) was collected for each woman; regression analysis was conducted to identify the effect on female labor market participation of having a birth over the past two years.

Figure 4.12 Estimated Change in Employment Status after Having a Child in South Africa, 2008–11

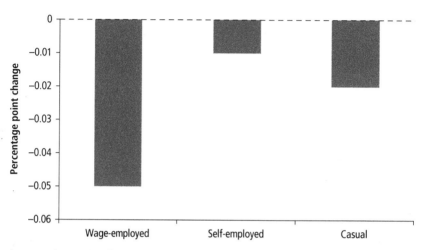

Source: Newhouse and Wolff 2013a.

The authors find a significant fall in women's employment and a corresponding rise in women's unemployment after the birth of a child. A woman in the sample is 8 percentage points less likely to be employed and 5 percentage points less likely to be employed in wage labor after having a child (figure 4.12). These estimates roughly translate into an eight-week reduction in women's employment due to the birth of a child. Sampled women are also 7 percentage points more likely to be inactive (out of the labor force) after the birth of a child (figure 4.13).

These findings suggest that having a child is associated with a substantial reduction in female labor force participation in South Africa: that is, the substitution effect associated with having a child seems to dominate the income effect. This may be because women who have a child are more vulnerable to losing their job than women who do not have a child due to the high opportunity cost of children in South Africa. This finding suggests that these results are unlikely to apply to most other African countries. With nominal GDP of more than US$384 billion, income per capita of more than US$8,000, and total fertility of 2.4 children per woman, South Africa is one of the largest economies in Africa and is advanced in the demographic transition (World Bank 2011b). Unlike many African countries, a very small percentage of the South African labor force (only 6 percent of working men and 4 percent of working women) work in agriculture. Moreover, over 60 percent of women are either unemployed or inactive, irrespective of the number of children they have borne.

Figure 4.13 Estimated Change in Labor Market Participation after Having a Child in
South Africa, 2008–11

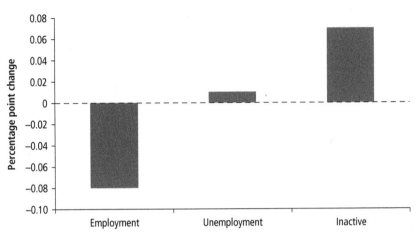

Source: Newhouse and Wolff 2013a.

Other distinguishing features of South Africa are generous insurance coverage
and social welfare programs as well as a small informal sector.

In their analysis of Tanzania, Newhouse and Wolff use data from the smaller-
scale 2008 and 2010 Tanzanian National Panel Survey. Similar to the South
African analysis, they gathered information on employment history, birth
history, and household characteristics (expenditure, household-related assets,
and consumption per household member) and conducted a regression analysis
to identify the effect of a birth on labor market participation among Tanzanian
women.

The Tanzanian results also suggest that the birth of a child contributes to
a decline in women's employment. In addition, having a child weakly reduces
a woman's chances of being wage-employed or self-employed; however, the
estimates from the analysis are too imprecise to determine whether the effect
is significant. This imprecision is most probably a result of the small sample
size, which leads to inconsistent measurement of the parameters of interest, and
other inconsistencies between data waves that are likely induced by changes in
the questionnaire format and survey design.

Savings and Investment Payoffs

In addition to the jobs payoffs, the demographic transition can potentially
increase individual and national saving rates. At the macro level, higher saving

rates can lead to higher levels of investments and faster economic growth. At the household level, they imply higher self-insurance and income protection.

The demographic transition usually increases saving rates through three main channels. First, income per capita may rise as more public and private resources are put toward education. Second, saving rates become positive when individuals are working and peak in mid-career (Modigliani 1990), such that changes in age structure affect aggregate saving rates even if individual age-specific behavior remains the same. Finally, new cohorts of workers are expected to have fewer children and to live longer than older cohorts. Having fewer children may result in a shift from spending for elder care to financial savings, while a longer life span implies a greater need for savings to finance consumption during a longer period of inactivity during old age (Schultz 2004).

To what extent do these three channels operate in Africa? The analysis, which is based on macro- and household-level data, examines the determinants of saving in African countries. In line with the rest of the literature, the results suggest that the main predictor of saving is a country's income per capita. Hence, if the demographic dividend raises incomes, savings are expected to rise as well.

Africa, though, presents less evidence of a life-cycle pattern of saving. Indeed, other things equal, an increase in the share of workers in mid-career (proxied by a drop in the youth dependency ratio) does not lead to higher saving. Increases in life expectancy do not seem to have a significant effect on aggregate savings, further weakening the evidence in favor of a theory of life-cycle saving. Africa may simply be too poor for such saving to play a large role in capital accumulation. However, as incomes rise, the importance of age structure is likely to increase.[4]

The micro evidence from African household surveys is less conclusive. African data on income are rarely reliable, rendering it impossible to compute accurate saving rates. One reason for this patchiness is the high level of subsistence farming and self-employment in informal enterprises, which often feeds into very low estimated income for African households. In fact, in many household surveys, a majority of African households report expenditures far greater than income (implying negative saving). While a household may well run down its assets when suffering a negative shock, the practice cannot be as widespread and persistent as the data suggest; otherwise households would have enormous and rising debts, which the data do not show.

Even for the few African countries where income data and the observed distribution of savings seem more plausible (Malawi, Mozambique, and Uganda), there is no clear relationship between saving and age structure. The negative effect of children and youth dependency ratios, however, is not always significant. Moreover, the age of the household head does not seem to affect saving rates after controlling for other factors. Hence, there is no evidence in the African countries with credible data that, as age increases, savings increase, peaking in mid-career and declining toward old age. The results for many

African countries do show, however, that household income is the main driver of household saving. Other things being equal, higher-income households in Sub-Saharan Africa have higher saving rates.

Although they are increasing, aggregate saving rates in Africa have been consistently below those in other regions of the world (figure 4.14), largely as a result of high youth dependency and high fertility.

Several studies have analyzed the determinants of aggregate saving rates using cross-country data. The main framework driving these studies is the life-cycle hypothesis (LCH; see Ando and Modigliani 1963; Modigliani and Brumberg 1954). The LCH assumes explicitly that life span is finite and structured and that income and consumption exhibit systematic variations arising from the life cycle, characterized by the succession of pre-working, working, and retired phases. According to the LCH, the working-age population contributes positively to savings through efforts to smooth consumption over their life cycle, and the dependent population (too young or too old to work) contributes negatively to savings through their consumption (Hassan, Salim, and Bloch 2011).

Leff (1969) was the first to test the LCH empirically. The past four decades have seen marked changes in our understanding of the effect of age structure

Figure 4.14 Savings as a Share of GDP in Select Regions, 1990–2010

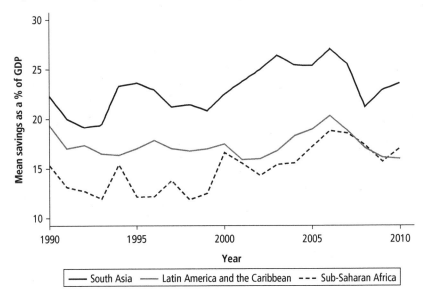

Source: Robalino 2013.
Note: GDP = gross domestic product.

(dependency ratios) on savings (see Hassan, Salim, and Bloch 2011). For developed economies, the predictions of the LCH seem to be verified, particularly the effect of the old-age dependency ratio on savings (Graham 1987; Koskela and Viren 1992; Masson, Bayoumi, and Samiei 1998; Miles 1999). However, the international evidence for other economies is mixed.

Some studies confirm the effect of young- and old-age dependency ratios on savings. For instance, Doshi (1994), Edwards (1996), Loayza, Schmidt-Hebbel, and Servén (1999), Masson, Bayoumi, and Samiei (1998), and Thimann and Dayal-Gulati (1997) find that higher young- and old-age dependency ratios have a significantly negative effect on private savings.

However, Bailliu and Reisen (1998) and Ul Haque, Pesaran, and Sharma (1999) find no statistically significant effect of both young- and old-age dependencies on private savings. Similarly, Ozcan, Gunay, and Ertac (2003) find no significant effect of old-age dependency on household savings. Analyzing the macroeconomic implications of aging in Brazil, Jorgensen (2011) finds that an increase in the old-age dependency ratio has, so far, led to an increase in the private saving rate. A recent analysis for 19 Asian countries finds no statistical effect of age composition of the population on saving rates after accounting for endogenous lagged savings (Schultz 2004).

Bloom et al. (2007) argue that the effect of age structure and life expectancy on life-cycle savings depends on the policy environment. They find large effects in countries with no government pension system or with mandatory real saving. However, they also find that demographic factors play a small role in aggregate savings in countries with universal pension coverage, pay-as-you-go systems, or high replacement rates (the ratio of the pension to final earnings). Pay-as-you-go systems involve making contributions that may seem like saving to individuals, but at the aggregate level such systems may be backed by little actual wealth.

The analysis here uses cross-country panel data on saving rates, working with a large sample of countries—including many from Sub-Saharan Africa—and a long time period to explain gross domestic savings, including savings from the government, firms, and households. It is assumed that savings are affected by the level of income of the country, its young- and old-age dependency ratios, the fertility rate and life expectancy, and other controls such as the balance in the current account. Table 4.2 reports specifications in which only contemporaneous variables affect saving rates.

The effect of income per capita is robust across specifications. In all models, higher income per capita is correlated with higher savings. The young- and old-age dependency ratio depresses savings in the world sample, but, when the analysis is restricted to countries in Sub-Saharan Africa, this effect disappears or even reverses, consistent with the idea that the LCH cannot explain saving behavior in Africa. A majority of households, particularly in rural areas, might

Table 4.2 Determinants of Saving Rates in the World and in Sub-Saharan Africa, 1990–2010

Indicator	World (1)	Africa (2)	World (3)	Africa (4)	World (5)	Africa (6)	World (7)	Africa (8)
GDP per capita growth	0.351*** (4.77)	0.319** (3.23)	0.499*** (4.74)	0.447** (3.06)	0.353*** (4.32)	0.355** (3.27)	0.515*** (4.67)	0.471** (3.04)
Young-age dependency ratio	−0.303*** (−7.03)	−0.115 (−1.05)	−0.131** (−2.94)	−0.016 (−0.16)				
Old-age dependency ratio	−0.675*** (−4.58)	2.398* (2.32)	−0.473*** (−5.21)	2.304* (2.30)				
Current account			0.601*** (7.70)	0.429*** (3.93)			0.632*** (7.70)	0.399** (3.55)
Life expectancy			0.151 (1.70)	0.201 (1.32)			0.051 (0.57)	0.207 (1.27)
Fertility					−2.230*** (−6.82)	−3.478** (−3.14)	−1.056* (−2.08)	−1.978 (−1.55)
Constant	45.890*** (10.76)	10.820 (0.73)	25.073** (2.93)	−4.466 (−0.32)	28.618*** (17.83)	36.488*** (4.92)	22.748** (2.90)	19.607 (1.28)
Number of observations	2,720	840	2,714	840	2,719	840	2,713	840
Number of countries	132	40	132	40	132	40	132	40
R^2	0.230	0.194	0.505	0.395	0.170	0.197	0.476	0.362

Note: t-statistics are in parentheses. Robust standard errors are clustered by country. Year dummies are included.
*$p <.05$, **$p <.01$, ***$p <.001$

rely on precautionary saving to manage risks rather than life-cycle saving. Even in the case of precautionary saving, other informal mechanisms for managing risks, such as support of the community or family or the purchase of land or animals, are not captured by the data on savings. Myopia and psychological biases might also explain why individuals do not save more in early and mid-career, as the LCH suggests they should be doing.

In columns 3 and 4 of table 4.2 the current account balance and life expectancy are added as explanatory variables. A high current account surplus is associated with higher savings. Life expectancy, which may capture the need to save for retirement, does not appear to be significant in either sample.

Table 4.3 reports results for households headed by urban wage earners. This approach avoids some of the difficulties in calculating income for farmers and the self-employed. In Kenya, there is some evidence of life-cycle saving, with rising age of the head of household initially correlated with saving, but then declining. This is not, however, the case for the other six countries in the sample.

The major effect for them is, once again, income. High-income households have high saving rates, while low-income households have lower saving rates. The share of children also seems to have an effect, as large numbers of children

Table 4.3 Household Saving Rates of Urban Wage Earners in Select Sub-Saharan African Countries, 1990–2010

Variable	Kenya (1)	Malawi (2)	Mozambique (3)	Uganda (4)	Côte d'Ivoire (5)	Ghana (6)	Sierra Leone (7)
Gender (male = 1)	0.188*** (4.101)	0.229* (2.962)	0.150 (1.858)	-0.092 (-0.814)	0.311*** (2.988)	0.106*** (3.793)	0.315*** (6.014)
Age	0.043** (2.569)	-0.061** (-5.156)	-0.012 (-2.659)	0.046 (0.828)	0.024 (0.921)	-0.017 (-0.899)	-0.048* (-3.059)
Age^2	-0.000** (-2.257)	0.001* (3.814)	0.000 (0.864)	-0.000 (-0.560)	-0.000 (-1.348)	0.000 (0.851)	0.000 (2.058)
Lower income	-0.892*** (-18.503)	-0.676** (-7.353)	-0.775** (-4.705)	-0.590*** (-5.405)	-0.850*** (-14.778)	-0.792*** (-11.336)	-1.458*** (-23.975)
High income	0.544*** (12.525)	0.661** (8.140)	0.714*** (24.940)	0.582*** (5.231)	0.577*** (9.838)	0.632*** (9.905)	1.766*** (121.677)
No education	-0.034 (-0.644)	0.026 (1.170)	0.258** (4.880)	0.237** (2.608)	0.280*** (4.292)	0.096 (1.684)	0.005 (0.043)
High education	0.019 (0.263)	-0.073 (-0.706)	-0.069** (-4.419)	-0.195 (-1.001)	0.015 (0.389)	-0.088 (-1.527)	-0.101 (-0.585)
Never married	0.072 (1.225)	0.042 (0.686)	-0.081 (-0.748)	0.118 (0.522)	0.266*** (5.722)	0.400*** (6.681)	-0.178** (-3.482)
Polygamous	-0.035 (-0.381)	0.190 (1.049)	-0.050 (-0.698)	-0.335 (-1.957)	0.137 (0.826)	-0.588** (-2.557)	0.050 (0.224)
Living together	-0.211*** (-3.129)		-0.079 (-2.304)			-0.029 (-0.928)	0.055 (0.123)

(continued next page)

Table 4.3 (continued)

Variable	Kenya (1)	Malawi (2)	Mozambique (3)	Uganda (4)	Côte d'Ivoire (5)	Ghana (6)	Sierra Leone (7)
Divorced or separated	0.021 (0.258)	0.202 (1.090)	0.302*** (12.596)	−0.020 (−0.118)	0.140** (2.480)	0.204** (2.319)	−0.382 (−1.758)
Widowed	−0.069 (−0.655)	−0.032 (−0.248)	0.345** (5.969)	0.024 (0.085)	0.171 (1.064)	−0.242 (−1.130)	0.444* (2.447)
Own house (yes = 1)	−0.165*** (−2.947)	−0.175 (−2.663)	−0.102 (−1.912)	−0.003 (−0.014)	0.064 (1.500)	−0.103* (−1.970)	−0.096 (−2.074)
Share of children [0–14]	−0.007*** (−8.327)	−0.001 (−1.330)	−0.002 (−2.088)	0.009** (3.198)	−0.004*** (−3.897)	−0.003** (−3.071)	−0.005** (−3.188)
Constant	−0.632* (−1.978)	1.905*** (11.710)	0.101 (0.574)	−0.509 (−0.431)	−0.894 (−1.556)	−0.438 (−1.085)	2.933*** (10.865)
Number of observations	2,078	919	1,746	219	1,338	1,271	325
R^2	0.440	0.302	0.229	0.298	0.363	0.381	0.260

*p <.05, **p <.01, ***p <.001

in a household lower saving. This could be due to high consumption needs within households or to the perception that children are a substitute for savings to provide old-age care.

The general point is that, in African countries, both the level of income and the number of dependents affect household behavior. However, there is no evidence of a relationship between age and saving rates. It may be that the life-cycle model only begins to play a role in determining saving behavior at higher levels of income than are currently seen in Africa.

Modeling Economic Growth and the Demographic Dividend: Simulation Results for Nigeria

For more than half a century, economists and demographers have debated the extent to which reducing fertility in a developing country would affect economic growth and development. Following the example of Ashraf, Weil, and Wilde (2013), a demographic-economic macro-simulation model was con-structed to characterize the evolution of economic growth and development outcomes under a "baseline" scenario in which fertility falls slowly. This model aims to shed light on the debate by identifying the effect of fertility decline on economic growth. Like Ashraf, Weil, and Wilde (2013), this analysis specifies the channels through which fertility affects economic outcomes and extends their model to include key previously ignored channels, including (1) the effect of fertility on savings, (2) the effect of a more realistic two-sector model, (3) the effect of fertility on health, and (4) the effect of market imperfections, which are prevalent in the developing world. Adding these channels is important to providing a more comprehensive understanding of the relationship between fertility and economic growth.

Once the baseline outcomes have been determined, it is possible to compare them to alternative outcomes in which fertility declines more rapidly over time. These baseline and alternative scenarios are useful for simulating the economic implications of the demographic transition under varying fertility rates.

While maintaining much of the core structure of the model of Ashraf, Weil, and Wilde, the revised model allows for three additional effects. The first is a Malthusian effect where population numbers lead to pressure on fixed resources, particularly land. The second is a Solow effect, in which rapid popu-lation growth reduces the ratio of capital to labor. The third is a mechanism through which saving rates respond to changes in the age structure, although the magnitude of this effect may be mitigated by international capital flows that depend on the return to capital. In the model, changes in age structure due to fertility decline can change both labor supply per capita and labor productivity. In particular, fertility decline can reduce the time costs of child care, leading to more labor supply, particularly for women. The model is also enhanced by adding the effect of investments in education and a channel in which health, proxied by height, improves when fertility declines. This improvement may come from improvements in the timing and spacing of births or through higher health investments per child.

More important, allowances are made for inefficiencies in production. This may be particularly important in Africa. The first inefficiency allowed is a risk premium or tax on investment. Another is inefficient allocation of resources. A two-sector model was also run to examine population effects on sectoral composition. Rather than a simple aggregate production function, the model allows for an agriculture sector that requires land and where output is divided equally between workers and for a modern sector that requires capital and pays workers their marginal product. This structure means that the agriculture sector has lower labor productivity than the industrial sector. This opens up an additional channel for population effects: rapid population growth may force workers into the low-productivity agriculture sector. Finally, allowance is made for a natural resource sector (such as oil) that can provide output exogenously.

This structural framework is useful for identifying and analyzing the channels through which fertility declines may affect economic growth. The model parameters are based on estimates from micro-level studies as well as baseline data on population and economic indicators from Nigeria to ground the simulations, but the data and parameters can be adapted to the context of any African country. Details of the model are available in Canning, Karra, and Wilde (2013).

Results from the Macro-Simulation Model

Figure 4.15 presents the changing pathways of fertility under three possible scenarios. Under the high-variant scenario, total fertility declines by 2.91 children per woman, from 5.61 children per woman in 2005–10 to 2.70 children per woman in 2095–100. The total fertility rate under the medium-variant scenario is the same as the total fertility rate under the high-variant scenario in 2005–10 and then begins to decline at a faster rate, differing by 0.25 birth per woman in 2010–15, by 0.40 birth per woman in 2015–20, and by a fixed 0.50 birth per woman from 2020 onward. In a similar fashion, the low-variant total fertility rate is projected to be the same in each time period, and the difference in fertility between the low- and medium-variant scenarios is the same as the difference in fertility between the medium- and high-variant scenarios.

Figure 4.16 presents the evolution of total population under each of the three fertility scenarios. By these estimates, population in the low-variant scenario will be 10.6 percent lower than population in the medium-variant scenario and 19.6 percent lower than population in the high-variant scenario in 2050.

Figure 4.15 Fertility under High-, Medium-, and Low-Variant Scenarios in Nigeria, 2010–2100

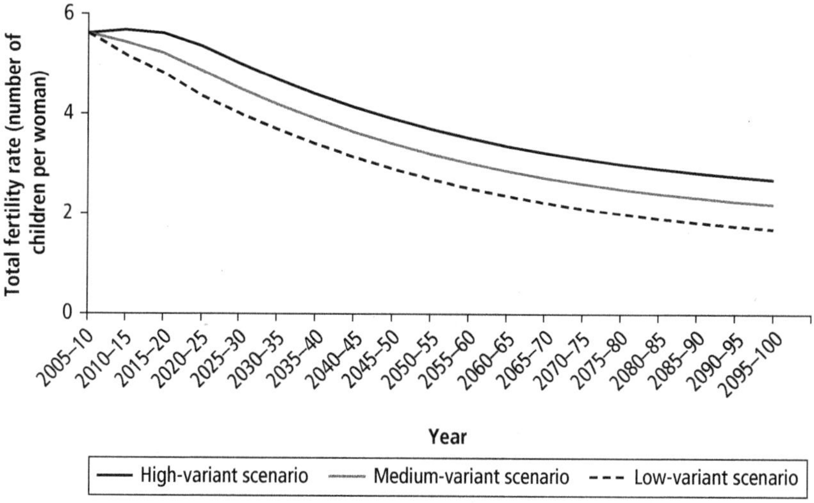

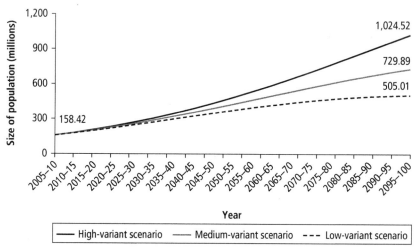

Source: Canning, Karra, and Wilde 2013.
Note: The period covers July 1 of the first year to June 30 of the second year.

Figure 4.16 Size of Population under High-, Medium-, and Low-Variant Scenarios in Nigeria, 2010–2100

Source: Canning, Karra, and Wilde 2013.
Note: The period covers July 1 of the first year to June 30 of the second year.

Results from the Two-Sector Economic Model

Figures 4.17 and 4.18 present the path of income per capita and output per worker per sector, respectively, against the share of workers in the manufacturing sector as a percentage of total labor supply. Each of these paths is presented under the three fertility scenarios. In accordance with Ashraf, Weil, and Wilde (2013), 2010 is the starting year for the simulation because it is the last year before total fertility rates in each of the three scenarios start to diverge.

Figure 4.17 indicates that reducing fertility from the baseline high-variant to the alternative medium-variant and low-variant levels of fertility results in an increase in per capita income of 21.1 and 37.7 percent, respectively, over a 90-year time horizon. Additionally, because fertility rates are lower in the alternative scenarios than in the baseline scenario for the entire period examined, per capita income across the three scenarios will continue to diverge. In the high-fertility scenario, income per capita is projected to be just over US$9,000 by 2060 (compared with just US$2,000 today), while in the low-fertility scenario it is projected to be more than US$13,000 in 2060. The low-fertility scenario raises the growth of income per capita by about 0.7 percentage point per year.

Across the two sectors the level of output per worker is consistently highest in the low-variant fertility scenario (figure 4.18, panel a) and lowest in the high-variant fertility scenario (figure 4.18, panel c). In all three scenarios, output per

Figure 4.17 Income per Capita under High-, Medium-, and Low-Variant Scenarios in Nigeria, 2010–2100

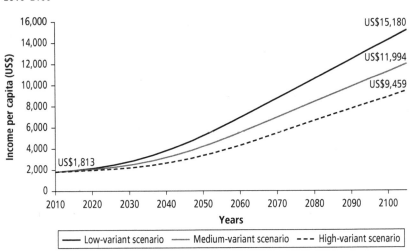

Source: Canning, Karra, and Wilde 2013.

Figure 4.18 Output Level per Worker, by Sector, under High-, Medium-, and Low-Variant Scenarios in Nigeria, 2010–2100

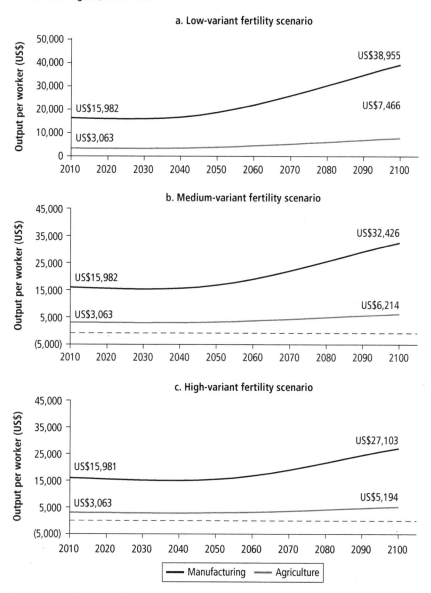

a. Low-variant fertility scenario

b. Medium-variant fertility scenario

c. High-variant fertility scenario

Manufacturing   Agriculture

Source: Canning, Karra, and Wilde 2013.

Figure 4.19 Share of Workers in Manufacturing under High-, Medium-, and Low-Variant Scenarios in Nigeria, 2010–2100

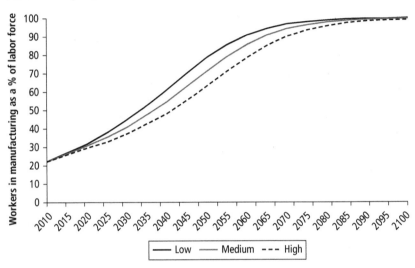

Source: Canning, Karra, and Wilde 2013.

worker is higher in manufacturing than in agriculture. Moreover, beginning around 2040, output per worker begins to grow faster in manufacturing than in agriculture, reflecting the increasing productivity in manufacturing and the consequent shift in labor away from agriculture. Figure 4.19 further illustrates this transition by portraying the increase in the share of workers in manufacturing as a percentage of total labor supply.

While all three fertility scenarios indicate a labor transition away from agriculture and toward manufacturing, the rate at which this labor transition occurs varies considerably by fertility scenario. In particular, the share of workers in manufacturing increases the fastest and remains the highest in the low-variant fertility scenario over the time horizon.

Policies to Reap Africa's Promising Economic Dividends

To harness the demographic dividend, policies are required that both hasten the transition to smaller cohorts and enable cohorts to be productive. The number of policies and their prioritization will need to be nuanced for each country, depending on the state of its transition and its economic environment.

The challenge in most of Sub-Saharan Africa lies in engaging the large youth cohort in high-productivity formal sector jobs rather than in informal, low-productivity, low-wage jobs in agriculture or household-based enterprises. In higher-income countries such as South Africa, a large youth cohort can mean high youth unemployment. But in most Sub-Saharan countries, the large informal sector results in low unemployment rates, but with youth employed in low-productivity jobs.

One approach to harnessing the youth dividend is to increase the competitiveness of production in African countries and to expand exports and jobs in the formal sector. Despite low wages, much of Africa is not highly competitive in international markets due to government failures, high barriers to trade, lack of infrastructure, and lack of skilled manpower. Since most jobs are in the informal sector, policies can seek to raise the productivity of the informal sector. At the same time, policies can seek to increase the competitiveness of exports, which will expand the formal sector (World Bank 2013).

Raising agricultural productivity requires land policies that improve land titles and increase productivity—for example, policies that make credit available for investment in new farming techniques. It also requires policies that improve the skills needed to adopt high-productivity methods of farming and the infrastructure needed to connect farms to markets. Large numbers of informal household enterprises provide consumer services and consumables. Since these enterprises are outside the usual system of regulation, they may face harassment from the authorities. But they can also offer potential growth opportunities. By providing household enterprises with operating security and official recognition, governments can enable them to enter the formal sector eventually and to abide by formal regulations. This process may involve allotting official spaces to informal enterprises operating in cities and providing legal access to public infrastructure services such as water and electricity. As in the agriculture sector, the provision of financial services and skills can help informal enterprises to grow.

Prominent features of the demographic transition in Sub-Saharan Africa are a youth bulge and higher labor force participation of women. Both can be addressed in part by employment policies ensuring that youth and particularly young women have appropriate labor skills. But the sheer size of the growing labor force means that youth and female employment policies in themselves will be inadequate. While the demographic transition ensures the labor supply side of growth, labor demand is needed to turn the transition into a demographic dividend.

In addition to increasing the opportunities for employment, Sub-Saharan Africa needs to prepare for the second demographic dividend by increasing savings for retirement. This effort requires setting up low-cost savings schemes accessible to workers in the informal and formal sectors and directing the boost in savings toward productive investment, eventually replacing foreign funds as the main source of investment financing.

Countries in Africa need to ensure that appropriate financial instruments and regulations are in place to capture and allocate efficiently the potentially higher flow of savings that may occur later in the demographic transition. There is also a need to expand the coverage of social insurance programs. Today, less than 10 percent of workers in Sub-Saharan Africa are covered by contributory social insurance. This situation is unlikely to change over the short and medium terms. Indeed, part of the problem is that the contributory Bismarckian systems are targeted at employees in medium and large enterprises in the formal sector, which employ only a small minority of African workers.

Noncontributory health insurance and social assistance programs (for example, cash transfers and public works) are needed to help families to manage short-term risks, such as the risk of unemployment, falling commodity prices, and disability or disease. Both cash transfers and public works programs have been successfully adopted in low-income countries (Grosh et al. 2008; Subbarao et al. 2012). In addition, countries such as India have been able to expand noncontributory health insurance to the poor by relying on new information and communication technologies (World Bank 2011a).

There is also room for governments to promote voluntary savings, encourage self-insurance for short-term risks, and provide income protection during old age. These programs should be targeted at youth entering the labor market, as they have the time to build savings. The general strategy in this case would be to offer different types of incentives, including financial incentives, to motivate savings. Recent work in Kenya, for instance, suggests that making savings tangible, providing information and reminders, and matching contributions could be considered. These matching contributions could be of two types, ex ante or ex post: the government could make the transfers first, but take back the money if the individual does not contribute his or her share, or it could make transfers into savings accounts after individuals have made their deposits (Hinz et al. 2012).

For these programs to work, transaction costs have to be low. Individuals should not be required to travel to urban centers or to wait in line to enroll. Enrollment can take place through mobile agencies and aggregators (such as cooperatives). Mobile technology can also be used to facilitate payments and withdrawals—Kenya's Mbao pension plan is one example (Kwena and Turner 2013). Part of the incentive to enroll in these voluntary programs would also be that, regardless of savings, the government would guarantee a minimum amount of income during old age. This amount could be flat or, ideally, reduced in proportion to the amount of savings accumulated at the time of retirement, but at a low marginal tax rate (Holzmann, Robalino, and Takayama 2009).

Such programs need to be sustainable. While the costs may be low in the short run, the population as a whole will eventually age, putting strains on pay-as-you-go systems, favoring systems with mandatory but real saving of contributions. Such systems would also boost saving.

While population aging is not a major challenge for most African countries at this time, African governments need to be able to address three current and likely future issues: retirement, savings, and health care. Of particular concern are social security systems that encourage early retirement and financially penalize a longer working life. Labor market participation of the elderly is quite responsive to social security incentives (Gruber and Wise 1998). At present, public pension systems in Africa are poorly funded and strongly encourage early retirement. Moreover, these pension systems have limited impact at the present since they only apply in the formal sector (Holzmann 2005), but economic growth will increase the coverage of these systems and shape the incentives (and disincentives) to work at older ages. In any case, reforming these pension systems, setting up mechanisms for saving for retirement, and creating access to health care for the elderly should all be addressed before the population ages much further.

Africa's working-age population will continue to grow. Will that growth produce a demographic dividend or a demographic disaster? With the right policies, Africa's labor markets can provide productive work for a rapidly growing workforce, helping Africa to reap a tremendous demographic dividend to propel its economic takeoff.

Notes

1. In this section, statistics on investment, savings, FDI, ODA, and remittances are based on three-year moving averages.
2. Some caveats exist when inferring a relationship between structural transformation and TFP growth in Sub-Saharan Africa. Agriculture is highly seasonal, and agricultural workers may not be continuously employed, confounding efforts to measure their productivity. With many African households engaged in both agricultural and nonagricultural activities, this can be especially problematic. In addition, TFP growth is not necessarily slower in agriculture than in other sectors. The few studies that compare TFP growth of the agriculture and nonagriculture sectors provide inconclusive evidence. For example, Block (2010) suggests that TFP growth is highly nonlinear over time.
3. The data on labor market outcome are from the International Income Distribution Survey (I2D2). The I2D2 is a harmonized collection of household and labor surveys from 1990 to 2010 constructed and maintained by the research group of the World Bank. The data set is described in detail in Montenegro and Hirn (2008). The data on population are from the Health, Nutrition, and Population Statistics of the World Bank. The data base contains country population estimates by gender and five-year age group from 1960 onward. The time period was chosen because data on labor market outcomes are generally available beginning in 1990.
4. There is a perceptible negative correlation between fertility and savings in Africa, supporting the hypothesis that households tend to substitute children for savings.

References

Ando, A., and F. Modigliani. 1963. "The 'Life Cycle' Hypothesis of Saving: Aggregate Implications and Tests." *American Economic Review* 53 (1): 55–84.

Angrist, J. D., and W. N. Evans. 1996. "Schooling and Labor Market Consequences of the 1970 State Abortion Reforms." NBER Working Paper 5406, National Bureau of Economic Research, Cambridge, MA. http://www.nber.org/papers/w5406.

———. 1998. "Children and Their Parents' Labor Supply: Evidence from Exogenous Variation in Family Size." *American Economic Review* 88 (3): 450–77.

Arbache, J., and J. Page. 2010. "How Fragile Is Africa's Recent Growth?" *Journal of African Economies* 19 (1): 1–24.

Ashraf, Q. H., D. N. Weil, and J. Wilde. 2013. "The Effect of Fertility Reduction on Economic Growth." *Population Development Review* 39 (1): 97–130.

Assaad, R., and S. Zouari. 2003. "The Timing of Marriage, Fertility, and Female Labor Force Participation in Morocco." University of Minnesota, Humphrey Institute of Public Affairs; University de Sfax, Faculté des Sciences Economiques et de Gestion (Tunisia). http://www.mafhoum.com/press4/136S27.pdf.

Bailey, M. J. 2006. "More Power to the Pill: The Impact of Contraceptive Freedom on Women's Life-Cycle Labor Supply." *Quarterly Journal of Economics* 121 (1): 289–320.

Bailliu, J. N., and H. Reisen. 1998. "Do Funded Pensions Contribute to Higher Aggregate Savings? A Cross-Country Analysis." *Weltwirtschaftliches Arch* 134 (3): 692–711.

Barro, R. J., and G. S. Becker. 1989. "Fertility Choice in a Model of Economic Growth." *Econometrica* 57 (2): 481–501.

Becker, G. S. 1985. "Human Capital, Effort, and the Sexual Division of Labor." *Journal of Labor Economics* 3 (1): S33–58.

Block, S. 2010. "The Decline and Rise of Agricultural Productivity in Sub-Saharan Africa since 1961." NBER Working Paper 16481, National Bureau of Economic Research.

Bloom, D. E., D. Canning, G. Fink, and J. Finlay. 2009. "Fertility, Female Labor Force Participation, and the Demographic Dividend." *Journal of Economic Growth* 14 (2): 79–101.

Bloom D. E, D. Canning, R. K. Mansfield, and M. Moore. 2007. "Demographic Change, Social Security Systems and Savings." *Journal of Monetary Economics* 54 (1): 92–114.

Browning, M. 1992. "Children and Household Economic Behavior." *Journal of Economic Literature* 30 (3): 1434–75.

Buffie, E., A. Berg, C. A. Pattillo, R. Portillo, and L.F. Zanna. 2012. "Public Investment, Growth, and Debt Sustainability: Putting Together the Pieces." Mimeo, International Monetary Fund, Washington, DC, March.

Canning, D., M. Karra, and J. Wilde. 2013. "A Macrosimulation Model of the Effect of Fertility on Economic Growth: Evidence from Nigeria." Working Paper, Harvard University, Cambridge, MA.

Cho, Y., and B. Tien. 2013. "Compilation of 29 SSA Countries." Background paper for this book, World Bank, Washington, DC.

Chun, H., and J. Oh. 2002. "An Instrumental Variable Estimate of the Effect of Fertility on the Labour Force Participation of Married Women." *Applied Economic Letters* 9 (10): 631–34.

Cruces, G., and S. Galiani. 2007. "Fertility and Female Labor Supply in Latin America: New Causal Evidence." *Labour Economics* 14 (3): 565–73.

Doshi, K. 1994. "Determinants of the Saving Rate: An International Comparison." *Contemporary Economic Policy* 12 (1): 37–45.

Easterly, W., and R. Levine. 1997. "Africa's Growth Tragedy: Policies and Ethnic Divisions." *Quarterly Journal of Economics* 112 (4): 1203–50.

Economist. 2011. "The Sun Shines Bright." *The Economist*, December 3.

Edwards, S. 1996. "Why Are Latin America's Savings Rates So Low? An International Comparative Analysis." *Journal of Development Economics* 51 (1): 5–44.

Gindling, T. H., and D. Newhouse. 2014. "Self-Employment in the Developing World." *World Development* 56 (April): 313–31.

Goldin, C. 1994. "The U-Shaped Female Labor Force Function in Economic Development and Economic History." NBER Working Paper 4707, National Bureau of Economic Research, Cambridge, MA.

Graham, J. W. 1987. "International Differences in Saving Rates and the Life-Cycle Hypothesis." *European Economic Review* 31 (8): 1509–29.

Grosh, M. E., C. del Ninno, E. Tesliuc, and A. Ouerghi. 2008. *For Protection and Promotion: The Design and Implementation of Effective Safety Nets*. Washington, DC: World Bank.

Gruber, J., and D. Wise. 1998. "Social Security and Retirement: An International Comparison." *American Economic Review* 88 (2): 158–63.

Hall, R. E., and C. I. Jones. 1999. "Why Do Some Countries Produce So Much More Output per Worker Than Others?" *Quarterly Journal of Economics* 114 (1): 83–116.

Hassan, A. F. M., R. Salim, and H. Bloch. 2011. "Population Age Structure, Saving, Capital Flows, and the Real Exchange Rate: A Survey of the Literature." *Journal of Economic Surveys* 25 (4): 708–36.

Hinz, R., R. Holzmann, D. Tuesta, and N. Takayama. 2012. *Matching Contributions for Pensions: A Review of International Experience*. Washington, DC: World Bank.

Holzmann, R. A. 2005. *Old-Age Income Support in the 21st Century: An International Perspective on Pension Systems and Reform*. Washington, DC: World Bank.

Holzmann, R., D. A. Robalino, and N. Takayama. 2009. *Closing the Coverage Gap: Role of Social Pensions and Other Retirement Income Transfers*. Washington, DC: World Bank.

Iacovou, M. 2001. "Fertility and Female Labour Supply." ISER Working Paper 2001-19, Institute for Social and Economic Research, Essex.

IMF (International Monetary Fund). 2012. *Regional Economic Outlook: Sub-Saharan Africa*. Washington, DC: IMF.

Jacobsen, J. P., J. W. Pearce III, and J. L. Rosenbloom. 1999. "The Effects of Childbearing on Married Women's Labor Supply and Earnings: Using Twin Births as a Natural Experiment." *Journal of Human Resources* 34 (3): 449–74.

Jorgensen, O. H. 2011. "Macroeconomic and Policy Implications of Population Aging in Brazil." World Bank, Washington, DC. https://openknowledge-worldbank-org.ezp -prod1.hul.harvard.edu/handle/10986/3292.

Kim, J., and A. Aassve. 2006. "Fertility and Its Consequence on Family Labour Supply." IZA Discussion Paper 2162, Institute for the Study of Labor, Bonn. http://papers.ssrn .com/sol3/papers.cfm?abstract_id=910227.

Korenman, S., and D. Neumark. 2000. "Cohort Crowding and Youth Labor Markets (A Cross-National Analysis)." In *Youth Employment and Joblessness in Advanced Countries*, edited by D. G. Blanchflower and R. B. Freeman. 57–106. Chicago: University of Chicago Press.

Koskela, E., and M. Viren. 1992. "Inflation, Capital Markets and Household Saving in the Nordic Countries." *Scandinavian Journal of Economics* 94 (2): 215–27.

Kwena, R. M., and J. A. Turner. 2013. "Extending Pension and Savings Scheme Coverage to the Informal Sector: Kenya's Mbao Pension Plan." *International Social Security Review* 66 (2): 79–99.

Leff, N. H. 1969. "Dependency Rates and Savings Rates." *American Economic Review* 59 (5): 886–96.

Lewis, W. A. 1954. "Economic Development with Unlimited Supplies of Labour." *The Manchester School* 28 (2): 139–91.

Loayza, N., K. Schmidt-Hebbel, and L. Servén. 1999. *What Drives Private Saving around the World?* Washington, DC: World Bank.

Lundberg, M., N. Sinha, and J. Yoong. 2010. "Fertility and Women's Labor Force Participation in a Low-Income Rural Economy." Paper presented at the fourth annual Research Conference on Population, Reproductive Health, and Economic Development, Cape Town, South Africa. http://www2.econ.iastate.edu/faculty /orazem/TPS_papers/sinha_et_al.pdf.

Lundberg, S., and E. Rose. 2000. "Parenthood and the Earnings of Married Men and Women." *Labour Economics* 7 (6): 689–710.

Masson, P. R., T. Bayoumi, and H. Samiei. 1998. "International Evidence on the Determinants of Private Saving." *World Bank Economic Review* 12 (3): 483–501.

McKinsey Global Institute. 2010. "Lions on the Move: The Progress and Potential of African Economies." McKinsey Global Institute, New York.

Miles, D. 1999. "Modeling the Impact of Demographic Change upon the Economy." *Economic Journal* 109 (452): 1–36.

Modigliani, F. 1990. "Recent Declines in the Savings Rate: A Life-Cycle Perspective." In *The Collected Papers of Franco Modigliani*, 107–40. Cambridge, MA: MIT Press.

Modigliani, F., and R. Brumberg. 1954. "Utility Analysis and the Consumption Function: An Interpretation of Cross-Section Data." In *Post Keynesian Economics*, edited by K. K. Kurihara, 338–436. New Brunswick, NJ: Rutgers University Press.

Montalvo, J. G., and M. Reynal-Querol. 2005. "Ethnic Diversity and Economic Development." *Journal of Development Economics* 76 (2): 293–323.

Montenegro, C., and M. Hirn. 2008. "A New Disaggregated Set of Labor Market Indicators Using Standardized Household Surveys from around the World."

Background paper for the *World Development Report 2009,* World Bank, Washington, DC. https://openknowledge.worldbank.org/handle/10986/9033.

Newhouse, D., and C. Wolff. 2013a. "Fertility and Female Labor Participation in Africa." Background paper for this book, World Bank, Washington, DC, May.

———. 2013b. "Youth Cohort Size and Youth Employment in Africa." Background paper for this book, World Bank, Washington, DC, May.

O'Higgins, N. 2001. *Youth Unemployment and Employment Policy: A Global Perspective.* Geneva: International Labour Organization. http://mpra.ub.uni-muenchen.de/23698/.

Oosthuizen, Morné. 2013 "Maximising South Africa's Demographic Dividend." Development Policy Research Unit, (DPRU) Working Paper, School of Economics, University of Cape Town, South Africa.

———. forthcoming. "Bonus or Mirage? South Africa's Demographic Dividend." In *Exploring the Generational Economic,"* edited by Concepcio Patxot, Ronald Lee, and Andrew Mason. *Journal of the Economics of Ageing,* special issue.

Ozcan, K. M., A. Gunay, and S. Ertac. 2003. "Determinants of Private Savings Behaviour in Turkey." *Applied Economics* 35 (12): 1405–16.

Pradhan, E., and D. Canning. 2013. "The Effect of Educational Reform in Ethiopia on Girls' Schooling and Fertility." Unpublished mss., Harvard School of Public Health, Department of Global Health and Population, Cambridge, MA.

Robalino, D. 2013. "Saving in Africa." Background paper for this book, World Bank, Washington, DC.

Rosenzweig, M. R., and T. P. Schultz. 1985. "The Demand for and Supply of Births: Fertility and Its Life-Cycle Consequences." *American Economic Review* 75 (5): 992–1015.

Rosenzweig, M. R., and K. I. Wolpin. 1980. "Life-Cycle Labor Supply and Fertility: Causal Inferences from Household Models." *Journal of Political Economy* 88 (2): 328–48.

Sachs, J. D., and A. M. Warner. 1995. "Natural Resource Abundance and Economic Growth." NBER Working Paper W5398, National Bureau of Economic Research, Cambridge, MA.

———. 1997. "Sources of Slow Growth in African Economies." *Journal of African Economies* 6 (3): 355–76.

Saxena, A. 2013. "Demographic Transition and Aging in Sub-Saharan Africa" Background paper for this book, World Bank, Washington, DC, March.

Schultz, T. P. 1978. "The Influence of Fertility on Labor Supply of Married Women: Simultaneous Equation Estimates." *Research in Labor Economics* 2: 273–351.

———. 1990. "Testing the Neoclassical Model of Family Labor Supply and Fertility." *Journal of Human Resources* 25 (4): 599–634.

———. 2004. "Demographic Determinants of Savings: Estimating and Interpreting the Aggregate Association in Asia." Working Paper 901, Yale University, Economic Growth Center, New Haven, CT. http://www.econstor.eu/handle/10419/20778.

Subbarao, K., C. del Ninno, C. Andrews, and C. Rodriquez-Alas. 2012. *Public Works as a Safety Net: Design, Evidence, and Implementation.* Washington, DC: World Bank.

Temple, J. 1998. "Initial Conditions, Social Capital, and Growth in Africa." *Journal of African Economies* 7 (3): 309–47.

Thimann, C., and A. Dayal-Gulati. 1997. "Saving in Southeast Asia and Latin America Compared: Searching for Policy Lessons." IMF Working Paper 97110, International Monetary Fund, Washington, DC.

Ul Haque, N., M. H. Pesaran, and S. Sharma. 1999. "Neglected Heterogeneity and Dynamics in Cross-Country Savings Regressions." Cambridge Working Paper 9904, Cambridge University, Cambridge, MA.

Welch, F. 1979. "Effects of Cohort Size on Earnings: The Baby Boom Babies' Financial Bust." *Journal of Political Economy* 87 (supplement, October): S65–97.

Westeneng, J., and B. D'Exelle. 2011. "The Influence of Fertility and Household Composition on Female Labor Supply: Evidence from Panel Data on Tanzania." DEV International Development Working Paper 29, University of East Anglia.

Wong, R., and R. E. Levine. 1992. "The Effect of Household Structure on Women's Economic Activity and Fertility: Evidence from Recent Mothers in Urban Mexico." *Economic Development and Cultural Change* 41 (1): 89–102.

World Bank. 2009. *Youth and Employment in Africa: The Potential, the Problem, the Promise.* Washington, DC: World Bank.

———. 2011a. *Social Protection for a Changing India.* Vols. I and II. Washington, DC: World Bank.

———. 2011b. World Development Indicators 2011. Washington, DC: World Bank.

———. 2013. *Youth Employment in Sub-Saharan Africa.* Africa Region Regional Study. Washington, DC: World Bank.

Young, A. 1995. "The Tyranny of Numbers: Confronting the Statistical Realities of the East Asian Growth Experience." *Quarterly Journal of Economics* 110 (3): 641–80.

———. 2012. "African Growth Miracle." NBER Working Paper 18490, National Bureau of Economic Research, Cambridge, MA.

Index

Boxes, figures, maps, notes, and tables are indicated by *b*, *f*, *m*, *n*, and *t*, respectively.

Environmental Benefits Statement

The World Bank Group is committed to reducing its environmental footprint. In support of this commitment, the Publishing and Knowledge Division leverages electronic publishing options and print-on-demand technology, which is located in regional hubs worldwide. Together, these initiatives enable print runs to be lowered and shipping distances decreased, resulting in reduced paper consumption, chemical use, greenhouse gas emissions, and waste.

The Publishing and Knowledge Division follows the recommended standards for paper use set by the Green Press Initiative. The majority of our books are printed on FSC-certified paper, with nearly all containing 50–100 percent recycled content. The recycled fiber in our book paper is either unbleached or bleached using totally chlorine free (TCF), processed chlorine free (PCF), or enhanced elemental chlorine free (EECF) processes.

More information about the Bank's environmental philosophy can be found at http://crinfo.worldbank.org/wbcrinfo/node/4.